A Sober Year

Daily Musings on an Alcohol-Free Life

By Meredith Bell

Green Rabbit Media
GreenRabbitMedia.com
info@greenrabbitmedia.com

You can contact the author at sevendayssober@gmail.com

GreenRabbitMedia.com

Contents

INTRODUCTION

I quit drinking because my life was no longer manageable. I was in my thirties with a career, a family and a grab bag of various hobbies and community affiliations—and I was drinking myself to blackouts every single night. My life looked pretty great on paper but behind the scenes I was struggling with a one- to two-bottle-per-night wine habit, memory loss, outlandish behavior and bell-ringing hangovers.

I was keeping it together, but barely. And the drinking was making me so tired, confused and emotional that living up to my responsibilities was at best a struggle and at worst total failure. When I looked in the mirror I saw a woman destined to look back on her life and wonder what the hell just happened.

I wrote *A Sober Year: Daily Musings on an Alcohol Free Life* because it was the book I needed to read. It is not a program of sobriety or a replacement for rehab. Nor does it offer any medical help. It is simply a collection of daily thoughts, ideas, tips and philosophies I have gathered on my sober journey.

Sobriety has led me to discover new approaches to dealing with conflict, stress and fear. Sobriety has also opened my eyes to new forms of creative expression and discipline. I've re-learned how to be joyous and grateful. I've connected with divinity.

Finally getting sober after two failed attempts was painful, freeing, exhilarating and fraught with emotional land mines. I don't know that I will ever live a life where my addiction doesn't harangue me from the sidelines, but I do know that I now have the tools and resources to at least make it shut up so I can get something done.

I invite you to start the book where you'd like. Read your birthday first. Jump into your favorite holiday. Open it randomly. There are no rules here.

Thank you for your sobriety. It's not only a gift you've given yourself. It's a gift you've given to all of us. For that I am truly grateful.

Meredith Bell

January
New Beginnings

January 1

"Hope
Smiles from the threshold of the year to come
Whispering 'it will be happier'..." —Alfred, Lord Tennyson

Let's get happy. The New Year serves up a chance for change on a silver platter. It's *de rigueur* to have a resolution. In fact, this is the time people get sober, quit smoking and lose weight. Gym memberships skyrocket. But before we go all resolution crazy, let's take a moment to recognize the happiness our sobriety has already brought to us.

For me, every morning that I wake up feeling fresh and rested I am deeply grateful. Before, when alcohol had me in its grasp, mornings were a time to be dreaded and endured. Now when I awaken, I know that I can handle my anxieties and difficulties with a clear head and a tranquil spirit. Even without all of the accomplishments I have found in sobriety this is enough for me to know that every single day of this year will be happier than any of the days I experienced when I was drinking.

Sobriety does not promise an easy road. We are still going to encounter difficult people and circumstances. We may get sick. Our plans may not unfold quite the way we envisioned. We will be happier, though, in ways that is nearly impossible to express if you've never experienced it.

If you're new to sobriety this may not yet be apparent. If you've been around awhile, you're nodding your head. Let hope smile upon you in this New Year, knowing that your sobriety will deliver you another year's worth of happiness.

January 2

When I was drinking, seeing a sunrise usually indicated that events had gone terribly wrong the night before. Seeing a sunrise meant I was lost, late or in a stranger's bed. In fact, the last pre-sobriety sunrise I witnessed was after an all-night drive to get to a family reunion after my flight had been cancelled. I probably would have arrived long before the sun came up, but I kept exiting the expressway to find a liquor store that was open all night. When I finally got to my hotel room I toasted the sunrise with a bottle of Sonoma County Pinot Noir and stayed up for the rest of the day, drinking. Not my finest moment.

Sobriety has introduced me to the wonder of daybreak, and if I'm up for the sunrise now it usually means I'm on the way to the beach or I'm up for a yoga class—all good things! Embracing the stillness of those moments before dawn has taught me that I am able to create that stillness within my own heart, and use it as a touch point for serenity throughout the day (although sometimes getting up this early means that I need a nap later).

Even if I don't quite make the sunrise, my mornings have taken on a new meaning. Sometimes mornings find me reflecting on how my nights used to be, not because I want to beat myself up about my past behavior, but because I want to revel in the health and wellness I feel now. Before, I would cling to every moment of the night because I was grasping, in futility, for some kind of magical feeling that I was convinced was at the bottom of the next glass. Evening would transform into night, night would transform into morning and there I was, still feeling the raging despair and completely unable to function. Anxiety about the next day would take over (I would know that I was about to feel wrecked all day) and I would drink more in an attempt to stanch those dreadful fears.

If you are able, welcome some calm mornings into your sobriety. Celebrate the stillness that is only capable from a life lived without drugs or alcohol.

January 3

Author Paolo Coelho wrote, "*Once you decide you want something, the whole universe conspires to help you get it.*" In this time of new beginnings, you are invited to meditate on the things you want in your life, and then move through your new world as if you have been showered with blessings.

You've probably discovered lots of delightful things you want more of in your life. When I was drinking the best I could do was focus on wanting the next drink, waiting for the server to show up with my drink order or wanting a greasy burger right this minute to help me deal with my sickness. The universe had no problem delivering all of these things to me because I sent a clear and unalterable message that these things were my priorities.

If the universe will conspire to bring us the things that destroy our lives, my guess is that the universe is equally willing, if not more so, to bring us the things that create peace, wellness, happiness and joy.

This phenomenon is described in New Age circles as "The Law of Attraction." This "law" maintains that we are able to draw experiences to our lives as long as we are tapped into the same energy level. I'm skeptical about this description, and would like to offer that it's actually the "Law of Attitude." If your attitude is aligned with positivity, hope, success and joy you will naturally see and recognize opportunities that will help you achieve your goals. When I was drinking my attitude was aligned with bitterness, resentment, lack and escape. Naturally, I attracted more drinking.

Sobriety has shifted my attitude. I am continually looking for opportunities to learn how to be better—and I find them everywhere. My energy field hasn't shifted. My attitude has. Before I would look at an annoying family member and drink to dull my irritation. Now I see an opportunity to offer a healing conversation

10

to someone who may be in pain (or the very least a chance to learn how NOT to do things).

What would you like to ask the universe for today? How can you shift your attitude to see that it's already waiting for you?

January 4

"The one thing more difficult than following a regimen is not imposing it on others."—Marcel Proust

When the blurry haze of addiction clears, and we have discovered a new way of being in the world, it's so easy to see where others could benefit from the same revelations.

When I was first sober I was full of the zeal of the newly converted. I decided that everyone I ever knew drank too much, and that their lives would improve if they would quit. I proselytized to everyone who would listen. If I had thought of it I would have gone to the "public speaking" area of my local park to rain down hope on the wasted masses. I only had a sobriety hammer, and every problem was a drunken nail.

My enthusiasm was not well received. On several occasions I was told in no uncertain terms that it was time for me to keep my opinions to myself. Just because I had a drinking problem, I was told, didn't mean that Joe was sleepy because he drank too much the night before or Jane was forgetting deadlines because of her two-martini-a-night habit. Butt out, they said.

They were right. You may feel overwhelming exuberance for your new lifestyle but take my advice and keep it t yourself.

Maybe you have a family member who would be happier if he lost 50 pounds, and you think he can use your sobriety program for similar results. Perhaps a co-worker of yours would finally find the peace he seeks if he could stop his destructive relationship patterns, and now you know exactly what he should do because you're clear of mind. It's hard to resist sharing what you know. But there's a better way—a way that ensures you won't become "THAT sober person" who no one wants around anymore.

When you find yourself thinking about all the things others could do to better the lives of others, take a moment instead to consider your own next step. Could you change your diet, end a bad relationship, discover a new hobby, take a class or learn a new skill? The only person you have control over is you. Focus your energy on your own new beginnings, and lead by example.

January 5

"I love sleep. My life has a tendency to fall apart when I am awake, you know?"—Ernest Hemingway

When I was drinking one of my favorite times to sleep was after a day of suffering a painful hangover. I would slink home from work, pour myself a few drinks and tuck myself into bed early, falling into sleep like a corpse pushed off a cliff. I would engage in this pattern a few times a year. I would congratulate myself for having the best night of sleep ever.

In sobriety I sleep like this nearly every night. For the first month without alcohol I definitely suffered sleepless nights, sweating and agitation, but since then I have slipped off to a deep, peaceful sleep without incident.

If you haven't already discovered this, you will find that the deep sleep that is available to you when you embrace sobriety renews, refreshes and rejuvenates. Giving yourself the tools for a peaceful, heavy sleep is a gift you can give yourself every night.

Discover sleep hygiene. Sleep hygiene includes taking very specific measures to ensure that you experience the best sleep possible. The most important step is maintaining the same sleep schedule. Other measures include avoiding stimulants, getting proper exercise and keeping your bedroom at a comfortable temperature. I find that keeping my room clean and my linens fresh contribute to my sense of relaxation. I have trouble sleeping in a bed that hasn't been made, so I make my bed every morning.

A good night's sleep will not only make you feel good, it will also prevent you from exhaustion that may trigger you to drink. If you'd like to learn more about sleep hygiene, visit sleepfoundation.org.

January 6

Sober living delivers opportunities to your doorstep—opportunities you could never have imagined while you were using. Things that never interested you before may now seem exciting and invigorating. You may finally feel ready to achieve a goal you set for yourself long ago.

So many sober people I know have changed careers, found new loves, embraced travel, built successful artistic ventures, started families and learned new skills. One of my friends recently completed a 50-mile ultra marathon. The woman who was my AA sponsor now owns and operates a thriving landscape statuary business—and she makes the statues herself. A dog groomer got her nursing degree. A medical transcriptionist started her own clothing line. A waiter became a successful local actor. A homeless woman qualified for a mortgage. A homeless man now operates his own auto detailing service. A young girl with a fear of heights took a trapeze lesson. A mom became president of the PTA. I finished three books.

When asked, each of these people will say the same thing about their new ventures: "I never could have done this when I was drinking."

It's like magic. Get the alcohol out of your system and let the opportunities take its place. Close the bottle and open your mind. Fill your now-sober time with following your dreams. You'll be amazed—it's almost impossible not to succeed when you're sober.

Now you know. Keep your eyes open for the chance encounters that may introduce you to new ways of being, thinking, behaving, learning and creating that you were once too foggy to recognize. The universe is opening doors for you; it's up to you to go through.

January 7

Every day is an opportunity to make a change. By simply deciding not to drink today, I offer myself to the world in a way that I never could have before: present, real and ready to rise to any challenge.

When I evolved deeper in my sobriety I discovered that I was making decisions in a completely different way. Instead of looking for the easy way out or trying to cover up a long series of lies and screw-ups, I began approaching my problems directly and honestly.

One of the most obvious examples of this is how I now approach work screw-ups. My poor little drunk ego was way too sensitive and special to actually admit when I made a mistake. I had no problem with coming up with convoluted reasons why projects weren't delivered properly. I missed a deadline? The vendor sent the info late. The meeting didn't happen? My contact bailed. The information wasn't posted online? My Internet connection was down.

Flash-forward to sobriety and you'll see a whole new version of work Meredith. If the deadline passes and I am not done, I tell the truth about forgetting the deadline or my inability to manage my vendors. If a meeting gets cancelled I reschedule or Skype. If I fail to post important data online... Well, I don't let that happen anymore.

In fact, I don't let any of these things happen anymore. I find that forcing myself to be honest also forces me to do what I'm supposed to do. Admitting that I "forgot" something is way too embarrassing.

This was not something I actively pursued; it happened as naturally as falling down the stairs when I'd had too much to drink! Somewhere along the line I learned that being a grown up meant facing my mistakes, awkwardness and discomfort head-on, rather than using some tired old coping mechanism to protect my

16

egomaniacal inner child. Eventually, I found that I had fewer screw-ups to manage, and that my mind felt more like a glassy pond than a raging river.

January 8

I often find myself comparing the person I want to be and the person I am. This is because I now have the opportunity to fully express every aspect of my personality that was previously held captive by my destructive addiction. In every moment I ask myself, "Is this who I am? Is this who I want to be?" And then I make adjustments to reflect a new and better choice. In your sobriety you are also able to decide who you want to be and then make the decision now that brings your actions in alignment with your new values.

I look to my role models for ideas on how to improve. I read books by authors I admire in order to glean some of their brilliance. I watch documentaries about people who have achieved the things I'd like to achieve so I can follow in their footsteps. I try to absorb healthy habits from those who have gone before me. This work— this constant learning—is how my desire to become better expresses itself.

This was not always the case.

When I was drinking I had no room in my heart for advice, good examples or inspiration. Social media was my nightmare and my obsession. I could not get through a day without seeing what my "friends" were up to and becoming absolutely twisted with resentment. They had better houses, better cars, better kids, better yards, better trips, better jobs... Every wonderful thing they had meant there was one less great thing for me to have. My social media contacts were my role models, and it was a dysfunctional relationship. And I certainly wasn't becoming a better person.

I have learned that there is enough for all of us. What I may lack in square footage, I make up for in creativity (or insight or whatever...). I may not be in Thailand right now, but I have satisfying work that I love. I am striving to be better, and that meant I had to look elsewhere for inspiration.

Find role models that lift you up. (And don't EVER meet them—that's a post for another time.) Whether it's Oprah, Cheryl Strayed, Tony Robbins, The Rock or Amy Schumer, take from them the lessons that will help guide you on your own path to wellness. Search for the words, films, stories and events that show you a new way of being. (And maybe turn off your Facebook page.)

January 9

There are no overnight successes. Every expert, every superstar and every winner you see on TV, on the Internet or in magazines started as a beginner.

When I decided to learn how to figure skate, my lessons were scheduled during the same time the professional skaters practiced their routines. I can't begin to tell you how embarrassing it was for me to be out there learning simple swizzles while accomplished skaters were jumping, spinning and racing all around me. I honestly felt that I would never get there even if I devoted all of my extra time to my new sport. It's so easy to get discouraged when you are a beginner surrounded my excellence.

My brilliant coach continually reminded me that all of these skaters began skating when they were three or four years old, and they are now in their thirties and forties. That's several decades of dedication, early morning training and heartbreak (and glory) at hundreds of competitions.

Don't let anyone's seemingly instant success discourage you from taking on a new path. For every moment you see a person basking in the limelight, know that they spent a thousand moments alone, unseen and unappreciated, putting in the work no one else was willing to do. When you decide to bring a new challenge into your life, know that you won't be perfect right away but that you should do it anyway.

January 10

The Buddhists embrace the concept of "beginner mind." This is the idea that we are to approach every moment with fresh eyes, an open heart and a willingness to learn without allowing our past experiences to influence our thoughts. Sobriety not only allows you to experience beginner mind—every second that you don't drink offers infinite hope—but beginner mind is a requirement for success.

When I started out as a copywriter I was indignant at my editor's revisions. I was the expert, of course! How dare this person question my decision to write that headline or insist on that slogan?

In sobriety, I decided to re-read everything I wrote as a person who was seeing my words for the first time—a beginner. Perhaps my readers knew what I was talking about right away, but I often discovered that I was writing from a viewpoint of assuming they were already on the same page. When I started approaching my words as if I was a beginner trying to explain a point to other beginners my writing became clearer and—surprise—I got fewer requests for revisions.

Whether you are starting something new or you are involved in the same old rehashed dramas, take a moment to slip into beginner mind to see if you can let go of any expectations. What you learn may surprise you.

January 11

Learning to cope without alcohol is a highly creative endeavor—one that requires developing new approaches to old problems. After an impossible day at the office I could no longer achieve instant equilibrium with my drink of choice. I had to really think about how I was going to spend that time. I was very disheartened to find that those hours don't just fill themselves. Plus, I had no buffer for all of the things that were happening around me that I didn't like.

It's no secret that our relationship problems, our personality defects and our anxieties don't vanish when we stop drinking. What sobriety offers us is a chance to solve these issues by trying something more than drowning them. In order to keep from plunging head first into the anxiety zone I had to move my body, get absorbed in a creative project or let myself have a good old-fashioned cry.

The grace of sobriety is found in every single moment. We can decide for ourselves, in each second, how we are going to rise to or hide from life's challenges. The calendar year drops a huge catalyst for change right into our laps, but it's also important to remember that you can put the drink down and hit restart button any time, anywhere and in any moment that calls for a new beginning.

January 12

People often claim that fear of failure is what makes them afraid of getting sober or trying new ways of living. I think it's equally possible that fear of success makes it difficult to embark on a new journey.

For me, fear of sobriety was an equal dose of both. I deeply feared the humiliation that would accompany my inevitable failure. I feared snickering behind my back and judgmental gossip. I would, in fact, go on to get sober and fail. No one laughed. Most of my friends were relieved to have their drinking buddy back.

I also deeply feared what my life would be like if I succeeded. Would I become self-righteous, boring and cloistered? (For a while, yes.) Would my life be devoid of excitement? If I was able to exert the self-discipline to stay sober what other things would people require me to do? What would I expect of myself?

If we succeed at *something* people might expect us to succeed at *everything*. If we succeed at something all of the excuses we've leaned on for years will no longer serve us. If we succeed at something we might have to give up our self-image as a victim. When we succeed we open ourselves to a whole host of new experiences that may change our perspectives in unpredictable ways. When we succeed we are asked to leave our old, destructive patterns behind. When we succeed we have to admit that we are worthy, we are capable, we are competent.

You're ready for success. What are you *really* waiting for?

January 13

"When you arise in the morning, think of what a precious privilege it is to be alive—to breathe, to think, to enjoy, to love."—Marcus Aurelius

Your mornings are what you make them. Sure, we have responsibilities to our families and our jobs that can often make mornings feel hectic and rushed. But if you change your perspective on mornings you may find that this is a prime time to center yourself for the rest of the day. I found that, once I'd cleared the possibility of a crushing hangover out of my life, I was able to wake up earlier and have some time for myself before the day really shifted into gear.

Morning is my time to have tea, read the news, go for a run or even take a long bath. I find that this time allows me to approach the rest of the day with a calm heart, no matter what the demanding hordes throw my way.

It goes without saying that this was not always the case. Even after I had been sober for several months, I would still lie in bed staring at the ceiling and waiting for my existential angst to pass. I have always desperately wanted to be a morning person, but I just...wasn't. So I did what I do and found an expert.

Hal Elrod is the brains behind a movement called Miracle Mornings®. The premise is exactly what you'd expect: when you manage your mornings, you manage your life. He starts with a simple six-minute strategy that looks like this:

Minute One: Silence
Minute Two: Affirmations
Minute Three: Visualization
Minute Four: Journaling

Minute Five: Reading
Minute Six: Exercise

His philosophy is that if you can launch your day like this (and a little earlier that you usually do) you will give yourself ample space to succeed and thrive. You can learn more about his amazing journey and this simple practice at halelrod.com.

January 14

Before electric light became the norm in the developed world, people spent a good portion of the day quite literally in the dark. Far from being a problem, people used this time to dine by candlelight, play games, converse with family and otherwise wind down. Another interesting fact is that before electric light people would tuck in early, wake up in the middle of the night to gather in the kitchen for a snack or work on writing projects and then go back to bed until daybreak.

Now that our homes are bright enough at night to be seen from space, we've created the expectation that nighttime is another extension of the daylight hours, time that can be used doing laundry, making phone calls, finishing up business, making lists, cleaning rooms and any other manner of busy-making work (like drinking).

Now that you're sober, try being a bit old fashioned about the dark. Create a space in your evenings to unwind, to be with the people you love and forget about doing more. Go to bed early. Read in bed. Use this time to shake off the cares of the day in order to prepare for another day of being present, in the moment and sober.

January 15

"I remember talking to someone early on after I was sober about how I suddenly felt awkward at parties. They said, 'Well, you're supposed to. Everyone feels awkward at parties.' It's an appropriate feeling to feel." —Craig Ferguson

I used to break out in a sweat at the mere *thought* of feeling awkward. I believed that it was a requirement to be in control of every situation and that being awkward was for sissies. As a result of this brilliance the moment I felt awkward I would slug back some alcohol and my awkward feelings would transform into confidence, then bravado, then silliness. If I didn't pass out shortly, the feeling spectrum would morph into anger, depression, bad decisions and criminal negligence. Anything's better than being awkward, right?

Wrong.

Be awkward. All new beginnings require moments when we're not quite sure what to do, think or say. Rather than trying to avoid looking, being or feeling awkward, remind yourself that awkwardness is a signal that you're opening yourself up to experiencing life in a different way. Embrace awkwardness at every level of your sober journey. Admitting to yourself that you don't know what to do—that you don't always have the answer—will free you in ways you couldn't possibly imagine.

January 16

Weekends can be both a blessing and a curse for sober people. Many of us face the weekend with a combination of fear and delight: fear that we may find ourselves in situations that will prompt us to drink, including parties, get-togethers or total boredom, and delight that we now have vast stretches of time to fill with new experiences.

It took me a few times to get sober, but each time I quit I was confronted with these terrible weekends of unstructured time. Once I got over the pouting, I threw myself into so many activities I would collapse into bed exhausted at the end of the day. I was afraid of having time to think or to process my own experience. I didn't want to feel painful feelings so I ran myself ragged to avoid doing so.

I remember waking up one Sunday, heading to an Ashtanga class at 5 am, meeting up with friends at for 7 am breakfast and then heading out for a 13-mile hike at 9:30. After that I made a big lunch from scratch (salad, fish and potatoes), cleaned my house (including scrubbing the baseboards), finished three loads of laundry, completed a work spreadsheet, reheated some leftovers, did another 30-minute yoga DVD and fell into bed—where I read Anna Karenina for an hour.

This is not a healthy way to spend a Sunday. It's too much. One of those things would have been enough.

Discover new ways to fill the time that you would have spent drinking. Take a slow walk. Cook a small meal. Lie down for a nap. Release yourself from the pressure of having to have each minute perfectly planned and take your free time as it comes. Relax and breathe into each moment that you don't have anywhere to be, nothing special to do... Be wary of over-filling your day. Be busy, but be balanced. It is in these quiet moments, engaged in the simplest activities, that our soul informs us of our true purpose.

January 17

"I think in terms of the day's resolutions, not the year's."—Henry Moore

New beginnings come in all sizes. From accepting a big challenge like running a marathon or deciding to take a short walk this afternoon, each new beginning comes with its own discoveries and rewards. The point is that you made the decision to start anew. Go at your own pace and pay attention to how you're feeling every step of the way.

In my new book *The Sobriety Handbook: What You Need to Know to Get Sober and Stay That Way* I discuss the process of facing fear—and taking it slow. We'll talk about fear later in the year, but I believe that new beginnings can be handled in the same way.

If you decide to try something new there's no need to go all in at first. What I mean is that if you want to be a runner you don't have to run ten miles on day one. If you want to learn to kayak there's no need to spend $3000 on equipment. If you want to quit smoking, you can go cold turkey but you don't have to. There are methods for stepping you off slowly, with support and gentleness.

Embrace your new beginnings, but go slowly if that feels right. Do your research. Find the right teachers. Read the source materials. Plan a strategy. Your new beginning, if it's the right one for you, will be patient while you ready yourself for the challenge.

January 18

Making great and sweeping changes in your life rarely requires an earth-shattering moment, and if that's what you're waiting for you may be waiting for an awfully long time.

I believe there are no epiphanies. So many people are waiting for a lightning-bolt-from-the-sky moment to make a significant change. We see it all the time on television and in movies: the hero witnesses an event, experiences something traumatic or is given a piece of information that *changes everything*. This is not what happens in real life.

In real life change happens over time, in small moments, daily decisions and repetitive action. If you're waiting for an epiphany to grasp on to your new beginning, stop. Your new beginning is happening in this tiny moment, right now. Always in *this moment.*

January 19

When I gave up drinking, I gave up my attachments to certain friends and family members. I also gave up my system for rewarding myself. Gone were the celebratory cocktails. I also lost my ability to be with some people. I lost a sense of who I am. Who am I if I am no longer the life of the drunken party?

This does not make me special. When most people give up alcohol they give up a lot more. Sometimes it's the bad habits that come along with drinking that go by the wayside, like smoking or late-night junk food. Sometimes you lose friendships, social networks and opportunities to be with other people. And sometimes quitting drinking means saying goodbye to our only coping mechanism.

Although this is a struggle it's important to remember that by giving up unhealthy behaviors you're making room for more positive relationships and experiences to come in to your life. It's very much like clearing the clutter out of your closet. When you get rid of all the old, smelly clothes, the things that don't fit or are now out of style, you make room for new things that express the person you are now.

The beauty of this kind of giving up is that no one is taking anything from you against your will. You are cheerfully (sometimes), willingly and peacefully releasing yourself from the habits, cravings and behaviors that keep you locked in to an unhappy life. This is not the same as giving up something at gunpoint. This kind of letting go comes from maturity, intelligence and hope. Like the young person who leaves their hometown to strike out on their own, this new beginning can unfold with infinite possibilities.

So, yes. Your life will not look the same. You may not have the same job or friends. You spend less time with certain family members, have a new home or new hobbies. You've given up the old; it's time to welcome the new.

January 20

One of the reasons people avoid taking on a huge change like sobriety is that they are incapable of admitting they don't know something.

This has been true for me since I was a kid. I remember times where I took charge of a team or a plan and insisted I knew all the answers when really I had no idea what I was doing (and our team or plan failed miserably). When I was in the fifth grade a teacher asked if anyone in my class knew the Mexican Hat Dance. I raised my hand, and found myself being ushered into another classroom to teach those students how to do it. I had never done a Mexican Hat Dance in my life. The teacher realized this very quickly and ushered me out of there fast.

Not only was I unable to admit I didn't know anything, I would insist I knew things I didn't when it wasn't even called for! This was a young alcoholic in the making, people.

I have since mended these ways, and I freely admit that I know nothing. Maturity helped with that, along with sobriety, but in sobriety I have developed the confidence to simply say, "I don't know."

It's perfectly fine to admit you don't know something or that you don't understand it. When faced with something new that you don't understand, ask someone who does. Research online. Take a class. Find out everything you can. Admitting that you don't know something is a gift that can lead to a very fulfilling journey of discovery if you follow the thread.

January 21

"You can't cure obesity by buying bigger pants."—Mr. Money Mustache

I have done so many things to manage my drinking. I tried slamming drinks early and switching to water. I tried alternating water and booze. I tried not drinking until 10 pm. I tried drying out at a spa (the first thing I did when I got home was drink). I tried drinking so much that I would disgust myself and never do it again. I moved. I bought numerous hangover remedies and detoxifying teas. Basically I was trying to cure myself by making allowances for my alcoholism, rather than addressing the alcoholism itself.

This practice isn't limited to alcoholics. We're overweight so we buy bigger clothes. We're in debt so we borrow more money to pay our bills. We don't have the stamina to walk to the store, so we drive ourselves there when the answer is to walk more, not less.

If you find yourself making changes to accommodate a problem or an inconvenience, stop and reevaluate. Don't be the person who builds a new garage because they have ten cars. Get rid of some of the cars.

In your newly sober life, what problems can you eliminate rather than accommodate?

January 22

"A man of courage flees forward in the midst of new things,"—
Jacques Maritain

Just like we talked ourselves out of getting sober on more than one occasion, we can talk ourselves out of trying new things with a variety of tried-and-true excuses. You don't have enough time. You don't have enough money. You aren't naturally artistic/athletic/intellectual, etc. When you decide to invite change into your life, ignore those old excuses and do it anyway.

I missed out on so many things because of this tired way of thinking. I was (and still am, if I am being honest) fearful of challenges. As a kid I quit anything when it got difficult. As an adult I wouldn't event start. I preferred to stay in my own little bubble, preferably with a full bottle of wine.

I missed trips to Europe with the excuse that I had to work. I passed on a once-in-a-lifetime bike trip because I didn't think I could keep up. I failed to show up for an important audition (I thought I would be an actress...) because I didn't have the right outfit. These excuses made sense to me at the time. They won't fly anymore.

Now that I refuse to fall prey to my excuses I have found that the world expands to help me find the time, arrange the time off, redistribute the money and locate the teachers I need. If you really want something stop making excuses and let the world rearrange itself to accommodate your desires.

January 23

"You cannot step in the same river twice."—Heraclitus

Whether we have gotten sober or not we are not the same person we were a year ago, a month ago or even a moment ago. Literally speaking, our cells regenerate constantly. Your liver is brand new every 150 days. Your lungs are only about two months old. Every two to four weeks you get a whole new suit of skin. Your body is continually being reborn all the time.

This is uplifting news for those of us who have suffered damage from a daily dose of toxins, but it should offer you a perspective on change you may not have had before.

Physically, mentally and emotionally, every moment offers an opportunity for a new beginning. Just because you made a bad decision a year ago, a month ago, a day ago or an hour ago you don't have to make the same decision again. We are offered infinite choices in every moment. Let this knowledge empower you to begin again, and again, and again and then again.

January 24

Is everyone still talking about their New Year's resolutions? I love making resolutions. I have not only made some sweeping life changes as a result of the New Year, but I also got sober in January.

But let's put all that aside for a moment. I believe in goal setting as a way to enrich your life, but I also believe that time spent in reflection is just as important. So let's also spend some time this month making some New Year's Realizations.

Take some time away from your goal-oriented resolutions to look deeper inside yourself. Be alone with your thoughts. Sit quietly. Achieve stillness. Consider what all of these changes your life mean to you on a soul level. How proud of yourself are you?

By allowing yourself to touch base with your innermost desires you might find that your life begins to change organically, that your thought processes become more in line with your ideals and that you are naturally taking yourself in a new direction without the "must accomplish X by X" mentality that adds so much extraneous pressure. Your resolutions push you toward a goal; your realizations may lead you to your bliss.

January 25

"Character is the ability to carry out a good resolution long after the excitement of the moment has passed."—Cavett Robert

What a thrill! What a rush! The excitement of newfound sobriety can create feelings of vitality and energy like you've never had before.

This is wonderful, but eventually your enthusiastic feelings will simmer down. This is not a reason to veer off course, however. Simply look at these relaxed feelings as the comfort that comes with getting to know a new process, a new habit or a new skill a little better.

When I first started figure skating at age 36 I fell head over heels in love (fortunately not on my face) with the sport. I went to the rink as often as I could. After a while, though, my enthusiasm waned. I still loved skating, but I wasn't daydreaming about it all the time like I was when I started. I kept going, though. I've been skating now at least once a week for six years, and I've found that even though my initial excitement has worn off those feelings have been replaced with a deep sense of accomplishment. I'll never be an Olympic skater, but I have made actual improvements all because I allowed my new beginning become a very fulfilling habitual practice.

You're going to reach a more stable emotional plane with your sobriety. Enjoy the all-out excitement while you can and then prepare yourself to enjoy the security of knowing your sobriety is part of your new routine.

January 26

Sometimes we're forced into a new beginning by something that is out of our control. Our partner leaves. Our company lays us off. Our kids move out. The judge says we must attend AA meetings or go to jail.

I was laid off while I was going through a divorce. My dog died at the same time. I drank through all of it, and there's not a single aspect of any of it that improved as a result. In fact, all of those dark feelings were there waiting for me when I finally sobered up.

Be careful with your sobriety when tragedies occur. Take the time to check in with yourself to explore your anger, your sadness and your disappointment. Remember that taking a drink or using drugs will not improve the situation.

Your choice to stay sober is something you *can* control.

You may not be able to control what you feel from one moment to the next, but you can control how you treat your body. Instead of falling back into old patterns remember that you have the option to take a nap, go for a walk or call a friend. When the situation is out of your hands, take a moment to remind yourself of all the things you *can* manage. Focus on those things to keep yourself centered and sober.

January 27

"If we are facing the right direction, all we have to do is keep on walking." —Unknown

By getting sober you know—without me hammering it home—that you are now facing the right direction. You reached your saturation point, literally and figuratively, and you know that the only way to save your life is to dry out. Now what?

I failed the first two times I tried to get sober. There are thousands upon thousands of reasons why, not the least of which was that I did not surrender to my new beginning.

Rather than diving into my experience with my full head and heart I created a rigid framework of behavior in order to force an outcome. I had a very ill informed picture in my head of what a sober life looked like, and I held myself to an impossible standard. Ultimately I drank again because I tried to manhandle the experience rather than letting it unfold.

I believed that a sober person was a perfect person. I required myself to be thin, goal-oriented, perfectly put together, smart, savvy and successful. I wrote lists and I checked them off. I made myself stressed and sick from trying too hard.

In my new, successful sobriety, I no longer manipulate experiences to match my preconceived notions. I have no preconceived notions. I point myself in the sober direction and keep moving. If I gain a few pounds, I go with it. If I must go out to the mailbox without brushing my hair then so be it. If I make a mistake I admit it and move on.

When embarking on a new adventure like sobriety, don't force the outcome. Surrender to the journey to become who you really are, not who you think you're supposed to be. When we try to control outcomes we invite frustration and disappointment, and we close ourselves off from possible opportunities. When you launch any new beginning, simply take it one step at a time and savor everything that happens along the way.

January 28

"Face the facts of being what you are, for that is what changes what you are."—Soren Kirekegaard

Humans love turnaround stories. I'll admit to being glued to *The Biggest Loser* each week in order to witness people at their worst being transformed to their best. Similarly, I adore stories about low-bottom addicts who metamorphose into spiritual leaders, entrepreneurs or movie stars. Like most people, I also revel in tales of high school nerds becoming bazillionaires, ugly ducklings turned supermodels and the wheelchair-bound who learn to walk.

In truth, these types of stories are not the norm. The reason they get any publicity at all is because these transformations are extremely rare.

This is not to say that change does not happen; indeed it does, every single day. However, most life-changing transformations are not necessarily visible to those around us.

I've been sober for quite some time, but there are many people in my life who do not know that. The change in me is not visible from the outside the way losing 300 pounds is. The change I have undergone is in my approach to problems, my willingness to serve and my desire to at least try to do the right thing.

It's not always necessary to undergo a massive outward transformation in order to have a new beginning. Sometimes we're adjusting an attitude, bringing a fresh perspective or finding a new approach to something we're currently doing. Take a few moments to reevaluate your current projects, hobbies, habits or goals to see if any opportunities for change exist within the current framework of who you already are.

January 29

If you're feeling annoyed with someone it's probably time to take a long look in the mirror.

One of my most beneficial new beginnings in sobriety was the understanding my frustration with others' behaviors was a reflection of my own frustrations with myself.

Hallelujah! When I was drinking my daily annoyances were legendary. My frustrations were the catalysts that launched a thousand quips. Others' misdeeds were the material for my hilarious drunken storytelling.

The problem is that I got sober and was left with nothing but a bunch of people and behaviors that pissed me off. Knowing I had to work through these feelings in order to maintain a sane sobriety, I spent a lot of time writing about, studying and trying to understand my triggers. My un-scientific study pointed out, glaringly, that the stuff that bugged me the most was the stuff that I either did myself or wasn't doing at all.

My boss was always on my back about the quality of my work. This annoyed me because her work ethic was puritan-on-steroids, and I envied the way she held herself to high standards. My stepson's unwillingness to do his homework irritated me because it reminded me of all the years I wasted getting wasted in school.

If you find someone annoying, bothersome or difficult you have an opportunity to learn more about your own personality. When someone is really getting under your skin, take a moment to consider whether or not their actions are holding a mirror up to your own behaviors. Take note. Our "enemies" can often be our greatest teachers.

January 30

When you face your life without alcohol you have the opportunity to bring your best self to every situation. Whether it's a celebration, a gathering, a conflict or a challenge, when you are sober you open yourself up to participating in all of life's events in a way that is real, authentic and validating.

But that doesn't mean that every event is going to go well for you. Early in my sobriety I was invited to a meeting by one of my clients. It was a gathering of all of their vendors, and the idea was that we would brainstorm ideas for promoting the company's products. I showed up, bright-eyed and bushy-tailed and ready to dive in to the creative process.

As far as I was concerned it went great. However, the next day my partner called and chastised me for dominating the conversation and not supporting her when others attacked her ideas.

I did not like this, but I realized that since I was clear-minded and sober I was able to really hear what she was saying, provide her with the encouragement she wanted and then adjust my approach for future meetings. I may not have completely agreed with her assessment but I could understand why she felt the way she did. As a result, we moved forward, I didn't beat myself up too much, and we approached these meetings much differently in the future.

Although this experience did not go exactly like I thought it should, it showed me that drowning in my disappointment wouldn't have helped anything. In fact, diving into a bottle would have fanned the flames of my anxiety and sown the seeds of doubt. No matter what, sobriety is always the better option.

January 31

"What the caterpillar calls the end the rest of the world calls a butterfly." —Lao Tzu

Without endings there would be no beginnings. When I was drinking I was caught up in putting off endings as long as I could. When I saw the full bottle of wine in front of me I was aglow with the magic of possibilities in each sip; when I saw that the bottle was about to run out I would be on the verge of panic. Knowing that this was my weakness, I made absolutely sure that I always had plenty of new ones to open.

Similarly, I held on to relationships long past their expiration dates. My first marriage probably never should have happened, but I could not bear the idea of ending it.

Now that the dust has settled, it's easy to look back on the divorce and realize that it was one of the best things to happen to me. I'm stronger, wiser and more self-assured than I ever would have been if I had stayed. It's very easy to see how getting sober and ending the madness of drinking has helped me evolve into a kinder, more open and serene person—but it's hard to have that perspective when you're teetering on an ending.

Endings are inevitable whether we force them or they are forced on us. Have faith that a new beginning is on its way because you deserve something better.

February
Learn to Love Yourself

February 1

One of the traps I fell into when I was drinking was the idea that I was "rewarding" myself with an evening of cocktails.

Promotion at work? Pop a cork (or six).

Season premiere of Breaking Bad? Martini time!

Got some bad news? This six-pack ought to cheer me up.

Most often my "reward" turned into a blackout evening followed by a crushing hangover.

In sobriety I've learned that I deserve *real* rewards. Good news is celebrated with a trip to the coast. An accolade gets a healthy, home cooked meal.

Bad news sends me to a restorative yoga class or into a hot bath with an uplifting book. Really bad news delivers me into the healing hands of a massage therapist. Sometimes I take a nap.

Let's face it: it's not really a reward if it damages your body, mind and productivity. Real rewards nourish the body and spirit, and elevate your being. Take care of yourself when you get good news, bad news or no news. Drinking was never the reward you thought it was.

February 2

In the movie *Groundhog Day* Bill Murray's character experiences the same day over and over again. It's maddening for him, going over and over the same exact experiences with absolutely no change in the outcome. It's exactly like being caught in the trap of addiction. Life can become sickeningly predictable: drinks now, drinks later, finding more drinks when the drinks or drugs run out. Wake up feeling poisoned and start all over again...

I accepted this way of living for years. And, like Murray, I knew there was a better way but it took me several years to accept that it was I who needed to change. No amount of trying to shape my external reality or control the outcomes helped me move forward. I had to accept that I was the problem—not my job, not my spouse, not my parents—me.

It isn't until Murray learns how to love and care for others that he's able to break the cycle and move forward to February 3. After months of aggravation he breaks this painful, irritating series of events by becoming a better person. Break your own cycle by learning to love yourself and by prioritizing your own health and serenity.

February 3

If you've been your own worst enemy it's time to invite yourself to become your own best friend. Ponder the chicken-and-egg scenario of addiction. Did you become an addict because the voices in your head convinced you that you were unworthy, stupid, alone and unlovable? Or did you start talking to yourself this way after your addiction took hold?

I think for many of us it's a combination of both. I had low self-esteem because I didn't understand that I had to work for things, (I thought the world owed me a beautiful life just because I was here) and I didn't understand that the only way to build self-esteem was through accomplishment. Instead, I chose to wait for people to hand me success, acclaim and applause. When these things didn't arrive, not only did I develop scorn for others, I also developed a good bit of scorn for myself. When I added drinking to the mix my thought patterns morphed from misunderstanding to outright malevolence. I hated myself, and the voices in my head convinced me that I was right to do so.

Now that you're sober the voices in your head can go to work for you rather than against you. Talk to yourself like you would talk to a sick friend. Make yourself feel better. Be a cheerleader. This could be awkward at first (and the voices will probably struggle against this new positive attitude, but do it anyway.) Singer/songwriter P!nk wrote a lyric that says: "Change the voices in your head. Make them like you instead."

You are lovable, worthy, talented and unique. You are sober. You are committed to making the real change required to have the life you deserve. It's time your inner voice started shouting that from the rooftops.

February 4

Embracing sobriety is a massive accomplishment. You've made a choice to face your life on life's terms with no chemical crutch. Sticking with sobriety in this drinker's world, where liquor is not only widely available but widely acknowledged as a *privilege*, is a feat so monumental that most people *never even try*. Sit with this idea today.

When I am surrounded by people merrily living it up while passing around the bottles of Côtes du Rhône, I often have to take a moment to speak to myself the way I would talk to a friend in the same circumstance. I don't beat myself up for becoming an alcoholic—I reaffirm my sobriety. I congratulate myself for facing my problems head on rather than continuing to hide behind a bottle. It's what I would do for any close friend—or even someone I hardly know.

How would you respond to a friend or loved one who overcame huge obstacles and succeeded? Would you write them a letter of congratulations, send them a memento or tell them how proud you are? Be your own best friend by reveling in your ability to take on this challenge. Cheer yourself on. Celebrate your success. Pat yourself on the back and then pat yourself on the back again. You are a shining example of self-love overcoming self-destruction.

February 5

What can you do that no one else can? Can you run four miles without stopping? Can you quote your favorite movie line-for-line? Write a perfect poem? Make a flawless meal?

While you were using, you probably ignored these talents in favor of escaping from your terrible reality. We all have something we can do better than anyone else, but addicts only see what they can't do, what they failed at or what they could have done better.

Make a list of the things you can do to see if you can inspire some latent pride in yourself. Remind yourself that your talents are unique, that your contribution to the world is a special, individual stamp that only you can offer. Your sober self can build on these talents to shape your world to become exactly what you want it to be.

February 6

Magazines, television shows, Facebook... These things conspire to make us feel really rotten about ourselves. When you see your friends and favorite characters doing impossibly wonderful things with their perfect families it's hard to imagine that they feel the same anxieties and pressures that you do. Remember your social media friends are sharing their highlight reel and not the behind-the-scenes messiness that every life entails. Debt, relationship troubles, health difficulties—these are the real problems every human deals with on a daily basis.

Sometimes when I am sitting in my bathrobe on a Saturday morning, dishes piled in the sink and the kids doing god-knows-what, I'll come across a post from someone who decided to spend an extra week in Paris just because they were having such a good time. To distract myself I'll put on a TV program and find myself feeling resentful that the characters on my favorite shows have such lavish homes. To really put the cherry on top, I'll get an email from a family member who scored a huge investment in their new company.

I may be sober, and I may be doing the work to take care of my side of the street, but sometimes I go out of my mind wondering why others seem to have so much material joy and I don't. I mean, *what the hell am I doing wrong*?

Here's my advice if you struggle with the same mania: don't get caught up in the highlight reels of other people, especially famous people who have teams of specialists who are devoted to making them look flawless, glamorous and fulfilled. Find the things in your life that are impossibly wonderful though they may seem small to others. If you have a roof over your head, delicious food, a handful of friends or a comforting spiritual practice, then rest assured that you are doing better than the vast majority of the seven billion people who share the planet.

Plus, you have your sobriety, a gift that will bring you more satisfaction and serenity than any other accomplishment. Your behind-the-scenes IS your highlight reel. There's simply nothing better than a life lived sober.

February 7

"To control the breathing is to control the mind. With different patterns of breathing, you can fall in love, you can hate someone, you can feel the whole spectrum of feelings just by changing your breathing."—Marina Abramovic

One of the first things you notice when someone is angry is their deep, huffy breathing. You can also tell if someone is bored when they sigh, if they are in pain by their panting and if they are asleep by the slow, regulated breath of the very relaxed (or snoring!).

I'm anxious by nature and, as a result, I am also a very shallow breather. I take short, quick breaths. I know this because part of managing my mental state means understanding how to manage my breathing. Once I understood that my anxiety could be controlled by the length and depth of my breath, I realized that I could change my moods, reactions, irritations and anything else by drawing in oxygen slowly and releasing it completely. Honestly, it works for any uncomfortable state of mind.

When you're feeling defensive, anxious or frightened, take a moment to notice your breathing. When your breath stops, so does your ability to face your problem head on. If your breathing is rushed and skittish, that's a clue to that your inner state is chaotic. Throughout the day, monitor your breath to get a clear indication of how you feel about the things that are happening to you. After you slow down and deepen your breath, then decide how, and if, you should react. It's a loving, gentle way to bring yourself back into the moment, especially if you're feeling tempted to drink.

February 8

Out-of-control drinking is an obvious form of self-sabotage. In my personal experience, I was so worried that people wouldn't like me that I would get drunk and act horribly just to make sure they wouldn't. I also had a pattern of getting plastered the night before a big trip, important presentation or family event so that I would be panicked, sick and dull with a hangover. I never brought my best self to any situation when I was drinking.

Now that you're sober, you've eliminated a huge form of sabotage. But what other patterns have emerged? Do you make sarcastic jokes at other people's expense? Do you take shortcuts on projects that you know your boss will catch? Do you talk yourself out of accomplishing goals? Do you blame others when things go wrong in your life, rather than finding a way to make things work?

In this month of self-love, get out of your own way. Identify the new self-sabotaging patterns that you may or may not have and discover all the ways you can help, rather than hurt, yourself. I promise, you're your own worst enemy.

February 9

One of the things most alcoholics (and most *people,* in my opinion) have in common is an overwhelming feeling that everyone is looking at them, judging them and thinking about them. Feelings like these can make even the most confident person feel challenged throughout the day, but for us it's especially daunting.

One of the most self-loving things you can do is to realize that no one else is really worrying about what you do, say, wear or anything else. They are so busy worried about how they come across to others that judging you is probably the last thing on their minds.

One of my co-workers called me in a panic after a meeting. She wanted to know if she had come off overly defensive during an exchange. She was so worried about how others perceived her that she stayed up all night drinking and worrying, and then was so hungover she even came in to work late the next day. I literally had no idea what she was talking about. I was still thinking about everything I had said and how I looked that I didn't even give her presence in the meeting a second thought. In my opinion, she wasted a whole night getting wasted and worrying over something no one remembered.

When was the last time you walked away from a normal human interaction thinking about and judging the other person? Rather than noticing that the other guy had goop in his eye, you were probably concerned that you still had your lunch in your teeth. Now that you're sober and no longer dangling from the chandeliers, most people probably give you nothing more than a very pleasant passing thought. Stop worrying so much about what others think of you. Give yourself a break, be yourself and relax already.

February 10

So much of the drinking life is full of ugly sights. Toilet bowls. Dingy bars. Filthy convenience stores. Strange beds. When you're in the throes of an addiction it's nearly impossible to believe that there's any beauty in the world. In my case, my drinking was a direct result of trying to create beautiful experiences out of ordinary things. But I soon learned that drinking never elevated anything. Mostly I ended up face down in my own misery.

After I got sober, I found beauty everywhere. I noticed things that had never caught my attention before like the birds that visit my patio, the summer sky full of clouds and kind interactions between people.

Seek out some beauty. Visit a museum. Go to a bookstore and leaf through some home design books. Drop by a botanical garden. Straighten out that print on your wall that has been off-kilter for months. Visit photography websites.

Beauty is all around you, and it multiplies. Invite some beauty in to remind yourself what a gift this sober life is.

February 11

Now that you're sober you should insist on exceptional experiences. That means creating your own positive reality no matter what the situation. All of us deal with life's little annoyances: traffic, long lines at the grocery store, messy kitchens and irritating phone calls. But we can approach all of these experiences with an unwillingness to accept anything less but the very best possible outcome.

For example, you can make your commute pleasurable by keeping your car clean and pretty, putting on some useful audio books and slowing down to enjoy the scenery. You can mitigate the unpleasantness of long lines at the grocery store by planning your shopping time when the stores are less crowded or making sure you have a detailed list—and then sticking to it. I keep a book in my purse to read while I'm standing in line.

Your aggravating home messes can be remedied by creating a 20-minute block of time each day where you put things away, rinse those dishes and make your bed. Phone calls with recalcitrant customer service reps are always helped by creating a connection with the person on the other end of the line. Ask them how they are. Find out where they live. You'll find that if you approach anyone with kindness rather than defensiveness they'll practically bend over backwards to help you.

Exceptional experiences are your birthright, but more often than not they come from within. What experiences are on today's list that deserve your best self? How can you make sure you have exceptional experiences all day long?

February 12

"Don't own so much clutter that you are relieved to see your house catch fire."—Wendell Barry

Whether you're sober or struggling, everything in your life will improve if you make room for positivity. I mean this in the most literal sense possible. Cluttered closets, junky drawers and piles of laundry trap the energy flow in our lives and keep us stuck emotionally and spiritually. When we're drinking, our physical surroundings often reflect our inner chaos. If we can physically attack the mountains of mess, we not only create organized spaces that feed our well being, but we also create additional space around which the positive energy can move and thrive.

One of the first things I did when I finally came out from under my drinking rock was to attack what had been named "Laundry Mountain." Between the four of us who shared the house we had created a pile of clothes worthy of its own name, hiking trails and volunteers. It was bad.

At first I committed to staying on top of the laundry, and that worked for a while. Then I realized that part of the problem was that we all had way too many clothes and towels. Why was I washing 150 pairs of socks and 22 towels every week? I identified this problem and sorted out the things we no longer needed. It took about a year to get this situation completely handled but now we each have one towel apiece and far fewer clothes. Laundry Mountain has gone the way of the dodo bird.

Take a look around your home to see where you can make room for change. It can be a small step: one tiny corner, one closet or one drawer. Make room for yourself in your own life and you'll be surprised at the gifts that are hiding under all the chaos.

February 13

Despite the modern world's insistence that we run, run, run, taking time to be idle is a significant priority for your self care. Between work, school, kids and an array of other adult responsibilities, you do enough. When you prioritize down time, you have a chance to revitalize and renew—giving yourself much needed energy and peace with which to fully enjoy your life of sobriety.

Idleness is defined as doing nothing. Sit. Be. For those of us with the monkey mind of addiction this seems impossible! The mind will trick you into thinking you're lazy or unproductive. Ignore this and keep doing nothing. With practice, you'll find that this idle time results in calmer nerves, creative solutions to problems and a detachment from the idea that it's more important to "do" than to "be." Busy is good, and it's great to be involved in fulfilling activities, but we're not here to just do more. We're also here to *be* more.

February 14

St. Valentine lost his head for love, or, more accurately, for his deep, principled faith in Christ. Emperor Claudius demanded that St. Valentine renounce this odd, threatening religion, and he refused. As a result, St. Valentine violently perished for his beliefs.

Today's Valentine's Day bears no resemblance to the holiday's true origin. Today, we are awash is a flurry of cards, chocolates, flowers and other pithy romantic gestures. These mementos are fun and very sweet, but on this Valentine's Day, let's consider the profound peace that arises from adhering to newfound beliefs regardless of what others think or threaten you with.

Your sobriety is a deep and soulful journey. It's an interior process, and those around you who are not on the same path may be very defensive or dismissive when they see you embracing a notion that runs so counter to the accepted beliefs of society.

St. Valentine was brave in the face of criticism (to say the least). I am not asking you to get your head lopped off, but I am suggesting that you take a page from his book and stick to your guns when challenged. Your friends and family are in no position to make judgments on your behalf of your health. Only you know how alcohol drained, demoralized and damaged you. Make your sobriety your absolute priority on your journey to self-love.

February 15

Cooking and enjoying food are often considered acts of love, but when we're drinking our food consumption is rarely self-loving. Purdue University released a study that shows that alcohol arouses the centers of the brain that crave salty, fatty food. This explains why you were more likely to order a triple cheese pizza than sauté some greens when you were boozing.

Programs that address alcohol abuse are crucial for helping you clear your system of booze, but what about learning what you need to *put back in*? To be truly self-loving you should learn to feed your appetites properly. Incorporate some salads, fruits and grains into your diet. Read the labels on any packaged food you buy so that you are aware of the sodium, fat and corn syrup levels. Flip through cookbooks to find nourishing foods that are easy to make, in season and feature health-giving veggies and fruits. Proper nutrition is an easy, affordable way to show yourself a little love this month, and maybe you'll learn a new recipe or two.

February 16

That little kink in your shoulder. The stabbing pain when you bend your knee just so. That itchy spot between your fingers. If you've been ignoring any health issues, now is the time to face them head on—even the ones that may have been caused by your drinking.

Show your body a little love this month by making an appointment for a checkup. Tell your physician what you've been dealing with physically and emotionally. Point out all of your symptoms, even the weird ones, and let your doctor determine which ones need to be sorted out. It's better to know than not to know. Even better, you may find simple relief for some of the physical problems that have been plaguing you. Taking care of yourself is an act of self-love, but it also shows those around you that you care about them and want to be at your best for a very long time.

February 17

Loving yourself after you've spent years engaging in behavior that wasn't very lovable is a sea change. For most addicts the idea of self-love is hokey at best, distressing at worst. If we're so lovable, why did [fill in the blank] happen to me? Why did I [fill in the blank]? Why did [fill in the blank] leave, break up with me, die, ignore my calls, refuse to accept my apology?

If you're resistant to this month of learning to love yourself, I suggest you do it anyway.

Let me repeat that: even if you believe in your heart of hearts that you are completely unlovable, *love yourself anyway.*

Like any love relationship, sometimes it's best to take it slowly. If you can't look in the mirror and say, "I love you," to yourself, then spend 15 seconds repeating, "I am lovable." Do it until you squirm and then do it some more. Next time, spend 30 seconds remembering something nice you've done for someone. Nice things can range from being polite to the cashier at the corner store to petting a neighbor's dog or saving ten people from a burning building. Remember these kindnesses, and if you find that they are few and far between, go out and create some more.

You are loving, you are *lovable.* If your past behavior hasn't borne that out, you have a chance every single moment of every single day to change your present. Start now.

February 18

The chilly winter months are a lovely time to treat yourself to some cozy loving-kindness. Being outdoors in the blustery wind, wet snow and early darkness can feel punishing to anyone. If you can, transform your home into a warm, welcoming environment to heal yourself from the bitterness of winter.

Light a fire, burn some scented candles and soak in a bubbly tub to get the chill out of your bones. Put the ingredients for a stew in the slow cooker and savor the melded flavors. Read a wintry book. (My favorite is *Wuthering Heights*.) Make hot cocoa from scratch. Tuck yourself into bed early. Use the weather as a reason to slow down and warm yourself from the inside out. These small gestures reconfirm to your body and soul that your self-destructive days are behind you.

February 19

When I feel most unlovable, I take a moment to consider whether I am behaving lovingly. If I'm snapping at the kids, bitching about my neighbor or cursing someone for stealing MY parking space, I am not putting myself in a loving frame of mind.

I find that if I pause and shift my attitude toward one of loving others I feel more lovable myself. I try to do something kind for someone else. Sometimes it's as easy as baking cupcakes as a surprise for the family. Other times, it's a bigger gesture like donating my time to raise money for my local parks. When I begin to behave lovingly, my heart always opens to reveal the most lovable parts of myself.

February 20

The Sufi Poet Rumi, who famously wrote about love, once suggested, "Judge a moth by the beauty of its candle." What this means to me is that we are a reflection of the things we are attracted to. When I spend too much time mired in all the unloving ways of the world I try to turn my attention to the kindness, beauty and generosity that is also present. For example, I have a very unhealthy attraction to competitive reality shows where the contestants say ugly things, sabotage one another and start fights for no reason. (It's true! I can't get enough of this garbage.) But mostly these shows leave me feeling empty.

When I feel icky after watching women throw wine in each other's faces, or reading about how one superstar or another is on some dirty downward spiral, I know that I am not being attracted to a beautiful candle. To balance myself out, I seek out more uplifting entertainment. The poetry of Rumi is one example. I also adore the natural art of Andrew Goldsworthy. Sometimes, I take myself to a lake and quietly watch the birds and the ripples on the water. I'll listen to classical music, or a read a blog that centers on simple living or spiritual messages.

When I surround myself with love I begin to see the love within myself, and it grows outward, inward and all around me.

February 21

"We cannot swing up a rope that is attached only to our own belt."—William Ernest Hocking

Many addicts think that they must do everything on their own, and that asking for help is a sign of weakness. I always felt that everyone else had been handed a guidebook to living and I was absent the day the book was handed out. I was not only fearful and resistant to asking for help, but my false pride kept me from being able to admit I didn't already have all the answers.

Allowing others to help you is a radical act of self-love. When you open yourself up to this belief, you'll find the helpers everywhere. People will want to walk your dog when you're out of town, loan you the books they're reading and invite you over for dinner. Some brave souls will babysit the kids so you can get to that movie you want to see.

Long before I got sober, I had an experience that alerted me to the importance of allowing others to help. A friend of mine was visiting from out of town. I had had a particularly terrible day at work and was feeling very low (and very excited about the wine that awaited me at home). When I walked through the door, I was greeted by the most inviting smell of food cooking in the oven. My friend had taken the initiative to make dinner for me, and walking in to a home where someone was working on a kindness *just for me* overwhelmed me to the point of tears. I realized that no one had made dinner for me since I had gotten married five years before.

This gesture, so small really, was so touching. I realized that I had been trying to do everything myself: working, cleaning, keeping my marriage together, being otherwise perfect in every way... I can't say that I immediately started asking everyone in my circle for help, but I do realize that this was the experience that started the tables turning.

Allow others to help you. Return the favor. Build a cycle of giving and receiving love and it will turn and turn and turn.

February 22

When I first entered a sobriety fellowship I was really put off by the amount of hugging involved. People hugged me when I walked in, they hugged me when I spoke up and they hugged me on my way out the door. At one point I counted the hugs and realized that I had been hugged 12 times in one hour. That's a lot of hugging.

During my drinking days I was a strict non-hugger. I would shake your hand or give you a kind pat on the shoulder, but if you were getting a hug from me I was probably giving you the Heimlich maneuver.

After I sobered up, I remembered a time in my early twenties when I was painfully lonely. I lived in an apartment by myself in an unfamiliar city, worked in an office with one other guy who was always on the road. My best friends were literally Ross, Rachael, Chandler, Phoebe, Monica and Joey from *Friends*.

Out of sheer desperation I joined a local amateur choir. Before one rehearsal the director asked us to turn to the person next to us and rub their shoulders. When the gal next to me put her hands on my neck and started rubbing, I realized how long it had been since I had actually been touched by anyone, much less hugged or greeted warmly. I made my way through the rehearsal, but I cried all the way home. Shortly after, I discovered alcohol as a barrier to the disturbing realization that I needed non-sexual human connection. We are animals that simply need touch.

Nowadays I'm a pretty big hugger. I find that this simple act of reaching out to others in a comforting way helps those around me, but it also makes me feel loved in return.

Hug someone today. It won't kill you. It might save you.

February 23

"It's easy to love yourself when you feel good enough, when you feel special enough, when you're loved enough, when you have enough money and you're appreciated." —Debbie Ford.

If you've been following this month's theme about how to love yourself, it's possible that you've experienced an eye-rolling moment or two. Most of us don't succumb to addiction because we feel good, special, loved, financially secure and appreciated. The reality is that we have all probably been made to feel bad, average, unloved, broke and ignored for most of our lives.

Deciding that we are going to love ourselves often isn't enough. We learned that when we gave up our addiction our checklist of problems was still all there, waiting for our rapt attention. Sobriety solves a lot of things, but a light switch it ain't.

The good news is that self-love is closer than you think if you are willing to look for it from the *inside out rather than the outside in*. If you're still seeking external sources for good feelings, loving kindness, financial security and appreciation, you're barking up the wrong tree. Self-love comes only from within, and no external circumstances, whether you perceive them as positive or negative, can alter it.

Your self-love may build quickly or slowly. But if you build it *from within* by your responsible behavior, loving gestures toward others and rational problem solving, it will be built on a solid foundation that no external earthquake can shake.

February 24

There's a difference between solitude and isolation. In my drinking days, I craved the "solitude" of my quiet evenings at home, just me and my bottle(s). I "needed" this "me time" to refresh and renew for the next day of setting the world on fire (i.e. overcoming my blistering hangover).

This was not solitude. Solitude is time spent alone where you delight yourself with your favorite things: a hot bath, a spy novel or a walk in the woods. Solitude is time spent in thoughtful reflection or prayer. The silence found in solitude offers access to the deepest parts of your soul, and it is deeply healing and profoundly refreshing on an emotional and spiritual level.

Isolation is sheltering yourself from intrusion from the outside world so no one can nose into your business. Isolation is not answering the phone after 5 p.m. because you don't want to have to answer to anybody about anything. Isolation is drawing the blinds so your neighbors can't witness your activities. Isolation is a fear- and anger-based response to being overwhelmed.

Are your moments of "solitude" actually isolation in disguise? Be honest with yourself about that question, and you'll uncover a crucial clue on your journey toward self-love.

Embrace solitude. Banish isolation.

February 25

Our inner critic serves a vital role in our maturity. It's the guiding force that tells us when we've said too much, or not enough. It's the check valve that lets us know that our behavior may be unethical or dishonest. It is the mirror that reflects the perceptions of others.

An angry inner critic is not useful. At all. My personal inner critic is plain rude, using language I wouldn't condone in my presence under any other circumstances. Words like "stupid," "ridiculous," "dirty," "conceited," are dropped into its daily diatribes.

When your inner critic goes off the rails, stop at nothing to shut. it. up. You would never allow someone to speak to your friends or family the way your inner critic speaks to you, so treat it like an unwelcome guest and show it the door. Then make it offer a sincere apology, in writing if you can. Channel that inner critic and write yourself a well-deserved apology for speaking to yourself in such a deleterious manner.

Replace your critic's vocabulary with encouraging words like "clever," "charming," "funny," "expressive" and "compassionate." Accept nothing less than the most positive critiques, and your critic will begin sing your praises.

February 26

There's a funny line in one of my favorite comedies about how smiling "tricks your brain into thinking it's happy." Charlie Chaplin's song "Smile" encourages us to grin even if our hearts are breaking. Even Little Orphan Annie says you're never fully dressed without a smile.

I think we can all agree that a genuine smile is an attractive feature. But I would like to propose that you deserve something better than a beaming expression. Rather than forcing a smile, allow your inner peace to express itself on your face. Relax the muscles around the eyes and temples. Unclench your jaw. Unstick your tongue from the top of your mouth. Breathe slowly and deeply. Look into people's eyes.

Self-love, the kind that comes from within, creates an enormous reservoir of serenity. Don't force it to your face, but don't hold it back either. You may find that your carefully nurtured, meticulously maintained self-love results in a beautiful expression that outshines even the most dazzling smiles.

February 27

Learning to love yourself means learning to trust yourself. People with addiction problems can rattle off a laundry list of reasons why they don't trust anyone, least of all themselves. So often we come from abusive, neglectful backgrounds. People took advantage of or discarded us. Perhaps we were bullied or subjected to mind games by people who were supposed to love us. Naturally, since our examples of proper behavior were untrustworthy, we learned to be untrustworthy as well.

We've all promised ourselves we would "not drink today" after awakening with a nasty hangover, only to find ourselves drunk again that night. We swore we'd show up to the [wedding, graduation, retirement party, birthday celebration] only to arrive drunk or, worse, not at all. We betrayed the public trust by drinking and driving—and engaging in other dangerous behavior.

You're sober now, and just like you have to work to re-build the trust of your loved ones, you have to learn to trust yourself again. This is a simple process. Not easy, but certainly simple.

Here's how: Keep your promises to yourself. Keep your promises to others.

It's slow, but powerful. Like building a savings account one dollar at a time, the benefits are incremental. It may not seem like much right this minute, but over time you will have built up a tidy little nest egg. Keep your promises day by day, no matter how big or how small, and over time you will have built a solid foundation of trustworthiness—and one more reason to love yourself.

February 28

When I finally got sober I found myself overwhelmed with compassion for others. I realized that if this terrible affliction could happen to me—if I could damage my career, ruin a marriage and obliterate friendships for alcohol—that so many bad things could happen to other good people.

At first I cried for other people all the time. My friend was having a tough time with her boss? Sob. A colleague lost her father to cancer? Weep for hours. A stranger at the vet had to put his dog down? Inconsolable.

My emotions were on the pendulum swing back from totally dulled to painfully sharp. It was rough going there for a while, but now that I am balanced out, I love the newfound, compassionate me.

If you allow yourself to create compassion in your own life, you will not only love yourself more (because you are able to be compassionate!), but you will feel less anger toward others, harbor fewer resentments and maintain emotional balance.

When I find myself getting worked up about someone in line who is moving too slowly, or a person in a meeting who won't let go of their argument, I am able to remember that we all have pain and suffering that we are dealing with. I know the agony of alcoholism, but you'd never know it from looking at me. I try to use this awareness to react kindly to behavior that is otherwise irritating. I have no idea how painful this other person's life is. Who am I to be put out by their behavior?

When I tap into my wellspring of compassion, I create space of love around me, as well as within. And frankly, I like myself better when I feel kindness instead of anger.

Bonus!
February 29
(Only read this every four years.)

Leap Year! Before I got sober this special day would have provided a perfect excuse to have a few extra rounds. But if you're reading this on Leap Year, I ask you to instead reflect on the past four years and what's happened to you.

What obstacles have you leapt over on the way to your sobriety? Why did you decide that sobriety was a healthy choice? What have you accomplished in your sobriety that you never would have dreamed of while drinking? What about sobriety has surprised you?

Interview yourself like you're trying to get to know someone you find fascinating. You are fascinating. Your journey is totally unique and personal to you. On this Leap Year, use the extra day to shower yourself with an extra 24 hours of love and care.

March
Stormy Weather

March 1

"The enemy is fear. We think it is hate; but it is fear."—Gandhi

Fear is the most insidious state of mind. On its wide spectrum, ranging from little daily worries to tantrums and raging outbursts, fear pollutes nearly everything we say, think or do. The human ego is a very fearful creature.

Fear keeps us from forming intimate friendships. It weakens our ability to be compassionate. Fear can manipulate us into making self-seeking decisions, damaging our chances of success and even convincing us that we don't deserve happiness. Fear is the foundation of all of our selfishness, misguided beliefs, emotional imbalances and anger. Look at any negative emotion in your life or any situation that disrupts your serenity and trace it back to its beginning. I guarantee you that you will find fear at the root of every problem in your life, even your addiction.

Let's try an example.

Credit card debt = spending more than I earn (fear of not having enough) = need to purchase goods to look a certain way (fear of being judged) = unwilling to accept the reality that I can't afford this lifestyle (fear of facing the truth that I don't make enough money) = refusal to create and manage a budget (fear of facing past mistakes) = continual anxiety over unpaid bills (fear of making a change) = continue to rack up debt (fear of not living life to its material fullest, fear of being uncomfortable).

Fear. It's everywhere. As sober people, we must understand that fear is everyone's governing force. But once you start facing down every single fear, whether it's yours or someone else's, you will find an incredible reservoir of peace, self-awareness, compassion and gratitude.

March 2

Here's the truth. You will never be able to escape fear. It's everywhere you look, from the obvious (rigid security at the airport) to the ever-so-subtle (your father's unwillingness to go to a doctor). As a person who suffers from an anxiety disorder, the first emotion I face the minute I open my eyes is a near-paralyzing terror. I am actually afraid to get out of bed *every single morning.*

This is true in spite of the fact that the life I have constructed in sobriety is filled with delight: beautiful music, soothing scents, warm interactions with friends and colleagues, writing, meditation, time to dream.... I am aware that I have a perfectly lovely life, and I am still scared shitless to put my two feet on the floor when I wake up.

I get the fear thing. I see it all around me when the kids lie about their homework because they are afraid of getting in trouble, to the person who screams at their server in a restaurant because they are afraid that their needs aren't being taken seriously.

Where do you see fear in your life? Are you afraid of leaving the house without washing your hair because you fear judgment? Or is it something more serious like a fear of breaking out of a negative relationship? Where is fear activating you and how are you responding? Where do you see fear in others?

March 3

"Never be afraid to try something new. Remember, amateurs built the ark. Professionals built the Titanic."—Unknown

Fear keeps us from having/doing/being all that we deserve. Nearly everything I regret in life came from a place of fear, my drinking included. I was so afraid of growing up and being responsible for myself that I married a man I didn't love so that I could be financially secure. (This did not work out.) I also turned against friends, spreading gossip or lies, because I was afraid that other people didn't think I was as smart/attractive/successful... (This never works out for anyone, by the way.) I also remember a time in college when I had the opportunity to take a Semester-at-Sea, traveling from port to port while learning all about other cultures. I didn't go because I was afraid no one else on the ship would like me. (I was very young, but I would give anything to go back in time and make a different decision.)

The job you didn't go for, the relationship you damaged, the opportunity you let pass you by—these are the byproducts of your deep-rooted fear. Now that you know this, you don't have to waste any more time regretting any past fear-based decisions. Make a different decision today.

March 4

Let's talk about the ego. Many people have a misconception of what the ego actually is. We think the ego is someone's personality or ambition. We use ego to describe a person's sense of himself, or as the thing that gets damaged when things don't go our way (my ego is bruised, that sort of thing). You may be surprised to find out that your ego is actually none of these things. Your ego is your human fear in its purest form.

When you make ego-based decisions, you choose fear-based decisions. When you act in a way that protects your ego, you are really sheltering your own fears. When you declare that your ego is in charge of your destiny, you are signing up for a lifetime of fear-based results.

If you are ever going to let go of the fears that drive you, you're going to need to unravel the Gordian Knot of your ego. The more you try to untie it, the harder it will clench. Much like your disease of alcoholism, the ego does not like change. The ego does not like to suffer. The ego does not like to lose. But keep at it. Gently, slowly, patiently face your fears, acknowledge then and replace them with love.

The problem with your ego is that it is nearly impossible for it to make a decision that is based in love, compassion or freedom. That's not its job. Its job is to protect its precious sense of control. It's your job to tap into that place deep inside you that radiates with a spirit of connection, giving, and kindness, and to release the stranglehold of the fearful ego on your life.

March 5

The enemy of fear is forgiveness. It's essential for peace and serenity of mind to bring forgiveness into every interaction. I find this particularly useful when dealing with difficult people. If I am able to shut down my fear-based reaction center (read: ego) I can stop struggling so hard against what I think the other person is "doing" to me. I can be in the moment, hear what they are saying, understand the fear that is driving them in this situation—and *let it go.*

For ultimate peace of mind, forgive each and every slight.

Forgive the person tailgating you (fear of being late, fear of not being important, fear of not having enough time/space/room in their life). Forgive your friend for forgetting your birthday (fear of letting go of what their ego has decided is more important, fear of not being the center of attention). Forgive yourself for being afraid to get out of bed in the morning (fear of facing responsibilities).

Feel the fear. Yours and theirs. Then forgive, forgive and forgive again.

March 6

"Worrying is using your imagination to create something you don't want."
—Esther Hicks.

Before I got sober, worrying was a way of life for me. I drank because I was worried; I was worried because I drank. My drinking contributed to new worries that I couldn't have even imagined when sober! My worries and fears were quite possibly the defining feature of my personality. Every decision I made was fear-based. I was desperately trying to hold on to "something" that I thought someone else wanted to take from me.

Sobriety opened up crucial space in my mind to discover and eradicate the mindset of fear in which I was mired. I realized, through meditation and making different choices, that I didn't have anything to worry about at all. Worrying never, ever changes outcomes for the better. In fact, worrying never changes outcomes, period. Only right action when the time comes, ethical dealings and forgiveness ever change anything.

March 7

Identifying your particular fears is such an important step in your sobriety and for living a life of serenity. Earlier this month, I showed how nearly everything we do can be traced to fear. But our fears manifest themselves differently in all of us. For example, I have no real fear of heights or spiders. But I am desperately afraid of running out of money, of people thinking I am a fraud and losing my health.

Here's how those fears present themselves in my life:

Fear of running out of money. I take on multiple jobs from a variety of sources to ensure that I will always be employed. I also fanatically save every extra penny so that I can pay off my mortgage early and I will never have to fear being homeless. I get very angry at my stepkids when they waste money, lose money or spend it on disposable things.

Imposter syndrome. This rears its head every time I turn in a project. I double, triple, quadruple check everything to make sure that I know what I am talking about. I try to ensure there are no mistakes. I am, to the very best of my fear-based ability, painfully honest about my failures and problems so I reveal everything before anyone can "find me out."

Health: Green tea to wash out built up toxins. Vigorous exercise. Organic food. Meditation. I do these things now because I enjoy them, and they contribute to my overall well being. But it all started because I had a fear that all the drinking I was doing was going to give me cancer. It's true.

I share these things with you only to jumpstart your own process. Take some time today to write down your true fears and all the crazy ways they manipulate you.

March 8

A very talented psychotherapist once explained to me that fear is a human's natural state. Throughout our existence on planet Earth, fear has served a very useful purpose. Fear of the dark was absolutely rational. Caution around wild animals was well founded.

But some very smart people have, over time, found ways to alleviate those external fears that would once trigger our fight-or-flight responses.

If you're afraid of the dark, turn on one of Mr. Edison's handy bulbs. If you would like to eliminate encounters with ravenous predators, don't camp. Stay home and luxuriate in your wolf-bear-tiger-tyrannosaurus-free environment. Polio is a thing of the past.

So what the hell are we still so afraid of, evolution-wise? Great question.

We're clever little creatures, but there are certain biological realities that we can't escape. We are wired for fear and always have been. But our forebears would probably encounter less real fear, stress and anxiety in a month than we take on commuting to the office in the morning. Driving is terrifying. So are mortgages and having to pay the rent on time. Getting sober is something that makes me quake in my boots even today because I am afraid something terrible will happen that will make me think taking a drink is no big deal. Our bosses are scary. Picking out food at the market is fraught with infinite perils. It's no wonder we're crazed out of our minds most of the time.

Until now, you've probably dealt with fear by drinking or using drugs. What's comi-tragic about that plan is that the drinking and drugs stack up a whole new set of fears that we invited in, like a vampire, when they were completely unnecessary.

Now that you know that your fear is often a trick of biology—a bit of chemical warfare unleashed by your ego—you can manage it from a rational perspective. Fear is not your personality. What you fear is not who you are.

March 9

Even if you don't feel openly fearful or anxious about something, fear can present itself in your body. Pay attention to the signals your body is sending you.

When your boss walks in the room, your shoulders tense up. When strolling through town alone, you wrap your arms around yourself to protect yourself from... smiles? Sitting in a class, you notice that your hands are clenched. Also, pay attention to your jaw. Clenching your jaw muscles is a sure sign you're being attacked by fear.

You can alleviate these fearful symptoms by noticing them. Occasionally I'll be sitting on a plane and I'll notice that my breathing is very shallow. I deepen my breath to feel better. At dinner I'll notice that I've got my napkin in a death grip, especially when the wine is delivered. Although I feel fine, my fear is still managing to control my physical being.

Be mindful of the signals your body is sending you. One major step toward managing your fear is being aware of all of the ways— physical, mental and emotional—it works to control you.

March 10

I run from fear. I physically run from fear. In fact the whole reason I took up running was to overcome the crushing fear and anxiety I felt as a result of my drinking. Fortunately for me running turns out to be a very effective fear-manager for everything, not just drinking-related woes.

Everyone knows that physical exercise is one of the best ways to manage anxiety and depression. But *knowing* something and *doing* something are totally different things *(...So says the woman who took years to get sober despite the fact that her life was in complete disarray.)* Today, I ask you to consider how you can get your butt off the couch.

Perhaps you already have an exercise regimen that works for you. That's terrific! If that's the case, use your exercise time as a time to address your fears. As I run along, I bring all my anxieties, tensions and fears to the front of mind and I sweat them out. Be conscious of your fears and discover how this affects your workout.

If you're not currently active, find something you like to do and then keep doing it. The gym is not the answer for everyone. I have never joined a gym and I never will because I know that I am not motivated in that way. Walking is the simplest thing to do, and the effect on your mood is instantly noticeable. Maybe you like running, bowling, skating, yoga, sit ups, tai chi, jumping rope, swimming, biking or croquet. Bring your fears along with you, give them a good, long workout and watch them bow to your strength and physical prowess.

March 11

"He prefers the security of known misery to the misery of unfamiliar insecurity."—Sheldon B. Kopp

If you're sober or even thinking about becoming sober, then you are well acquainted with the all-consuming fear of change. Personal change, especially when addictions are concerned, is next to impossible for so many people. At some point we all find ourselves at a precipice of misery. It's a misery that we know. We created it. It's comfy. But it's misery. We peer in and we decide: give up and dive in because it's what we know. Or we back up into the dark unknown, with the small hope that maybe, just maybe things will be better if we try a different pattern.

I'm going to share a story that illustrates the point. I met my friend Max for dinner. I hadn't seen him in about six years, and I was shocked to see that he had gained close to a hundred pounds. I asked him about his life (it was hard, and nothing was turning out as he planned) his job (dead-end,) his relationship (stressed because of the two other things) and then his weight. He told me that he knew his weight was an issue; that he had slowly been gaining weight because of his fast food diet. He understood that he was not okay physically or spiritually on this burger-and-lard-strewn path.

He found himself pulling into a fast food drive thru one evening and he consciously chose, in that moment, to give up. He actually made the decision to go through the drive thru, get the burger, eat the fries, suck down the shake... And in that moment he dove into his precipice. He told me he is aware of the decision he made, that he is not happy about it, but he doesn't believe that his life would be any different anyway. He's not willing to do the work of changing, and it's easier for him to not care than to shake his spirit out of its torpor.

90

I have gazed deep into the chasm of my boozing, carousing, exhaustion and insane thinking, and I decided to change. I waffled. I negotiated. I argued. I cried. I denied. I pouted. I fussed. I squirmed. But ultimately I decided to face the unknown, and so did you. You had your Max Moment and you made a different choice, despite the feelings of being unmoored, the grieving over the loss of time and the terror of trying to live differently every moment of every day.

You made the right decision. I can't promise you won't still feel fear. But I can promise you that you will feel. You will live. And you will thrive.

March 12

"How soon 'not now' becomes 'never'."—Martin Luther

Now that we know that fear is our driving emotion, it's fascinating to see all the little ways it sabotages our efforts. Did you put off getting sober for years? I did. Have you diddled around with a book you were writing but never finished? Do you have an easel, potter's wheel or sculpting tools in your garage sitting there, dusty and unused? How about a car you've been promising to fix up or a bathroom remodel that needs attention?

This is procrastination, and it is one of the most mischievous forms of fear out there. Procrastination, for me, is as cunning, baffling and powerful as my alcoholism. I face it every day, with every project or task, and sometimes it still wins.

Sitting down to work on this book, for example, brings up a flurry of other activities that *must be done right now.* Those counters aren't going to wipe themselves! Does the dog need to go out? Did I remember to put the laundry in the dryer? I can fill my whole day with a little of this and a little of that, until I'm too tired to sit down and do what it is that I am *really* supposed to do. (A few moments ago I got up to make a cup of tea.)

I procrastinate because I am afraid. I am afraid of feeling discomfort. What if the task is too difficult or it takes too long? What if I can't do it? What if I make a mistake? I am afraid of failing. Hello there, writer's block! I'm afraid of missing out. Are all my friends hanging out while I'm stuck here working/cleaning/fixing/addressing my myriad responsibilities...? I am also afraid of success. I am afraid that if I do something, anything well, I'll be asked to do it again and again.

I used to procrastinate by drinking. Once the drinking started there was no way I was going to attack my to-do list.

Your sobriety has probably revealed a few things you really want to do with your time now that you're not filling it with drinking. Is procrastination, that nasty fear-imp, keeping you from doing anything you want to do?

March 13

There are two very good ways to handle fear: take action or do nothing.

In the "take action" column you can place things like opening that unpaid bill, getting some exercise, addressing the rumor, being honest despite the consequences, making the expensive repair, taking the trip, learning the new thing, leaving the abusive relationship and shouting down the bully. You can also add learning more about sobriety, staying sober and walking away from the drink.

In the "do nothing" column let's put things like your fear that your mother will never change, that people are judging you, that you aren't good enough or pretty enough or smart enough... Don't do anything about your friends who are still actively addicted and don't want help. Don't do anything to make anyone like you more or to make yourself look good in their eyes. Don't try to convince your friend not to marry that person who is totally wrong for him/her. Don't even think of doing anything to change anyone else's personality, quirks or opinions.

Take action when your fears center on activities you can control. If you want to learn something, learn it. When you decide to buy something, save for it. If you want to clear the air about gossip, say your peace and count to ten.

But if you're scared someone will never change, or that they are about to make a terrible decision, there's usually not much you can do to affect them. When it comes to handling your fears, do nothing when there's nothing you can do.

March 14

You are safe. That's not something we normally hear. The media's sole purpose is to drum up convincing evidence to the contrary, and if you're anything like me you swallow it hook, line and sinker.

I'll linger over articles that have me convinced that the government is spying on me and that salad greens have been found to be carcinogenic. It's very easy to persuade me that the next big market crash is coming and that I will be forced to sell turnips on the street to survive.

When I get overwhelmed with the scary things that happen in the world, I take a moment to check in and see how I am doing *right now.* Am I sober today? Do I have shelter from the weather? Is there a bill due right this minute or anything else that is so important that if I don't address it immediately the Earth will spin off its axis?

The answer nearly 100% of the time is that everything is fine. That's because in reality we are all perfectly safe. We may suffer loss. We may feel physical and emotional pain. But that thing that makes us *us,* that being-ness that comes from somewhere other than biology can't ever be harmed or taken away. It's our core being, our spirit, our *soul,* if you don't mind religious syntax. The real you is safe. It is loved. And it longs to be at peace. Help it out once in a while by taking a moment to forget your fears and revel in gratitude.

March 15

In the sobriety fellowship I attend, I hear other alcoholics talk about their feelings of separateness, of being different and having to be self-reliant because they had no other choice. Relying on others can be challenging for anyone in this day and age (since we have become convinced that somehow we're all supposed to be Supermen or Superwomen), but for alcoholics it presents a whole new set of challenges. We feel alone, we always have, and the fear of reaching out to others is strong.

You are not alone. Aloneness is a myth we perpetuate to stay in our comfort zones, to paint ourselves as a victim and to create those deep wells of self-pity we alcoholics love to dive into.

You are not alone *figuratively*. There are countless other people in the world who share your same fears, desires, problems and struggles regardless of how specific your list is. You are not alone *literally*. Unless you live on hundreds of acres in the middle of nowhere, off the grid and growing your own food, you probably come into contact with several people every single day. One of the marvels of the modern era is the Internet, which effortlessly connects us with people who share our hobbies, concerns, problems and even fears in forums where we can communicate.

You are not alone. Every small action you take, each minute of every day affects someone, somewhere. Think about that. We turn on a light because someone at the power company is doing their job. Throwing a cigarette out of a car window can start a fire that blazes for days. Stopping for a pedestrian in a crosswalk can ensure that they arrive a few minutes early for their important job interview.

You are not alone. We are all connected in a web of humanity so great we couldn't possibly comprehend it from where we are sitting.

If you are struggling, reach out to someone. If you see someone struggling, reach out to them. It is through these human interactions that we discover how alike we all are, and how, truly, no one is alone.

March 16

Don't make decisions based on fear. There are usually plenty of rational reasons for doing or not doing something, so you can take fear out of your decision-making entirely.

Just this moment I experienced a fear of writing this passage. I wasn't really sure what I was going to say and if I actually had anything to say to begin with. I decided, because of my fear, that I was going to go check my Facebook page instead of writing.

I'm lucky that I caught myself. The decision to leave this page for that one was rooted in fear, and would not have been the right thing for me to do. For one, I may not have ever come back to finish.

This is a tiny moment, a miniscule example, of how fear can lead our decision-making. Fear can lead us to make small, bad choices like not going to yoga class this morning, all the way up to big ones like avoiding an important work project or, worse, having a few drinks because we're afraid of being left out.

Humans are emotional creatures so I don't suggest making all your decisions like an automaton. But if you're lingering in a bad relationship because you're scared to be alone or afraid to open those bills because you don't want to face your debt, ignore the fear and make the right decision.

March 17

Don't other people's fears seem irrational? I have a hard time believing some people are actually afraid of the things they say they are afraid of. I have one friend who is so afraid of snakes she won't go into any wilderness, anywhere, ever. Another person I know has a fear of bats so severe that any dark corner freaks her out. My stepson has a complicated relationship with heights, making going over bridges, hiking along bluffs or even climbing a ladder extremely challenging.

When it's not your fear, a fear of anything can seem a bit silly, can't it? I have what's commonly referred to as "bag lady syndrome." This is the fear that someday, due to circumstances out of my control (or my alcoholism), I will end up a bag lady living on the street. I finally confessed this fear to a friend of mine, in very serious, hushed tones, like one would if they believed they were sharing a deep, dark secret. She laughed it off, and said, "That's ridiculous. I would never let that happen to you."

"It's like being crazy," she continued. "The people who believe they're going crazy rarely are. Anyone who's afraid of being a bag lady is never going to let that happen to herself."

And in that moment, I heard how illogical my fear was. This tiny monster that I started feeding grew into something that was about to devour me, and my friend murdered it by laughing in its face.

Take some of your fears out of the closet today, dust them off and see if they are really as scary as you thought they were. Pretend that your friend, sibling or relative came to you with the same problem. How rational are some of those fears you've been nurturing all these years?

March 18

Conquer your fear! Overcome your fear! Face your fear! The only thing to fear is fear itself! (That last one always confused me...)

All this talk about going to war with our fears exhausts me. Instead, let's invite our fears in for tea. Find out where they're from. Ask a bit about their background, how they ended up here. See how long they plan on staying. Once you get to know your fears you may find them charming and harmless, like the new neighbors who moved in across the street.

March 19

"Bran thought about it. 'Can a man still be brave if he's afraid?'
'That is the only time a man can be brave,' his father told him."
— George R.R. Martin, A Game of Thrones

Our fears are merely energy waiting to be transformed into courage.

Think about where fear resides in the body. When my fears start to gin up, I usually feel an uncomfortable, almost electric, fluttering in my upper chest. I feel it any time I walk into a room full of strangers, every time I sit down at the page to write and in any situation where I am asked to do something I've never done before. This feeling is merely energy, and I can direct it any way I want.

I can feel the energy, attach emotion to it, and go curl up in a ball somewhere. Or, I can transform it into courage. As soon as I decide this physical feeling is courage in training, it feels different, more solid, more confident. I use it to move through the situation that scares me, do my very best, and come out on the other side proud of myself.

That doesn't mean that my outcomes are always perfect. But it does mean that I've had one more moment where bravery supplanted fear, and I got one more step closer to becoming the sober, confident person I've always wanted to be.

March 20

People are often fearful of something new because they don't know anything about it. Some call this "contempt prior to investigation," and I have been the victim of this way of thinking countless times.

A few years ago the company I worked for hosted a festival for our customers. One of the events was a mountain bike ride through the Napa Valley—arguably home to some of the world's most beautiful bike routes. I was asked to lead one of the small groups, but I was so fearful of looking stupid in front of these people, so afraid I would get them lost or that I wouldn't have the energy to complete the ride, that I spurned the offer. I pretended that I don't *do* that sort of thing and if they wanted someone to spend all day getting hot and dirty, they could find someone else, thank you very much. (If I am to be totally truthful, I planned on being very hungover the day of the ride.)

If I hadn't been so busy trying to prove to everyone that I was so much better than this whole thing, I would have realized that this was really a once-in-a-lifetime tour with professional bikes, skilled, knowledgeable guides and a gourmet lunch prepared by a famous chef. Far from arriving dirty and disheveled, our guests looked exhilarated, and the woman who took my place couldn't stop thanking me.

I've regretted my fear from ignorance ever since. In fact, I have taken up bike riding with a vengeance (wine country IS a wonderful place to ride). But I will never again get the opportunity to take that fantastic trip, all because my fear and my drinking kept me from investigating what it was really all about.

What opportunities are you missing because your fear keeps you from learning more about them?

March 21

If you're feeling angry feelings toward someone or something, take some time to get to the root of the fear behind it. Do this before it morphs into hate.

The most extreme form of fear transforming to anger is with hate groups that organize to violently attack a group they perceive as wrong, bad, different or as taking something from them. My guess is that if you are involved in this kind of activity, you're not reading this book. So let's stick to examples that may be helpful.

Recently I pulled my 12-year-old stepson out of private school for financial reasons. I simply wasn't able to keep up with the payments anymore and that fact, combined with my stepson's insistence that he would prefer the local middle school, made it pretty easy to decide to transfer him. We were both happy with this decision.

What I didn't count on was the vehement resistance from his school. Not only did they not transfer his records as requested, but on two separate occasions they insisted that I pay for the entire year, despite the fact that we were transferring.

I got angry. Ears steaming, nostrils flaring, foot stomping angry. Not only did they express no concern over the fact that my stepson was leaving the class, they were only concerned about putting the screws to me for money I didn't believe that I owed. My anger ruined a couple of perfectly nice, sunny days.

Knowing that anger is like drinking poison and waiting for the other person to die, I tried to figure out what the root of my issue was. Well, it was two things: One, I was afraid they would come after me for money I couldn't afford to pay. Two, I was afraid they judged me because I admitted I was struggling financially.

When I processed my fear in this situation, I allowed myself to feel a bit afraid and a bit icky. Then I realized that their reaction was based on fear, as well. The school is small, they have lost quite a few teachers in the past few months and new students aren't exactly banging down the front door (for the aforementioned financial reasons happening in my town). They were frightened that my son's departure would be one more loss that they may not be able to endure. Fear met fear and erupted in anger on both parts.

Anger is fear gone wild. Hate is fear gone completely off the rails. When you feel anger rising up, use this very important indicator to identify and work with the fear behind it. Once you get adept at that, you can identify the fear that creates the anger in others, and work to create the peaceful encounters you deserve in sobriety.

March 22

Although we may not choose what time to go to work, where the kids have to be, when to do the laundry or the other 1,000 things that demand our attention, we have remarkable control over how we actually spend our thoughts.

No matter what is happening around us externally, we have a rich internal life that includes revelations, opinions, thought processes, habits, resentments and, of course, fears. And this is a partial list. We can have hundreds of different thoughts, decisions and opinions fighting for recognition any given second.

So which ones are you going to single out and lavish with attention? Are you going to take those debilitating fears for a walk around the block so they can build up their strength? Maybe those resentments need a little dry material so they can grow from a tiny flame into a raging wildfire.

I'd like to suggest that you put joy and gratitude in a sunny window and watch them grow together. Your ability to forgive could use a bit of polish. Your capacity to bring peace and serenity would really like a day out doing something special just for you. How are you going to spend your thoughts today?

March 23

In Africa they say that if you see a lion crouching in the bushes and growling at you, run toward it.

The reason for this is that, when hunting, lions send the oldest and least agile of the pride to confront their prey. They roar that terrible roar. The roar frightens the prey; the prey turns and runs the other way—right into the waiting jaws of a handful of muscular, teenage lions perfectly adept at ripping things to shreds.

This is a great way to look at your fears. You see them there, waiting for you in the grass, with that old familiar roar. Head toward the beast. It's got no real power. Run toward it, and you'll most likely scare it to death. Your fear won't have seen this coming.

Better to run toward the fear you see, flying past it while it tries to gather itself, than to run blindly into a trap you set for yourself by avoiding the reality of what's in front of you.

March 24

Like everything in this world, fear isn't all bad. A healthy, balanced sense of fear, the kind you are close to having now that you're sober, is a tremendous tool to be used for good.

Fear that you'll drink again is what gets you out of the crazy party and home again to your warm tea and cozy bed. Fear of losing a good relationship can teach us to compromise, to be a better listener and to have more compassion. Fear that we're going to die one day gets us to Europe for that special trip, convinces us to paint the landscapes we love, write the book that's inside us or build the business we've always dreamed of owning.

Fear of getting sick and dying a miserable, unlovable drunk is what got me sober.

In my case, fear led me to my alcoholism and fear led me out. In sobriety, I work to continually balance healthy fear and irrational fear. I use the healthy fear to make my life work better. The irrational fears are my teachers. Diffusing them makes my spirit work better.

March 25

There are two kinds of people in the world: Those who have had their greatest fear happen to them, and those who are still afraid that it will.

Losing a spouse, losing a parent, losing a child, your own death—these are all fears that plague us. The house burning down, a cancer diagnosis, divorce... These are common fears and, fortunately, they don't happen to all of us, at least not in quite the ways we worry they will.

What happens to us when our greatest fear materializes? If you're alcoholic, first you find a support group to keep you sober. Second, you will find that your fear has morphed into something painful, misunderstood and deeply transformative: grief.

Nursing our fears about loss and pain are only useful insofar as they help us prepare for the possibility that they will come true. These fears are actionable in the most instructive way. Prepare detailed documents and wills that specifically address what will happen to you and your family in the incident of an accident. Get fire insurance and place your valuables in a fireproof box. Read about healthy, cancer fighting foods. Have a deep talk with your partner about what you both value in a marriage and make sure you both want to be there.

100% of us will experience grief at some point in our lives. You can prepare for this, too. Read books about grief. I personally love *How to Survive the Loss of a Love*, by Melba Colgrove, Ph.D., Harold Bloomfield, M.D. and Peter McWilliams. It's a great resource for dealing with death of a loved one, passing of a beloved pet or relationship breakups. Talk to a counselor about your fears of facing loss and grief.

Nothing can totally prepare you for the emotional impact of grief, but by reaching out now you can at least have some resources on which to rely.

Don't worry. Don't fret. Take action. Plan. Prepare. And sleep well at night knowing the thing you fear most will probably never, ever happen.

March 26

What would a life be without fear at all? The Buddhists call this enlightenment, and I have to think they know what they are talking about. To enlighten yourself can be interpreted as *making yourself lighter.* Fear can feel like a yoke around your neck or lead weights holding you in place.

I've always loved the image of the Boston Tea Party. All those revolutionaries faced a very real fear (the retribution of the British Crown). They started tossing those casks overboard anyway, without knowing that in the long run everything would work out. *They had no idea, and they did it anyway.* Their fear took a back seat to their desire to be fairly treated, and, if we must be honest, have a bit of a hissy fit. Their experience was a literal way of tossing their fears overboard and getting on with what's next.

Invite some enlightenment in. Throw your fears overboard and see what happens next. Everything will be fine. (And maybe even revolutionary.)

March 27

I don't fear death. I fear not experiencing everything I want to experience before I die. I fear physical pain. I fear being maimed. But I don't fear death itself.

When I was 13 years old my family was ejected from a raft during a whitewater rafting trip. I couldn't get out from under the raft and, in that moment, I knew I was going to die. As I accepted what I thought was an irrefutable fact, I was overcome by an incredible sense of serenity. I wasn't worried at all. I felt grateful for my time on Earth, and I relaxed into whatever was coming next. I released control.

I don't know how I got out from under the raft, but I do remember breaking the surface and swimming toward the shore. I was fearless. I had faced what I thought was death, and, assuming that was the worst thing that would happen to me that day, I took the moment and swam my face off. Obviously I survived.

None of us gets out of this alive. Our death is inevitable, and I think what delivers that heavy dose of fear is that you never know when it's coming and that it might *hurt.*

What I learned from my experience was that when I'm facing the inevitable, the thing that brings me a feeling of safety and peace is letting go. When my fears threaten to overwhelm me, I stop swimming against the flood and join in the flow. Amazingly, I always land on shore, refreshed, rejuvenated and ready for the next experience life throws me.

March 28

This is a fun game. When I am really struggling with fear-based thoughts, I approach my fear as if it is perfectly logical, realistic and reasonable. I then follow it to its inevitable conclusion. The process goes something like this:

- I have public speaking engagement tomorrow.
- I am afraid I will forget what I am saying, or that what I am saying is totally stupid. I am afraid that everyone in the room will judge me, say terrible things and that they will make fun of me.
- I make a mistake, and some of my facts are wrong. The crowd laughs hysterically and points. They are each leaning into each other, whispering words like "ridiculous," "stupid," and "unprofessional."
- People walk out, muttering that this was a total waste of time.
- A handful of rowdies standing near the buffet start chucking tomatoes at me.
- I flee from the room and run to my car. I ring my boss to get sympathy.
- She has already heard from our colleagues. She expresses her disappointment, says she's made a terrible mistake, and fires me.
- While heating a can of soup over a flame because my electricity has been turned off, I burn my hand. Not only can I not use the library computer for a few weeks, putting me behind in my job search, but the hand gets infected. I haven't seen a doctor because I no longer have health insurance.
- The infection is gangrene and they amputate my hand from the wrist down. I can probably still work as a one-handed writer, but it's going to be a lot tougher.

- The medical bills are tens of thousands of dollars. I file for bankruptcy. I lose my house.
- I am now a one-handed, unemployed woman living in my car. One winter night a friend allows me to park in her garage. I turn on the heat, and die in my car from carbon monoxide poisoning.

This process always makes me feel better because it's SO RIDICULOUS. It's okay to feel a bit anxious sometimes, but allowing yourself to be ruled by fear seems silly when you play it out to your worst-case scenario.

March 29

"You want to change your life? Control the only thing you can control: the meaning you give something." —Tony Robbins

Coddling our fears often results in a desire to control everything. Our parents are over-controlling because they fear for our safety, and we turn around and behave this way with our kids. We try to control our employees or our co-workers because we fear they will screw up and make us look bad or lose the company money. Our desire to control traffic results in anger that can lead to road rage.

Our fear-based controlling behaviors remind me of grabbing a fistful of water and trying to hold onto it by clenching tighter and tighter. Wouldn't it be easier to release your grip and cup the water gently in the bowl of your hand? You can make adjustments when it splashes over here or over there, but mostly you're allowing the water to rest lightly and be what it is.

If you manage fear by controlling things, making this shift could be very scary for you. Those of us who behave that way truly believe that if we let go for a single second the world will spin off into oblivion.

I am going to let you in on a secret: nothing you work to control is ever under your control anyway. Not for one second.

You have very little real control over the way life will unfold for you or for those around you. Your fretting, worrying, planning and anxiety may be appreciated (though most people find it annoying), but it rarely changes the outcome. So many moving parts are involved in every situation, and you will never predict all of them. So how can you possibly control anything?

Give up the illusion of control and you will be that much closer to a joyful, fear-free life. (And your friends and family will thank you for chilling out.)

March 30

My ego doesn't like all of this open communication about fear. My alcoholism is very bummed that I have been taking a step farther from it every single day. My ego wants be to be afraid. My alcoholism wants me to be sick. The two together are a dynamic duo that delivered blow after blow to me for years. I was afraid so I'd drink. I was sick so I'd drink. I was afraid of being sick and sick of being afraid, and I would drink to alleviate these fears.

This might be a pattern that is familiar to you, and the idea that you are thinking about sobriety or achieving sobriety is already a triumph over your fear-based life. If you can be honest enough with yourself to attempt to tame this beast, you can be honest enough to conquer all of your demons in whatever way works best for you.

What does a fear-free life look like? I haven't personally experienced a totally fear-free existence, and I assume it's different for everyone depending on the day anyway. Being honest about my fears is helping me overcome years of drunkenness. Facing my fears has opened my eyes to incredible experiences like learning to figure skate, taking up running, writing books and improving my relationships.

As we transition into spring, let some light in on your fears. The more light you shine, the more they'll scurry into dark corners and disappear.

March 31

"Thinking will not overcome fear, but action will."—W. Clement Stone

Transforming fear into love, kindness, or even neutrality is a lifelong process that could take your attention every single day. In order to be successful at managing our fears we must take continual action.

You already know about this. By getting sober you took action to overcome your fear of living without your addictive substance. You tackled your fear of the unknown by taking action to overcome it.

If you're a fan of the satirical news site *The Onion*, you may have seen an article that proclaimed something like "Best Cure for Depression is Sitting Around and Thinking All Day." I'm paraphrasing, but the point is that even the comedians know that to overcome negative feelings we have to *do* something.

You can attach actions to fears in a couple of ways. You can face them like you faced sobriety, seeking out help and wisdom to guide you through them. You can create a plan that has smaller steps and gives you small goals to achieve over time. For example, when I was first starting out in my career I was intimidated by speaking in front of my much older colleagues. I signed up for a public speaking club and I attended meetings every month, learning the skills I needed to overcome my fear.

Or, you can jump right in. Scared of heights? Time for a walk across the Golden Gate Bridge. Spiders make you squirm? Meet some people who keep them as pets and learn all the interesting facts about them.

Whether fast or slow, bullet-pointed or all-at-once, the only way to take control of your fear is to stop thinking and start doing.

April
Unleash Your Creativity

April 1

All humans are intensely creative. For over a decade my creativity manifested itself primarily in how I would choose to booze. I could create the most intriguing itinerary of food-and-wine-related fun. My parties—everything from Halloween bashes to baby showers—were bursting with boozy games, boozy party favors and boozy challenges. I created a game called Drinking Jenga. Each block had a different embarrassing drinking-related task on it and when you pulled it you had to do it. I was an endless font of fabulous drinking ideas, and I executed every single one.

Imagine if I had been able to channel that energy into work that actually elevates the spirit rather than smothers it? I wasted so much effort on getting myself effortlessly wasted.

Perhaps you weren't quite the Belle of the Booze Ball like I was, but my guess is that you spent countless hours devising ways to drink. Whether it was hidden or out in the open, the fact is that alcoholic drinking requires a lot of creative initiative. Hiding your drinking is like the wizard level of alcoholism. Finding places to stash the stash, remembering, when drunk, where the stash *is*... The emotional devastation of finding out that your hidden treasure is gone, having already been consumed by you... All Herculean tasks.

Drinking in the open is a little less daunting, but still exhausting. Talking people into staying out a little later with you, identifying the people in your office who are game for an after work cocktail and pretending like you're always having dinner parties to the cashier at your corner market are all genius-level creative endeavors.

If you begin to take a fraction of the effort it took to drink and channel it into a soul-feeding artistic effort, you will create something of such magnificent beauty you'll never be able to look at the world the same way again. Even if you think the result sucks (it won't) the process of change you will experience by *doing the work* will provide you with one more solid brick in your foundation of sobriety.

April 2

So many of our revered creative heroes have had substance abuse issues. Great performers like Billie Holliday and writers like Ernest Hemingway, F. Scott Fitzgerald and Jack London were all widely known for using booze in their creative processes. Artist Jackson Pollock was an art-world superstar and uncontrollable lush.

We can look at these examples and try to justify the use of chemicals in our own creative process, but if we dig a little deeper we'll see that substance abuse actually hinders most artists.

Billie Holliday died of a lethal combination of alcohol and heroin. Hemingway blew his brains out with a shotgun. Fitzgerald died of an alcohol-related heart attack (he claimed to have tuberculosis, which was suspected to be a cover for his drinking). Jack London perished after a morphine overdose. He was prescribed the drug to deal with the pain of renal failure, which was brought on by alcoholism. Pollock drunkenly drove himself and two other people into an oak tree.

There's nothing glamorous about addiction. There's nothing amusing or interesting about alcoholism. And there's nothing inherently creative about getting loaded. Anyone can toss back shots. But only a very few people can sing like Billie, write like Papa or paint like Pollock. Imagine all of the creative work these geniuses could have continued to contribute if only they had lived. Imagine the creative heights they could have reached while sober.

Your sobriety is destined to be the cornerstone of your creativity. Sobriety's calm serenity, its unwavering focus and its boundless energy will help you pull from the deep well of creativity that resides within you.

April 3

The only thing you need in order to start on a creative journey is a desire to discover what you are capable of. Your sobriety may already be nudging your spirit into new ways of being, and that's the perfect jumping off point for making your entire sober life a creative endeavor.

There are infinite ways to express creativity. The most obvious pursuits are writing, painting, drawing, photography, music, quilting, pottery—that sort of thing. But maybe the "artistic" forms of creativity aren't your bailiwick. You can also bring enormous creativity to a new business idea, organizing your home, cooking, managing your finances or volunteering. Get creative in your choice of a creative pursuit, and don't limit yourself to just the arty and crafty ones. From setting up systems that work to making pretty places, the world needs creative thinkers at every level.

April 4

When I first decided I wanted to be a writer (right about the same time I got sober the first time), I joined a writers group called The Red Room Writers Society. Led by a brilliant creative thinker named Ivory Madison, this group had a simple theory about writing that went something like this:

"Studying writing isn't writing. Reading about writing isn't writing. Thinking about writing isn't writing. Critiquing writing isn't writing. Only writing is writing."

This group of writers at every level, from beginner to bestselling authors, would get together and *write*. For one hour. At the end of the hour, we'd pack up our computers or pads of paper and go home. We didn't share our writing. At all.

You learn the most about any creative activity simply by doing it. If you want to learn to cook, go make a recipe right now. Then make another. And another. Think you have what it takes to make beautiful photos? Put this book down right now and go snap some pictures. You're probably also a financial genius who could make a killing on the stock market. Go invest something, any amount, and learn how the financial system works by participating in it.

Don't think. Don't justify. Don't rationalize. Stop reading about it. Just do it.

April 5

"I don't have time!"—Everybody

Here's a funny way to look at things. You have as many hours in every day as everyone else does. Each one of us gets a magical 24 hours every single day to do with what we can to bring ourselves joy and happiness.

If you think you don't have time to pursue a creative endeavor I am forced to ask you this: how much time did you spend drinking and using?

I haven't actually counted the hours that I spent shoving Gewürztraminer down my gullet, but it's safe to say that I spent at least five hours a day for about ten years doing nothing but drinking.

Five hours a day for ten years is just over 18,000 hours. The average 250-page novel is written in about 75 hours. In that time I could have written 243 books.

This is hyperbolic, of course, to serve the greater point. We do have time. Maybe it's an hour a day, or maybe we're lucky and have five hours a day. Maybe we have five minutes to brainstorm business ideas. Perhaps we can take the painting out of the closet, put it on the easel and mix the colors we'll use tomorrow. Maybe you could volunteer for service at your church or in your sobriety fellowship.

We all have the same amount of hours in the day. You have to decide, now that you're sober, the best way to use yours.

April 6

In her book, *The Creative Habit*, Choreographer Twyla Tharp talks about the importance of ritual in the artistic life.

What's refreshing is her take on the idea of ritual. Far from flailing about in the back yard, drumming topless on the beach or burying a cow's horn in the earth every harvest moon, Tharp believes that your *daily* ritual is the one simple thing that sets the jumping off point for the work of the day.

Every morning, she arises at 5:30, gets dressed in her dancer-y clothes, heads to the street outside her Manhattan home, hails a cab and goes to the gym for two hours. Every morning. After her workout she spends the rest of the day choreographing, dancing, listening to music or whatever creative endeavor she is called upon to do.

So the gym is her ritual? Makes sense. Working out is a great way to set the tone for the day. But that's not how she sees it. Her ritual is *getting in the cab*. It's simple, easy to reproduce the exact same way every day and foolproof. There is virtually no good excuse for skipping it. And that's why it works.

The strategy is so brilliant and effective in its ease, that it makes you wonder why we all don't do the same thing. Maybe you already do. In your sobriety have you incorporated a morning prayer or meditation into your day? Perhaps that could be your ritual. Maybe it's getting in the shower every morning, no matter what. I make my bed when I wake up, even on weekends. That simple thirty-second act makes me feel that I've closed a chapter and am opening another, more exciting one.

Maybe you can relate to this: before I got sober I had a ritual I wouldn't ever miss, even if I were being threatened at knife point.

My ritual was popping a cork. That satisfying sound signaled the end of my stressful workday and the beginning of "me" time. Was your ritual similar? The clinking of ice cubes, perhaps, or getting to the corner bar at a certain time? We've had rituals. And now that we're sober, it's time to start looking at ritual in a completely different way.

What ritual can you create that will help put you in a creative frame of mind every day?

April 7

One of the most glaring things I've noticed now that I am sober is how drinkers are always talking about what they are "gonna" do. I've been at countless parties, swirling around my club soda, listening to conversations devolve into utterly boring nonsense, mostly political. But what really gets my attention is how motivated people become to take charge of their lives when they're drunk off their gourd.

Recently I stumbled into an "I'm gonna" minefield. My host, who had three or four beers before I even arrived at noon, lamented his recent weight gain, which was significant. "I'm gonna start training for a footrace," he says. "I'm gonna cut down on drinking and start trail running," he exclaims. "I'm gonna get my bike out and ride it every day," he promises. But wait for it... Here's the kicker...

"But I guess I'll start tomorrow."

If you think I'm being a little harsh, keep in mind that this same host was "gonna" build a voice-over studio in his garage, send his headshots to casting agencies in order to get small acting jobs and take up martial arts again. The truth is that he will never do any of these things because he drinks instead.

Now that you're sober, you have no reason to be a "gonna." Don't talk about anything you plan to do. Do it, and the show off the magnificent results! It's always more interesting to talk to someone who has *already done something* than someone who *wants to do something*. Wantin' ain't doin'. Now prove it!

April 8

"It is almost impossible to be honest and boring at the same time."
—Julia Cameron

It's impossible to get sober without getting honest. One morning you woke up and saw yourself for what you really were: addicted. That moment of truth compelled you to straighten out and set forth on a journey that would change every aspect of your life.

If you're looking for creative inspiration, look for the honesty in what you want to express. Without honesty your work will never be a true reflection of who you are. Never try to do something a certain way because you think that's how it's done. How would *you* do it? What would *you* say? What rhyme would *you* create? Not your English professor, not your music teacher, not your next-door neighbor. You.

There is no way that anything you create from a place of total honesty will ever be boring. There is no way that you will fail on any path if you are honest from the get-go. It's not always easy, but it is simple. And the straight truth is never, ever dull.

April 9

To eat an elephant, so the saying goes, take one bite at a time.

It's easy to get overwhelmed when you have a big idea for a big project. Unfortunately what happens to most of us is that we see this huge responsibility looming before us and we run the other way rather than figuring out how to overcome it.

One bite at a time. Sounds like some other really good advice, doesn't it?

Eat that elephant one bite at a time. Paint your picture one stroke at a time. Write your song one note at a time. Complete your novel one sentence at a time.

When you feel overwhelmed by a project, or by life in general, step back and ask yourself what you can do right this minute to get yourself a tiny step closer to your goal.

What bite can you take right now?

April 10

I know a person who is a very talented artist. He can paint, draw and design beautifully. He rarely does these things, however, because he is more focused on getting his office perfect, his studio completed, or filling his workspaces with every imaginable gadget one would need to design a modern-day Sistine Chapel. His studio and all of his workspaces appear to house a professional artist, but he hardly produces a thing.

I know another person who is a writer. She has been writing fiction every day since she was six years old, and she reads about seven books a week. If you took away her office, she would write in the kitchen. If you took away her computer, she would write on a typewriter. If you took away her typewriter and paper, she would write with a pen on a cocktail napkin. Throw her on a deserted island, and she would write in the sand with a stick. And so on...

My one friend wants to *look like* an artist. My other friend actually *is* a writer (and she's published over 60 novels).

When you embark on your creative journey, as with your sobriety, check in with yourself to make sure you're doing the work and not trying to *look like* you're doing the work. If you find yourself obsessed with having the perfect laptop or chair before you get started, take a moment to find out if this creative endeavor is what you really want to do.

I'm all for high tech gadgets, beautiful workspaces and fancy thingamajigs, but don't let the appearance of work get in the way of your real work.

April 11

In November a group of strangers join together on the Internet for National Novel Writing Month (NaNoWriMo). Each person commits to writing a 50,000-word novel in one month flat.

Now, these novels don't always turn out well. I completed my 50,000-word novel during NaNoWriMo, and I can still smell it from here.

But what I learned was this: keep going. Finish no matter what, because completing something is the best feeling in the world.

I can always go back to my novel and spruce it up if I feel like it. The point is that I completed it. I actually *did* that. I didn't just *want* to do it. I didn't just say I was *going* to do it. I did it! And even though my effort will (probably) never win a Pulitzer, I learned everything more about persistence, tenacity, when to edit, when not to edit and follow-through than with any other experience of my life.

Pick a project. Give yourself a time limit to complete it. Then work like crazy to get it done. You'll be so proud!

April 12

No one ever achieved greatness without first falling on their face. Failure can be one of your life's greatest gifts as long as you allow it to teach you.

If you're in a sobriety program, it's likely that you've heard people introduce themselves as a grateful alcoholic. That's because they realize that this massive failure, their alcoholism, was the gateway to a life of gratitude, serenity and spirituality. They learned from their failure, and now they know the difference between a life of desperation and a life of inspiration.

I am a grateful alcoholic and I can also call myself a grateful failed artist. My paintings are a disaster. My writing has only been self-published (and I am deeply grateful for every single person who has ever read my books). I tried crafting, and had a disastrous experience with, a glue gun that has made me gun shy ever since.

But I learned something from each of those projects. I learned about color theory (and my inability to put it into practice) from my attempts at painting. My attempts at conventional publishing failed, but I learned incredible things about how to pace my stories, grab the reader's attention and include details that make a story come to life. I also learned that I should never be left alone with a glue gun.

Every success leaves behind a string of failures. The difference is that successful people use their failures to their advantage. They learn from them.

What have your failures taught you?

April 13

Suffer for your art as little as possible. After years and years of physical pain, emotional drama and spiritual sickness brought on by my alcoholism, I refuse to create suffering where there is none. That includes my creative pursuits.

I'm not saying don't pour your whole self into your endeavor. I am suggesting that the image of the suffering artist is a tired, outdated cliché. Even if you're exploring difficult topics through writing, painting, music, poetry or even quilting (I have a sober friend who refers to herself as a "blackout quilter"), find the bliss in our shared human and express it to its fullest. If you're bringing a creative mind to your service, volunteer work or a business venture, dig in to the enthusiasm of trying something new. Feel good about it. Don't suffer.

I invite you to be joyful, be brave and be ecstatic. I invite you to be sober for one more day, and to put aside your suffering. It's time you felt the rapture you deserve.

April 14

I attended a conference where the keynote speaker was Daniel Handler, a.k.a. Lemony Snicket, author of *A Series of Unfortunate Events*.

I have been to several writers' conferences, and they are all basically the same. Everyone is milling around trying to get in good with agents and sucking up to the published authors. There's always some sort of Q & A period with the keynote speaker and the same five questions get asked again and again.

1) How did you get published?
2) Where do you get your ideas?
3) Who are your favorite authors?
4) What are you currently working on? And finally...
5) How do you stay motivated to work?

Handler gave the most masterful response to this final question that I have ever heard. He said:

"Why would I have to motivate myself to work? I love writing, so motivation is very easy to find. If you, sir, are having trouble motivating yourself to write, perhaps you don't really want to be a writer."

If you've taken on a creative project that doesn't light your fire, why waste time trying to motivate yourself? It's possible that you like the idea of the project more than you like the work. Throughout your drinking you've already struggled enough trying to make square pegs fit into round holes. Now is the time to find the thing that gives you a sense of effortless joy. If you aren't thrilled by what you're doing there's no shame in putting it down and finding something else you truly love to do.

April 15

Tax day has arrived, and I'm thinking about how we pay for all of the choices we make. Some of us write a big check to the government, some of us get a check back, but somewhere in all the hullaballoo, Uncle Sam has taken a chunk out of our earnings whether we're paying attention or not.

For years I paid a drunk tax. I paid it literally by spending money on booze, which is always taxed at a very high rate. I paid it physically by expending wasted energy on being drunk, thinking about being drunk and recovering from being drunk. I paid it spiritually by draining myself so completely of any imagination, kindness and courage that there's no way I could have found a connection to the universe at that time.

Now that I am sober I pay much more attention to what I'm paying out. I harness my energy for creative projects. I foster compassion by being a better listener to my friends, family and children. I build strength and guts by challenging myself to be better, think better, act better and do better.

I am still taxed every single day. But the beauty is, now that I am sober, the tax I spend comes right back into my bank. I no longer waste my moments on resentment, anger and selfishness. Instead, I invest in love, patience and kindness. You should see how it grows.

April 16

Shortly after I got sober for real (the third try, if you must know) I joined a group of women who were reading *The Artist's Way* by Julia Cameron. Her brilliant book lays out a series of exercises and techniques that not only foster the creative process, but also reinforce the deep belief that we are all indeed artists. Her method is brilliant, and it has helped thousands of artists build foundations of creativity, confidence and imagination.

I had read the book before and had already incorporated a number of her methods into my writing process. At this point in my life I was less interested in growing as an artist (though still interested). I was more interested in growing as an athlete (I am a fanatic ice skater, runner and biker). As I futzed and fussed with this text, which I felt I already knew, I started thinking about the creative process for the athlete and how some of the same principles can apply.

Athletes struggle with the same self-doubt, ego pressures, fear of looking stupid and fear of failure. They also struggle with how to handle success, how to stay motivated and how to break through blocks and solve problems. Like artists, all of the hard work of being an athlete is usually done alone. Early morning runs. Practice through the night. Spending 17 Saturdays in a row perfecting a kick, a swing, a posture... Athletes and artists have so much in common. The expression of an artistic soul and the expression of physical exertion are both uncommonly beautiful.

Athleticism is as much of a building block of my sobriety as are my artistic projects. I try to bring creativity to my physical projects by adjusting a bit here or there, finding new routes, adding new figures... Now that I am sober, I find opportunities everywhere to express creativity. How can you look at your athletic practice more creatively?

April 17

Write like a motherf*cker.—Cheryl Strayed

Well, okay then. You can't read Cheryl Strayed's book *Wild*, her memoir of a transformational hike along the Pacific Crest Trail, without thinking that if this woman offers advice you should take it.

The advice I found from her, and it's emblazoned on T-shirts and mugs and all kinds of tchotchkes, is: "Write like a motherf*cker."

I'm not even entirely sure what it means, but there's something about the emotional force behind the words that motivates and inspires me. When I sit down at the page, I decide to write like a motherf*cker, and then I do just that.

What's funny is that if you had seen me three years ago and suggested that I should drink like a motherf*cker, I would know exactly what you were talking about. I would then *do it very well*, and wake up with nothing to show for my time except degradation, panic, physical pain and humiliation.

So I think I've made a bit of progress. At least now I have some words on a page.

What can you do like a motherf*cker? Draw? Paint? Sing? Sew? Run? Dance? Play? Pedal? Cook? Sculpt?

Pick something today and do it like a motherf*cker.

April 18

Before we become great at anything, whether it's singing, songwriting or sewing, you have to learn the basics. We learn the basics by copying what someone else has already done.

Getting sober is a radically creative act. And depending on how you initially went about it, there was probably some hardcore copying going on. I copied other sober people. I did exactly what they did because I lacked the imagination to do it on my own.

I copied until my own spin started to show through. Solid in the basic principles I learned by rote of how to be a sober person, my own personality, imagination, philosophies and twists started to shine. Eventually my sobriety became my own.

Copy artists you like or admire. If your favorite is Picasso, try out your own blue period. If you love Bob Dylan, try writing a folk song in his style. Copy the meter, the chords—all of it—until you find yourself discovering your own fingerprint.

Perhaps someone at work is getting positive attention you want for yourself. What can you learn from their behavior that you can incorporate into your own projects or behavior? How can you copy the successful people around you?

Fashion Designer Yohji Yamamoto says, "Start copying what you love. Copy, copy, copy, copy. At the end of the copy, you will find yourself."

April 19

I'm going to contradict myself over the next two days of April musings, but it's for the greater artistic good. Today I'd like to suggest ways for you to get inspired.

During my drinking decade, I always believed that the next drink would be *the one* that led to the lightning bolt. If I had another, stayed up a little longer, talked a bit more with this person or with that person, I would get the BIG idea that would change everything. Every ounce of my hope for creative inspiration was poured down my throat in the form of Chardonnay (and the occasional Viognier, for very special occasions). Guess what? The idea never came. And frankly, I wouldn't have had the energy to pursue it anyway.

In sobriety, not only do I have copious amounts of time that I have to fill with non-drinking, but I have the clarity to embrace the inspiration that surrounds me.

For example, I recently attended an art exhibit of works by a group of local developmentally disabled people. The work was stunning, and the stories behind each piece were so touching and real. Then, I noticed that some crafty folks had knit-bombed a few of our downtown signposts and trees. I read in the paper shortly after that that some clever soul had been putting up knee-high gnome paintings all over Oakland, and a poet had been placing hearts with inspirational sayings all over the city of Napa.

You can look at beautiful photos online, listen to music, read things you think may not even be interesting to you, only to find that pretty much everything is fascinating. You can take a walk and read the flyers at the local coffee shop that advertise drumming circles or Tai Chi classes or *plein air* painting groups. People are out there *doing stuff* right this very minute. There they are, waiting to inspire you.

April 20

Don't wait for inspiration. (I told you I was going to contradict myself.)

If I had waited for the stars to align, my job to be perfect and for all the stress in my life to evaporate before I got sober it never would have happened. Maybe some people have that experience, the one where the voice of God thunders from the heavens and points The Way. My experience is that there are no epiphanies, only small daily steps that bring you closer to your goal.

Our sobriety is a one-day-at-a-time experience. I wake up every morning and re-commit to this decision and, although it was white-knuckle there for a while, after time it became part of my daily life. No big whoop.

The most successful creative people work on their projects every single day. They may be in a shitty mood, the water heater is leaking or their kids are hell bent on making them miserable, but they sit down to the work anyway. They don't wait for the inspiration because they know that the inspiration comes out of the work.

There are two perfect examples of this in action. Charles M. Schulz, creator of the *Peanuts* comics, worked in his office seven hours a day, five days a week, no matter what. Over time, by showing up at the page every day with his pen, he crafted nearly 18,000 comics. Charles Schulz didn't become the king of comics by tearing his hair out, thrashing around and waiting for the voice of the universe to speak to him. He approached his work calmly and like a business, one day at a time.

Comedian Jerry Seinfeld has a similar outlook on the creative process. He has a yearlong wall calendar. Every day, he sits down to write new material. When he's done he marks a big red "X" over the day. His job is not to pour forth life changing material straight from the mind of the creator; his job is simply to make that "X." And after a while he has a treasure trove of material to choose from, all because he refuses to break that chain of Xs. He writes jokes one day at a time.

Don't wait to be inspired. Get started, don't break the chain and the inspiration will come.

April 21

"It ain't what you do, it's the way that you do it."—Sy Oliver and Trummy Young

Good luck finding an idea that's never been done before. There's nothing new under the sun, so they say, and that's mostly true. Originality in this day and age all boils down to execution.

Every single romance story has the *exact same plot*: boy meets girl, boy loses girl, boy gets girl back. The only difference is the personalities of the characters, the humor (or lack of it), whether there are vampires or zombies involved... Most pop songs are the same three chords. People have covered canvases with paint, animal parts, bodily fluids—you name it and an artist somewhere has tried to smash it onto the wall. Chefs have been screwing around with the same ingredients for hundreds of years, and so can you!

So forget having to come up with the next big thing. Do the thing that is authentic to you in the way only *you* can. The originality comes from inside you when you add your unique voice, eye, ear or palate to your project. Now that you're sober those quirks, traits and gifts that *only you have* should be yours for the taking.

April 22

One of my favorite personal finance philosophies is the idea that we achieve our goals incrementally. I latch onto this idea because I see that it *works*. I eschew the epiphany, the get-rich-quick-scheme and the lightning bolt of creativity. I believe in putting in a penny a day and watching it grow into a fortune over the next decade.

One of the most popular examples of this is the "Latte Factor." It's the idea that if you cut out your one $3.00 latte a day habit at the coffee shop, by the end of a year you will have saved nearly $1100.

This obviously works with sobriety, no question. I have a little counter on my smartphone and I check in with it every day to see how many, days, months and minutes I have been bone dry. It's satisfying.

Let's apply this idea to time that could be applied to creativity. What can you cut out that's stealing time from what you really want to accomplish? Is the two hours of TV a night something you forego in order to work on something that fulfills your soul? Could you take the train instead of drive so that you can spend that time doodling, writing or brainstorming? Do you head to the mall when you need a pick-me-up rather than picking up your guitar? Have you achieved level-200 brilliance at a video game when it's really your dream to develop an app that sells to millions?

Never underestimate the power of incremental work. A little time every single day will get you that much closer to your creative goals, your spiritual fulfillment or your dreams of business success.

April 23

An artistic temperament and addiction can go hand in hand. Outsized egos combined with constant rejection leads to pity parties, jealousies and resentments, which, as you know, leads to empty vodka bottles clanking around in the bin. It's no surprise that the creatively inclined lean on substances to help them cope. When you're that sensitive everything hurts.

But there is no proof that the addiction aids the creative process. It's possible that some of our greatest geniuses were actually hamstrung by their boozing, and they never achieved their full capacity. Sadly, we'll never know in most cases.

But we're here, we're creative and we're sober. And so are countless other creative, intelligent, successful people. As if I needed to convince you that sobriety is the cornerstone of creativity, here are few of my favorite creators who are completely clean and sober:

Julia Cameron, Author, The Artist's Way. From a rollercoaster life of writing on drugs and alcohol, a disastrous marriage to Martin Scorsese and a plunge into the tortured existence of a Hollywood climber, Cameron is now a prolific writer and a central figure in the creative recovery movement.

Warren Buffet, Billionaire. A famous teetotaler, Buffet channels his prodigious creative energy into creating massive wealth.

Jane Lynch, Funniest Person Alive. Star of *Glee* and amazing comedic actress in an array of hilarious films, Jane Lynch sobered up in her 30s and hasn't looked back.

Robert Downey, Jr., Actor. My love for Robert Downey, Jr. has continued unabated for nearly 25 years. We've been through a lot together. From his total meltdown to his jail time, I never waivered in my support, although my alcoholism really took off as his was getting addressed. He's been sober for years and he has not only regained his career, but he has become an international superstar. I still love him.

Tilda Swinton, Actress. So strange, so chic and so talented, Tilda Swinton has been one of my teetotaler heroes for years. Part of the reason I got sober was because I read she never drinks. It's weird to admit that, but it's true. If you've never seen her in the film *Julia*, watch it soon. If her performance doesn't make you glad you're sober nothing will.

Despite what you see on TV and on the Internet, there are thousands of sober people out there. They're sculpting, acting, writing, dancing, making money, growing businesses, inventing things... What are you going to create with your sobriety?

April 24

There's a new philosophy of parenting making the rounds on the Internet, and I think it applies perfectly to both sobriety and being creative in sobriety.

Called the CTFD Method, this inspirational program has been changing lives since its inception. For parents, it relieves pressure, builds stronger relationships and helps foster happiness for the whole family. I personally believe in this program so strongly that I have applied it to every single aspect of my life.

According to *Huffington Post* writer David Vienna, to use CTFD, follow these simple steps:

1. Calm the f*ck down.
2. There is no second step.

Easy, right? Let's all CTFD and get back to work.

April 25

Everyone and everything in the entire universe wants you to succeed. Whether it's your sobriety, finishing that knitted sweater, completing your first short story or taking your guitar to open mic night, every ounce of universal energy is conspiring to make you a success.

When was the last time you sat in the audience when a person who was obviously nervous was making a speech? How did you feel about that? Did you wait for them to screw up so you could poke the person next to you, point and laugh? Or did you earnestly wish them well, laugh a little too loud at their jokes to encourage them and applaud energetically to make them feel good when they were finished?

If you were in the first category, then boooo on you. That's mean. But I'm guessing that you were in the latter category. You wanted that nervous person to do well. You wanted them to succeed so everyone in the room could feel good and share in their success.

As you continue to move through sobriety with all of its pink clouds and dark pits, know that the creative process is very similar. Bring all of yourself to the page, the sewing machine or the guitar and feel the whole power of the universe surging behind you, urging you to succeed.

April 26

How did you handle your first few weeks of sobriety? Did you grab everyone you know by the shoulders and share with them your newfound bliss? Or did you keep it to yourself, nurturing your new sobriety like an orphaned kitten? Did you selectively share, revealing your sobriety only to people you know would be supportive, kind and helpful?

Cultivating sobriety requires many of the same processes as cultivating creativity. You need to be careful about sharing. Don't set yourself up for failure by taking on too much at once. (Do you really need to write, direct, act, sing and dance in your own feature film? How about we get some shots of the neighborhood to start out?). Be patient with your progress, knowing that some days are going to be easier than others. Choose to share your feelings about your art very carefully.

And most importantly, don't be too hard on yourself. You're transforming. Do you think caterpillars beat themselves up when turning into butterflies if it's not happening fast enough/the way they thought it would/or absolutely perfectly?

April 27

One of the best pieces of advice I ever got about sharing my creations was a college professor of mine who told me, in no uncertain terms, "Never be defensive about your work."

This little nugget has saved me time and again from engaging in pointless arguments about what someone else thinks about what I am doing. When someone else offers a critique about something I have created I use this method to listen. I don't need to defend or argue. I don't need to agree or disagree, I need to listen.

This advice has even helped me backtrack *before* I even decide to show my work to someone. If I feel that someone may give my work an unfair shake, if I already know them to be a bit negative or if don't trust their judgment, I don't share with them. I am careful about who sees my work while it is still in progress—just like I am still very careful when I choose whom I speak with about my sobriety. I don't mind people knowing I am sober, but I will not engage in conversation with those I know will try to talk me out of it, belittle me or brush me off because of it.

I am never defensive about my work because I don't put myself in a position to be.

April 28

Before I got sober I was overwhelmed by depression at the state of the world. The alcohol I was consuming made me more in tune to anxiety and sadness. I was stuck in repetitive cycle that left me feeling powerless to change myself, much less change the entire planet.

Becoming the change I wanted to see in the world (that old chestnut) was my first step on the road to recovery. Despite the fact that I was probably the biggest boozehound in my circle, I was acutely aware of how alcohol was affecting everyone around me. From the hangovers in the office that led to short-tempered encounters to the fragile relationships that broke under the weight of drunken flirting, I knew that alcohol was the foundation of all of the chaos I saw. I had to change in order to get out of that desperate lifestyle. It was the one small step that changed everything in my world.

It is no exaggeration that every single thing in my life is better because of my sobriety. Once the fog truly lifted I was able to see how, in my own small way, I could contribute to the world around me and alleviate some of the ills that were causing my pain.

Not only did I become the change I wanted to see in the world, but I also started creating the art I wanted to experience. I wrote the books I would have liked to read. I created the decorative spaces in my home that make me feel welcome and serene. I was able give my talents to volunteer organizations that needed my help.

What do you want to read/hear/see/wear/create/experience? What's stopping you right now?

April 29

No one is perfect, and neither are our role models. I have always had a cadre of role models to whom I look for how to act, be, create—whatever. I have business role models, behavior role models, creative role models and sobriety role models.

This is mostly a good thing, however I have found that sometimes my role model is such an expert at what they do, is so perfect in their execution and so flawless in their creation that just knowing they exist makes me not what to work on my project. Since they are so good, and there's no way I can match that, why even try?

One of my role models is a writer whom I will not name in order to protect her. She wrote a series of books that I found so inspiring that I would often open a page to see what wisdom I could glean in an instant from her deep spiritual writing. I have looked to her words for over a decade as one more guidepost to authentic living, the kind of real living I so profoundly crave.

Well, I came to find out that this author's word and her actions were two completely different things. She made a fortune on sales of her books, seminars and accessories—
which is wonderful! The problem is that when the money rolled in she disregarded everything she wrote about simplicity to embrace a sultan's existence: opulent homes, private jets, and a staff of nine people… All while promoting a philosophy of pared down, simple living.

Eventually she lost all of her money, I am sorry to say. I wouldn't wish that on her, and I'm not happy that she is suffering as a result. But I have learned that we cannot put our heroes on too high of a pedestal. We cannot allow their successes from discouraging us from accomplishing our own creative goals. You don't really know what's going on behind the scenes with any human. If their work inspires you, be inspired. Then *aspire* to create something equally as moving.

April 30

So many rules! Have a ritual, stay sober, create what you love, find role models but don't expect too much, copy stuff, work every day, blah blah blah!

Now that we've spent the month of April mapping out some strategies to flourishing creatively in sobriety, I have one last little piece of advice:

Don't be so hard on yourself.

Life is to be lived! Creative projects should be fun! The results are meant to inspire!

So you miss a day of working on something because there was a Real Housewives marathon on. Big deal. Maybe you haven't picked up your guitar in two weeks because you decided it was more important to exercise, meditate or nap during that time. That's all great too.

Just like in sobriety, it's good to have a framework that works. All of my suggestions are proven tactics to achieve your creative goals. Now, find the ones that work for you, stop beating yourself up for not doing every single thing perfectly, and create something magical.

May
Finding Serenity

May 1

May Day rites of renewal have been performed across the globe for centuries. Originating from an ancient celebration of the goddess Flora, most of these celebrations focus on flowers, beauty and the sensual joys of spring.

The spring after I first got sober was a feast for my senses. The way the light played upon smiling daffodil blooms, the cherry blossoms fluttering from the trees like pink snow, crape myrtle trees awash in a riot of fuchsia... These were all things I had either never noticed or chose not to notice because I was so caught up in my own celebration on bar patios, at boozy barbecues or by the pool.

In the United States, May Day is often celebrated by giving baskets of flowers to friends. These small gifts acknowledge the beauty of the world, the abundance of planet earth and the deep connection we feel to those closest to us.

Now that you're sober, you have the opportunity to acknowledge all of the gifts you've been given, and to revel in the idea that your sobriety is also a gift to others. Get out and connect. Pick some flowers in a meadow and put them in a jar on your desk. Send an email with some inspiring images to someone important to you. Go for a walk in your neighborhood and try to spot something you've never seen before. Most of all, take a moment to acknowledge your own renewal, your own gift to the world.

May 2

Creating a sober life is like giving birth to the best version of you. You are no longer mired in the destructive cycle of addiction, and you are free from the mental obsession that drove you to manifest terrible experiences in your life. You are a refreshed, rejuvenated you.

The danger of springtime, with its intoxicating weather, warm breezes and stirred up hormones, is that these delicious moments can lull you into a sense of security in your sobriety.

Immerse yourself in the abundance of spring, but continue to guard your sobriety. Remind yourself that one drink can send you off the primrose path and down a route that's filled with pitfalls. In this season of renewal, recommit to your sobriety and protect it with the intensity it deserves.

May 3

In your quest for sobriety you've had to unpack a lot of unpleasant feelings. Not only did you have to face the fact that you had become addicted to alcohol, but you had to shine a spotlight on some humiliating, dangerous and unhealthy behaviors. But in going through that difficult process you cleared away all of the junk and allowed the sun to shine in. What a relief!

The emotional process of clearing is necessary for growth, but I would like to suggest that the physical process of clearing is necessary for serenity. Look around your space. Is there a drawer you can't open because it's stuffed full? Is your closet collapsing under the weight of items you don't even wear anymore? Is the light in your fridge blocked by a stack of pizza boxes?

Let's do some spring cleaning! When you got sober, you cleared your life of things that no longer serve you. If your house is full of things you don't use, don't want and don't like, get rid of them. Simplify your day by creating a spot to keep your keys. Turn the items in your pantry with the labels out so you don't get frustrated when trying to find things.

You've cleared your mind of a very unhealthy obsession. Now, clear some actual space for that positive energy to thrive.

May 4

I love the simple living movement. At the same time I got sober I began to embrace the idea of simplicity as a key to happiness. Quitting drinking instantly simplified a lot of my life, and I saw the benefits instantly, if not emotionally, then certainly logistically.

Gone was the need to plan, finagle, cover up, lie and plot. Enter lots of free time that needed to be filled with something other than three bottles of wine and a *House of Cards* marathon.

I wanted to avoid replacement behaviors that might prove to be equally destructive, namely shopping. As a person who always looked outside of herself for ways to cope, I was in no way immune to the lure of retail therapy. But I knew, even before I started down that path, that having more, better, prettier, shinier stuff was not going to make me whole.

There are a host of simplicity gurus to whom I turned for advice through books and online. I discovered the tiny house movement, where people move into spaces most of us would consider closets. There's the early retirement movement that shows people how to reassess and recalibrate financial processes so that they can free themselves from jobs they hate. I also love the de-cluttering movement, which encourages getting rid of anything that isn't absolutely essential. The zero waste folks take this one step further and completely eliminate any products that create any waste or overage.

The process has been enlightening and en-lightening. The feeling of shedding excess baggage and focusing my time on what truly matters to me brings deep serenity and calm. Simplicity and sobriety have gone hand in hand throughout my entire process, and the result is that my life is simpler than ever—and more joyful, too.

May 5

The simplicity movement is nothing new. Economically speaking, we hit a simplicity cycle every few decades, usually as a result of some kind of downturn or market crash.

The vast majority of world religions have some form of simplicity at their core. Christ was a simple man who changed the world through loving kindness. The Buddhists believe that the world is ever-changing, and that grasping for material possessions leads you off the path to enlightenment (or at the very least you've attached your spirit to what is essentially meaningless). Even sobriety programs, which are often spiritual in nature, embrace the idea of simply following the steps and doing the next right thing.

Whether or not you decide to sell all of your personal possession and live off the grid (I am not suggesting that...) there are several ways you can simplify your life right now. Cancel your expensive gym membership (the one that makes you feel guilty all the time) and go for nightly walks instead. Do you have multiple kitchen implements cluttering up your cooking space? Do you really need five colanders, eight butcher knives and nine bottles of nutmeg? Are you involved in groups or organizations that complicate your schedule and that you don't enjoy anyway? What about your kids? Are they overscheduled?

Simplicity is sobriety's best friend. Without the complicated things that frustrate us and cause resentments we have given ourselves fewer excuses for drinking today.

May 6

By becoming sober you've joined a great experiment without even really knowing it. To be a sober person in this crazy time is extremely unusual. You've probably seen this in action around you. Everyone's having fun boozing it up and you are the big weirdo who doesn't drink anymore.

That's part of what I love about striving for simplicity. I've gotten accustomed to being a an oddball in situations where everyone is swirling and sipping, but I am still getting comfortable with the idea that I no longer want the "approved" material things that my friends and colleagues still seem so focused on.

I don't get invited to fashion show fundraisers anymore because I no longer find value in spending money on fashion. I like to look nice and be stylish, but I have other financial goals that seem more important now. I laughed at friend recently when she showed me her new diamond-studded watch and then looked at her phone to check the time. I would rather spend my Sundays at home now, reading a classic novel, practicing meditation and cultivating sobriety and the true meaning of my life than getting in a limo with my girlfriends and heading out to ten wineries.

I don't claim to have reached enlightenment, nor do I think this is necessarily the goal. But I do think I have identified the core of what it takes to be truly happy. My new happiness comes from shedding irrelevant things and turning away from external solutions.

I do this by reading, resting, ridding, reflecting and refusing to take on anything that tears me down rather than building me up. My happiness is inside, it's growing in strength every day and it's so very simple.

May 7

Drinkers are emotional people to begin with, and we tend to draw drama toward us like a tractor beam. In order to stay sober, and in order to have a life of happiness and serenity, I continually strive for emotional sobriety.

The basis of emotional sobriety is allowing yourself to feel uncomfortable feelings rather than bypassing them. I don't love this. It hurts sometimes. The anxiety threatens to overwhelm me. But I stick with it, and nine times out of ten, I come through it able to make a sane assessment of what happened.

For example, if I am driving and someone recklessly swerves in front of me, threatening my safety, I experience anger, fear, anxiety and indignation. Before, I would probably scream some obscenities at that person, and when I arrived at my destination I would spend several minutes recounting the horror and rousing people to my side. Victim victory!

I don't bother with this anymore. I have accepted that people drive like maniacs, so I actually take responsibility for this by scheduling trips during low traffic times when I can and leaving early enough so that I don't have to ever worry about being late. I see dangerous behavior and rather than ranting about it, I acknowledge it, separate myself from it and offer a little gratitude to the universe for keeping me safe. That's emotional sobriety in action.

This took some practice and a bit of big-picture thinking. The fact is that if someone is slowing me down because they are driving at a snail's pace, for all I know they are doing me a favor by keeping me out of some unforeseen danger down the road.

You are but a small drop in a vast sea, but your emotional sobriety can cause ripples of calm and serenity in ways you may never know about. Feel your emotions, but don't let them rule you. And don't every let anyone take your serenity away from you.

May 8

If emotions were simple they wouldn't get is into so much trouble, right? My reasons for drinking were purely emotional, and I managed to twist, shape and mangle those emotions to create excuses to have another drink.

But here's the secret: Emotions actually are very simple. It's how we react to them that overcomplicates everything.

If you're mad you have the option of just being mad. You don't have to do anything, tell anyone or react at all. You also don't have to overanalyze your anger, blame your childhood, blame your mother, blame the world or tell everyone around you how all of these things have combined to make you mad. Be mad for a while. Feel mad. Don't attach anything else to that anger, and after a while it will dissipate and you can sanely address the issue that threw you off kilter.

The same process works for an array of negative emotions. Anxiety is my biggest demon, and when I feel it raise its hackles I have to continually remind myself to feel it without attaching any outcomes to my feelings. When I am anxious I don't make decisions, I don't flip through my history with this emotion and get stuck somewhere thinking that it makes me bad, stupid, silly or wrong. (I do sometimes, ok, but this is a work in progress.)

Emotions are simple. Our reactions are complicated. Diffuse your reactions. Feel your feelings. Then take the next step, if any are required.

May 9

In the classic film *Citizen Kane*, we witness a man strive for and achieve success by every conceivable measure, only to long, on his deathbed, for the freedom and joy he found with his childhood sled.

Charles Kane used everything at his disposal to appease his enormous ego, but he discovered that true happiness couldn't be bought for any price. As alcoholics, we are familiar with this insane thinking, and we have certainly fallen victim to trying to soothe an internal problem with an external source. At first, alcohol seemed like the answer to the unrest within. We not only surrounded ourselves with our fix, but we chose companions who supported our insanity. Often, alcohol wasn't the only thing we used to try to tame our demons. Many of us concurrently fell prey to workaholism, shopaholism, eating disorders... Like Charles Kane, our appetite for "isms" couldn't satiate what was really making us hungry.

Charles Kane is trying to repeat that simple exhilaration of being on a sled. Look deep into yourself and see what touchstone for happiness exists is buried there. Did you love walking in the woods? Stomping in puddles? A day at the beach? Search for those simple pleasures and reconnect with them when you can.

May 10

Allen Carr writes in his brilliant *The Easy Way to Stop Drinking* that humans have everything we need internally to manage stress and create happiness. Putting something in our bodies to relieve stress or deal with emotional pain sounds really batshit bonkers when you say it out loud. It's the same with any sort of external solution: My mother beat me so I buy shoes. I was abused by an uncle so I whack myself in the head with a hammer. I wasn't able to finish high school so I poke my eyes with a pointy stick.

{Insert terrible thing} happened to me so I drink to the point of death's door.

It hardly follows logic.

If we are shot with an arrow, we pull it out and stanch the bleeding. We don't stand there, guts dangling everywhere, looking for someone to blame and pouring ourselves a drink.

We have inside us everything we need to heal ourselves. Simple breathing exercises are often enough to clear our minds of pain. A brisk walk heightens the senses and releases endorphins. Meditation has been proven to relieve stress and help to manage chronic pain. Talking to a professional with training in trauma can change your life.

Your past may be complicated, and your pains numerous. But you can choose how to respond. Choose ease. Choose an inner fix. Choose simplicity.

May 11

It's no coincidence that I used to refer to getting drunk as getting "wasted." I wasted my time, my money and my health. I ravaged, ruined and devastated my relationships. I diminished my potential. I became morally marred and defiled. All of these words are definitions of "wasted" in the Oxford English Dictionary, and when I looked it up I was surprised that my photo wasn't included.

When you chose to sober up, you chose to simplify your life in myriad ways. You've chosen not to be wasted, or to lay waste to your life, anymore. In a very literal way you've chosen not to add waste to landfills or throw your money away on something that provides no return on investment. If you're reaching for true emotional sobriety, you've chosen not to waste your energy on things you cannot change.

That we were so willing to be wasteful with our lives by drinking indicates that there are probably other areas of our lives where we are being wasteful. Do you buy vegetables with full intention of making a hearty soup only to throw them away two weeks later after they're all mushy and black? (Guilty.) Do you waste time in the same conversation with someone over and over with no resolution? (Guilty.) Do you waste your effort trying to fix a situation over which you really have no control? (Done that. Got the T-shirt.)

You're not wasted anymore. What waste can you rein in today?

May 12

When I was drinking I could never get enough alcohol into my system at once. I drank fast and I drank constantly. If I was at a party I was always on the move, dancing over here, chatting over there—a perpetual motion machine. Plus, I was most likely in the bathroom half the night because gallons of liquid and a walnut sized bladder... Well you get the picture.

Flash forward to sobriety and I have, of course, completely overcome this behavior and become a font of serenity, a touchstone of grace, a calming presence in a world of chaos... WRONG.

I'm still jittery and flittery. I still bounce from one thing to another. You should see me surf the Internet and scan TV stations at the same time. If a movie is longer than an hour and twenty minutes I think long and hard about the time commitment there. I simply hate sitting still that long. Thank heaven they outlawed texting and driving in California. This law has probably saved my life already.

I'm not completely sure if this behavior existed before my alcoholism or if it is a throwback to alcoholic thinking. I really don't remember. But I do know that I don't like the person it reminds me of.

In my quest for serenity and simplicity in this wonderful state of sobriety I try very hard to identify this manic behavior before it gets out of hand. Perhaps you don't share this. Maybe your throwback is anger, sadness or self-pity. Maybe you isolate. If you are currently sober and you feel yourself slipping into alcoholic behaviors, pay attention. Reach out for help. Get on your meditation cushion. Tell a friend. Don't allow your old patterns to elbow in on your new serenity. You're much too sober for that.

May 13

When I gave up drinking and embarked on a simpler life I paid a lot of attention to what grabbed my attention. What was I filling my head with on a daily basis? What was I spending my time on and was it worthy of the new, sober, energetic and happier me?

One of the first things I noticed was how much time I spent looking at the news. I get 100% of my news from the Internet, and my news-seeking pattern looked like one of those chickens playing tic-tac-toe. Peck here, get a treat. Peck there, no treat. Peck over here again—-treat! I looked for good news, bad news, hilarious news, weird news…

And guess what? None of it contributed to my serenity.

The news today is designed to titillate and enrage, not to inform. Headlines are meant to catch our eye by creating an instant emotional reaction. I found myself getting addicted to the "high" of a great headline, a scandalous occurrence or outrageous political situation.

So I had to stop.

I propose a news fast for anyone who is looking for greater serenity and clarity in their life. By tuning out the noise and choosing where you will put your attention, you will instantly embark on building a stronger inner foundation of awareness and peace.

I'm not suggesting that you run around ignorant and unaware of history unfurling before you. I'm simply saying that you can limit your access to the news. If you check a few times a week rather than 20 times a day (like I did) you will stay up to date but won't have the continual barrage of salacious stories working away at your brain like a person being pecked to death by ducks.

The most important thing in your life is your sobriety. Take a news fast and turn that valuable attention, opinion and need for gratification inward. The reward to you—and to the world around you—will be that much greater.

May 14

What is serenity? Some of us in sobriety are always asking the universe to grant it to us, but what is it, exactly?

Serenity can be defined literally as clear skies and calm seas. As a state of being, serenity is also referred to as "cheerful tranquility." But my favorite definition of serenity is "calm brightness and quiet radiance."

So that's great. We've got that. But how exactly does one achieve calm brightness and quiet radiance?

Like anything it takes practice. Professional athletes don't roll out onto the field at their whim and overtake the competition. They practice. Plumbers don't waltz over to some leaking pipes and instinctively "know" what to do. And the Buddha didn't wake up "all enlightened" one day. He had to practice getting into the state of mind that would lead to enlightenment. We have to practice getting into the state of mind that leads to calm brightness and quiet radiance.

That means letting go of the little stuff (and most of the big stuff). That means facing your feelings rather than self-medicating. That means doing the work every single day by meditating, breathing, processing and doing the next right thing. It means staying sober. Then, after you've practiced these things every single moment for a long time, like the gymnast who finally sticks that landing, you'll find yourself in a state of serenity without even trying.

Serenity takes practice. Practice serenity.

May 15

To truly savor an experience you have to slow down, be present and pay attention.

Have you noticed that your senses are sharper now that you're sober? Food tastes better. Music sounds more detailed. The sky's a little bluer. Maybe you feel temperature changes more acutely.

Invite yourself to slow down and really connect with what's happening. One of the obvious places to slow down is in your car. Take your time. Let people in front of you. Notice the weather, the sounds of the road and the animals and birds that you see on your way.

Take the time to savor your food. You'll discover flavors you may never have noticed. You may also discover that you digest your food better.

If you can, slow down with a work project. Don't miss the deadline, but pay attention to whether or not you are paying attention. Is your mind wandering? Are you watching the clock? Are you bringing your best self to the work?

Sobriety is a gift to be savored. How slow can you go?

May 16

Consuming is an obsession for the addict. How can I get it? Where can I get it? Who is going to do this with me? How fast can I get the substance in and who is going to get me more when I am done?

It seems obvious that sobriety would make many of us shift our obsession to food. We can still consume it. It's legal. It's a treat.

Unfortunately our new focus on food can turn out to be very unhealthy as well. Sugar intake tends to increase for the alcoholic since we are accustomed to ingesting so many sugar units a day. Fattening, over-salted processed foods become our new comfort. In my opinion, this is fine. For a while.

But the fact is that bad food can destroy your health just like alcohol or drugs. I encourage you to transform your energy around food into a process that serves your overall health.

Educate yourself on healthy, affordable food options. Teach yourself how to make a few simple things, like smoothies, that can boost your energy and give you a shot of healthy vitamins. Try one new thing a day that you think you might not like. By slowly introducing healthier items into your life, over time, you'll see some big changes. And the things you avoided might now be the things you love.

May 17

Keeping food simple is the best strategy for regaining your health in sobriety. It is so important to make sure you replenish your system with energy-building, tissue-repairing and inflammation-reducing foods to combat the damage you have done to your body.

There are lots of great books and cookbooks on the subject, but there's one very simple guide that everyone who eats should have on the shelf. It's called *Food Rules: An Eater's Manual* by Michael Pollan.

The great thing about this book—especially in our month of simplicity—is that it is undeniably simple to read, simple to understand and simple to implement. It is not a diet. It does not promise that you will lose weight, win a million dollars or find the partner of your dreams. It is, simply, 63 things to think about when shopping, cooking and eating.

Great ideas like, "If it came from a plant, eat it. If it was made in a plant, don't," and "Don't get your fuel from the same place your car does," are just common sense. Plus, these rules are deliciously easy to follow.

May 18

"Have nothing in your house that you do not know to be useful, or believe to be beautiful,"—Craftsman, Designer and Poet William Morris

I love this quote, and it is on my mind as I edit things from my life that no longer serve me. Out goes the duplicate garlic press. Away with the ugly statue I kept for who-knows-why. Ridding my space of things I don't use or that don't inspire me has made more room for the things that I truly love.

Sobriety comes along with a bevy of useful tools and beautiful experiences. I challenge you to take this wonderful, practical quote one step further and think about whether the way you spend your time is useful or beautiful. Are your thoughts useful or beautiful? Is the entertainment you choose useful or beautiful? Are the foods you eat useful or beautiful?

Edge out everything in your life that doesn't answer these questions, and watch your soul come to life with all of the useful, beautiful experiences that await.

May 19

When my sobriety was new I was convinced I would never have fun again. I imagined long stretches of time with absolutely nothing to do. And while I did (and still do) have some days where I am antsy about what to do with myself, I have committed to finding simple, affordable ways to have fun even when I am not really in the mood.

I have to admit that it wasn't that way at first. Newly sober, I flung myself into all kinds of pricey spa experiences, lavish dinners (with a serving of sparkling water, thank you very much), online shopping binges and all of the little luxuries one can indulge in without drinking. I figured I wasn't drinking anymore so I deserved to live it up!

After a few solid months of this behavior my wallet was empty and my heart was, too. These experiences didn't fulfill me the way I had hoped they would. I found myself feeling anxious, broke and wondering why what I was doing wasn't working.

I decided to simplify to see if that would help. Rather than going out for a very expensive meal I would try to find something special in a cookbook or online and make it from scratch for my family. I not only filled a few hours but I also learned something new. Before I book a spa treatment at an expensive getaway, I try an online yoga class to see if that calms my spirit. I also used to love spending the weekend at fancy hotels with beautiful pools. I have since discovered hidden, natural swimming holes around my town, which are cold, crisp, clean and usually completely empty.

I have visited all of our local museums (most have free days). I have spent countless hours walking from one end of my town to the other. I'll take my bike out for two hours to see how far I can go. I read. I write.

I do still get fidgety. I get bored. I get bummed about not being able to have a glass of wine. I am *human*, for heaven's sake. But I know now, even though I may forget in the moment, that the answer to my problem is to keep my activities affordable, accessible and most of all, *simple*.

May 20

"Trying to be happy by accumulating possessions is like trying to satisfy hunger by taping sandwiches all over your body."—George Carlin

I'm not always exactly sure what we're talking about when we talk about happiness. The idea of happiness as a sort of "destination" seems to be the one most of us agree on. Most people seem to agree that we "arrive" at happiness, and we're there when we have the house, the car, the jewels and the semi-yearly Caribbean vacation.

I tried this approach wholeheartedly, and threw myself into the idea that once I am "there" my anxiety will disappear, my fears will evaporate and my life will be filled with sunshine and roses. I hate to spoil the ending for you but it didn't work out that way. The more I accumulated the more I became fearful of losing, and the only way I knew to handle fear was to drink and then drink a little more.

Nowadays I don't think of happiness as an overt "feeling" like the giddiness one feels when you get the job, get the date or find the perfect frock. I imagine happiness to be a deep well inside me that is filled with choices. If I am forced to make a decision of any kind, I check in with this deep well. If the choice I am considering keeps the water still and calm, that is the way I go. If the choice seems to make the water churn and roil, I slow down and consider another solution.

The answer is almost never "get more," "let's go shopping" or "if I only had [insert material item here]. (Although when the answer is "get more bandages," "let's go shopping for something to fix the roof leak" or "if only I had a fire extinguisher," I tend to go with those...).

Happiness is a direct result of making choices that feed your internal hunger with service, kindness to others and unselfish giving. When you try to feed your internal hunger with external "solutions," it's like George Carlin says. You'll never fill up that way.

May 21

One of the catalysts behind my own sobriety is that I don't like being tricked. The alcohol industry spends millions to make billions, and those millions are all directed toward one goal: to get you addicted enough to their product and their brand that you will spend your hard earned dollars to have it.

Now we could accept this as capitalism at work and point out that no one ever forced alcohol down my throat—and these things are true. The only difference is, and the thing they leave out of all the marketing, is that alcohol is a viciously addictive substance, not only because of the social conventions around drinking, but also because it is chemically designed to be so.

When I got tired of playing the stooge to the alcohol industry I expanded my reach, and you can, too. Use your newfound sobriety to take control of your purchasing decisions like never before. Find out where your food is made. Read the labels on your clothes to see if you can find information about who is making them and under what conditions. Learn about chemicals that are harmful to your family and to the environment, and make sure the products you use are safe for everyone.

You're sober now, and you're nobody's fool. What can you do today to ensure that YOU are in charge of what you eat, wear, buy or use?

May 22

Being alone without being lonely is the simplest form of living. You don't have to put on the face you wear for your boss, or put up the wall you use to protect yourself from toxic people. You don't have to make interesting conversation or listen to anyone's complaints. You get to completely be yourself, do exactly what you want to do and experience life completely on your terms.

One of my favorite artists and writers is a woman who calls herself SARK, and she advocates taking yourself out on alone dates. It was because of her advice that I discovered, nearly 20 years ago, that I love dining out all by myself. (She also wrote a book called *How to Change Your Life Without Getting Out of Bed*. How can you not love this woman?)

It was my 22nd birthday and I was all alone in a new city. I had just gotten a new job and had a little cash flow for the first time in a while, but I had absolutely no one to celebrate with. I was feeling sorry for myself, and reading one of SARK's books in an attempt to cheer myself up, when I read her suggestion of dining alone.

I called a fancy place, told them I was coming in for my birthday alone and I got all dressed up. When I arrived they had a beautiful booth in the corner where I could see the whole dining room. I asked for a phone (this was in the days before cell phones) and I called everyone back home while I sat there and enjoyed a five-star meal.

I still love going anywhere by myself, and now that I am sober I can do so without worrying about how I am going to get home. Take yourself out. Do something YOU would love to do, and see what simple things you can learn in joyful solitude.

May 23

So much my drinking was an attempt to recreate some "magical" feeling I seemed to remember from my youth. I think this is true of a lot of us. We're grasping for the elusive enchantment that takes us out of the everyday and elevates our spirit in some indescribable way.

This actually works for a while, doesn't it? I remember the lovely feeling of wine washing over all of my troubles and painting the world with a delicious golden sparkle. The uninhibited feelings, the hilarious conversations, the impromptu dancing... Sure. It works. Until it doesn't.

Sobriety can be a painful mind game at first. Not only are we forced to give up on the idea that we can create magic simply and consequence-free, but the thing that allowed us to maintain this delusion has packed up and moved on to another sucker.

We are forced to recalibrate our desires, our self-image and our actions. We must find a way to live simply or it will be oh-so-simple for alcohol to get its claws into us again.

I have had to shift my definition of enchantment, and it's taken some time and careful attention. Rather than being swept up in a sea of numb delirium, I find that the magic is in the moment. It's the feeling of finishing a paragraph. It's the satisfaction of keeping my promises, and the joyful desire to continue to make decisions that are in everyone's best interests, not just my own. The magic is in choosing, every single moment, to be here now, sober, simple and willing to serve.

May 24

There's something to be said for wholesome living. While I was running around drinking everything I could get my hands on, smoking everything that could be lit on fire and attempting to be "sexy" by throwing myself into every liaison that looked good, so many people I knew where quietly working in interesting jobs, having families, buying homes and helping out around the community. Many have achieved great wealth. Some have modest earnings but spend their time playing music, having play dates and block parties or going on wilderness trips. Some spend their vacation time building wells in South American villages. Some of these savvy folks have won awards for service to their businesses, their communities and their churches. They send out holiday cards, which, apart from a couple of years in the 90s, is something I have never managed to do.

Facebook is great for throwing all of this in your face, by the way. I find myself looking at these people I knew, who grew up in the same town and went to the same schools, and wondering why it turned out so differently for me. I envy what appears to be their wholesome lives (we can't every *really* know, but I respond to the image they present), and I wonder how I can bring some of that wholesomeness into my own ravaged life.

There are two things I have to remind myself of when I get bogged down in the "I'll never be wholesome" swamp. 1) I can't judge myself by someone else's highlight reel and 2) It's not too late to get some wholesome.

I can't go back and magically create some kids I never had and community awards I never earned, but I can choose to read quality literature, watch films with zero explosions, create food that is healthy and pure and volunteer to help build a park in my community. When I feel itchy because of my decidedly unwholesome, unhealthy past, I pick up garbage in my neighborhood (this really helps). I make a detoxifying smoothie. I meditate and thank the universe for my health, my well being and my sobriety. Then, I am whole again.

May 25

If you go on a search for simplicity in your sobriety you'll find some surprising things. One of the most delightful things I have stumbled upon is *The Book of Idle Pleasures*, by Dan Kieran and Tom Hodgkinson.

Originating out of England by a group of contrarians that have opted out of modern society in pursuit of a more down-to-earth lifestyle, the Idler movement has been gaining quite a bit of steam. These philosophers, musicians, artists, farmers and writers invite others to join them in experiencing life in a way that doesn't require people to be cogs in a machine.

Although their ideas delve deep into every aspect of society and how it functions, this little book offers a wonderful way to be reminded of how simple—and how simply lovely—life can be.

See if your local library carries this little gem, or pick one up and keep it by your bedside. You'll soon discover the joy of "looking at maps," "sunbeams" and "forgetting," just like I did.

May 26

I used to live on acres of land in the heart of wine country. One of my favorite aspects of this kind of living was what I called "animal capers."

Every week something new would show up: a possum in a tree, a fox living under the house or finches nesting under the eaves. Some of the occurrences were tragic, like the adorable baby raccoon that didn't survive a vigorous shaking by my dog. But some were lovely, like the mama fox that surreptitiously led her kits out into the woods every night at sundown.

These days I live in a downtown area in a townhouse over a retail establishment. My front yard is a parking lot and a train depot; my backyard is a 20 x 20 patio with a view of my neighbors' bedroom windows. I miss having an outdoor space to call my own, but most of all I miss my animal capers.

I decided to do something about it. Taking my cue from the Buddhist advice to "start where you are" I created a greenscape on my patio, complete with a full-grown Japanese maple tree, and array of container gardens, creeping jasmine and trumpet vines, rose bushes and a fountain. I placed a large dish full of bird food next to the fountain and I waited to see if maybe some of our local birds would grace me with their presence.

I waited patiently for about 18 months before any birds discovered the little paradise I created for them. Now I have house finches, house sparrows, Anna's hummingbirds, dark-eyed juncos, California towhees, oak titmice and ruby-crowned kinglets that regularly visit my tiny patio. I even have a few scrub jays that are *thisclose* to being convinced to take a peanut from my hand.

If you want to create something special in your own life, simply start where you are.

May 27

When you were drinking or using you did everything in your power to disconnect from your experience. In sobriety those delicate connections start to repair themselves through service, prayer, kindness, meditation—all of those "next right things" that keep our raging desire to consume under control.

Today, I invite you to participate in an assignment. I invite you to feed those fragile connections by connecting with the world around you in ways you may not have thought of.

What kinds of trees are in your neighborhood? Can you name three of them? What types of birds are local to your area? Could you ID five of them? It's May and wildflowers are blooming all over this great land of ours. Do you know what any of them are and if they can be used for any medicinal purposes? Can they be eaten? What about the butterflies and moths you see flitting around? Do you know their names or life cycles? What types of food crops grow near you?

When you start identifying some of these things you see every day by their names, you feel a connection with them that goes beyond aesthetic appreciation. You'll discover all kinds of fun facts, interesting trivia and uses for the things you see in your world. And that's one more way to connect to your life, to others and to all the beings that surround you.

May 28

I used to love to get out the bottle of wine and start bitching. *My boss did this, my husband did that, and can you believe what so-and-so said to me?* I could spend hours and hours refilling my glass and filling my companions' ears with complaint after complaint after complaint.

After alcohol had completely demoralized me, and I was no longer in a position to complain about what anyone else was doing (or *their* bad decisions or *their* terrible relationships) something incredible happened: I stopped complaining. And guess what? Over time, I had far less to actually complain about.

Complaints solve nothing. Complaints breed more complaints. Stop complaining completely, and you'll start wondering what it was you spent so much time complaining about.

May 29

When you tell your life story are you the victim or the hero? If you are striving for sobriety I encourage you to start looking at yourself like a hero. The truth is that you have embraced a challenge that the vast majority of people never even attempt.

Someone very close to me is the victim in her own life. She is not an addict—she has never even had a drop of alcohol in her life—but her perception of herself is very similar to so many people I know who have fallen victim to alcohol or drugs.

This person is absolutely incapable of a) thanking people for their help b) apologizing for anything and c) seeing herself as anything other than abused, taken advantage of, lied to and tricked. She truly believes that everyone in the world is out to take something from her, and she lives in constant fear. She is a perpetual victim who is continually waiting for someone else to solve her problems. After all, someone else caused all of her problems so why shouldn't someone else fix them?

Her presence in my life, though draining at times, is such a gift. Through her shining, textbook examples of what not to do, I am continually reminded that I can choose to be my own hero. As I see her mired in her own victimhood I am inspired to look at my problems another way, claim my part in any conflict and work for a resolution from a position of kindness and understanding.

Take a look at where you're a victim in your life. Is there an opportunity to be your own hero?

May 30

"To give without any reward, or any notice, has a special quality of its own." —Anne Morrow Lindbergh

By getting sober you have already blessed the world with an incredible gift. Your clear mind, your healthy body and your evolving soul are creating ripples of wonder and goodness that you will probably never see.

When I got sober I fully expected the clouds to part, the angels to weep and creatures great and small to line up to pay their respects to my bravery, courage and grace.

Um, that didn't happen. I got a few reactions but none of them involved cheers, applause or even congratulations. I have been sober for quite a while now and this fact goes mostly un-discussed, unmentioned and unacknowledged, at least by those closest to me.

But that's OK. Anne Morrow Lindbergh's words offer a guiding principle for me, and I often refer to this quote when I am feeling like someone's trying to "get something" from me, when I think I have gotten a raw deal or that no one sees or appreciates all of the mind-blowing, amazing, earth-shattering stuff I doing.

It is always enough to just give. Give the world your sobriety. Give the world your kindness. Give the world your talents. And if no one sees it, hold those gifts deep in your heart and know that they are giving and giving and giving right back to you.

May 31

Your sober life is yours to create in any way you choose. Your clear mind, balanced emotions and eager heart are in the perfect position to guide you on a journey toward a life so beautiful you can hardly imagine.

Start by editing. You've filled up with so many things that don't serve you. Everything from your daily clutter to toxic relationships can be reevaluated to discover whether they have the beauty or usefulness you deserve in your new life. Simple fun awaits, as does a whole universe of animals and plants that are waiting for you to learn their names. You've slowed down to savor some meals, and realized that sobriety and giving while sober are their own rewards.

You're the hero of your own life. You know that complaints bring more complaints, and that to discover joy you need to start where you are. You're reading labels and enjoying delicious, simple foods as well as having a lovely time in deep, enriching solitude.

As the glorious, youthful joy of spring transitions into the mysteries of a sultry summer, I congratulate you on a month of simple living and simply living. Let's carry these ideas along with us as we grow in our sobriety.

June
June Tune-Up

June 1

June is filled with sunny fun, and it's a great month to be sober. Everyone seems to be in a better mood in June. We head out on vacations and spend days submerged in water at the beach, pond or pool. It's warm, but not quite that stifling heat of summer. In my book, June is near perfect.

I find it very easy to be grateful when the sun is shining and the breeze is warm, so let's start the month with some simple gratitude. (It's important to be grateful in the dark and dreary months, too, but why make this harder on ourselves than we have to?)

So many smart people swear by the gratitude journal, and I have to agree with them. When I first got sober and it was suggested to me that I keep a gratitude journal I thought it was the hokiest, silliest, most juvenile thing I'd ever heard. Stupid! Futile! Pointless! Or so I believed.

But like a good trooper willing to go to any lengths I did it anyway. Lo and behold—they were right. As I spent five minutes every evening jotting a little list of things for which I was grateful, I did start to feel better. Next, I started to feel lucky. Little by little, I got a bit more grateful for things. Then, I started to feel blessed.

It's one of the easiest ways to make your life feel rich and full. Even if you think this is the most cockamamie idea you've ever heard, try it. Gratitude, even the smallest amount, can radically shift your perspective.

June 2

During your June tune-up you may be following the suggestion to create a gratitude journal. I have already extolled the virtues of this simple item and have outed myself as a believer in its efficacy.

Here's some hard truth for you, though: I don't write it down anymore.

The deal is that I am a professional writer for a living. I write from the crack of noon all day long for companies that hire me to do so. I make my living by the sweat of my brow and the scratch of my pen, and quite frankly, I often don't have the energy to write another word at the end of the day.

But I still make a list every night. Long ago, when my anxiety was unchecked, unbalanced and very unsober I had a terrible time falling asleep. In order to calm my mind I gave it something to latch onto by creating alphabetized lists of things, like boys' names. I would think of lists that would look like this if they were written down:

A is for Anatole
B is for Buster
C is for Calvin
D is for Dudley
E is for Edgar...

...And on and on until I fell asleep. Some nights it was girls' names or countries, American cities, foods or whatever came up.

Now I do the same thing with my gratitude list.

A is for Almond Milk because I am lactose intolerant.

B is for my client B____ because they are so kind, creative and fun to work with.

C is for my newfound sense of calm and serenity.

The point is that you can do your gratitude list however you'd like. Write it down. Sing it in a song. Alphabetize it. Or do one and done. The only thing that matters is that the universe hears what you are grateful for so it can give you more of it.

June 3

There's a wonderful Internet meme called "First World Problems," and it's a perfect satirical reminder of how lucky most of us are to live the way we do.

First World Problems are defined as frustrations and complaints only experienced by privileged individuals in wealthy countries. Examples include getting frustrated at getting locked out of your building's private gym, the inconvenience of having to get dressed to pay the gardener and the indignation one feels when their purebred dog is mistaken for a mix.

I think about this every time I have the urge to bitch and moan about the farmers market being devoid of arugula, when my meeting time is changed to 9 a.m. or when my coffee cup doesn't keep my beverage warm long enough. And I laugh because it is laughable.

That I have a roof over my head, clean running water and a good job leave me better off in every possible way than the vast majority of the Earth's population. I am happy that someone is making fun of my silly little problems because that's all they are: silly little problems. I'm grateful for that.

June 4

I believe in miracles. It is a miracle that I am sober, and I will be the first to tell you I never thought this was possible. Never.

Every day that I wake up and can remember the night before is a miracle. Every minute that passes that I don't bend my elbow to tip another sip is a miracle. It is a miracle that I survived my drinking days at all, because I know many people with lesser issues and much bigger problems.

Sobriety IS a miracle. But that got me thinking. If I can have the miracle of sobriety, what other miracles are out there waiting for me? What miracles can I manifest by sending some thoughts in that direction?

What I discovered is that miracles do occur and our prayers do get answered, just not quite how we envision them. When I asked for the miracle of financial security I found myself getting assigned more work than I could realistically handle. When I asked for more ways to be of service to my fellow man, I envisioned being hired by some swanky environmental organization to write their newsletters and annual reports. What I got was an opportunity to work my butt off for a community organization that was practically falling apart when I walked in. When I asked to find the perfect pet for our household, we found him all right, and like all good teachers he challenges me every single day. When I asked for an opportunity to rest from all of my responsibilities, I fell and bruised my meniscus. Out of order for six weeks.

I am not on this planet to be coddled, pampered and played with. My life's journey is one of learning, growth and sober reflection. Every single thing that happens is a miracle so long as I choose to see it that way.

June 5

You know those people you love, respect and admire? They are your teachers. What about those folks who make you want to punch something? They are also your teachers. There are countless people you encounter in a day whom you don't even really acknowledge. Guess what? They are your teachers, too.

After making my gratitude list every night I thank the universe for my teachers. I give thanks for my dear friend Susan who has been dealt some very hard blows—and has handled her tragedies with such powerful grace, deep emotion and good sense. I am grateful for my acquaintance Jill who is so mired in her own —isms, problems and complaints that I want to shake her. I give thanks for the person who pointed out my mistake as well as the person who gave me praise. I give thanks for anyone who helped me get out of myself for one second to learn something about myself, and the world I inhabit.

Look out for your teachers. They are *everywhere*.

June 6

Being a believer in miracles, I am acutely aware of the blessings I have been given. Apart from my comfy home, a loving family and work that I actually enjoy I have lots of extra goodies for which I am truly grateful. I love the little birds that visit my patio. I have access to fresh veggies and an array of interesting local food. I own a handful of books that I read again and again, and they never cease to delight me. It may not seem like much to some people, but to me it's an embarrassment of riches.

Reminding myself to give miracles to others is something I am committed to in my sobriety. Sometimes it's a big thing, like putting my own ego aside to celebrate something that makes someone else happy (even if I perceive it as bad for me in some way, like my boss leaving the company). Often it's something very small like remembering to ask the cashier how they are doing today, and thanking them for their help. It can be an even tinier gesture like letting someone who seems to be in a hurry merge in front of me in traffic, or making my kids their favorite breakfast.

The point is that we can bring miracles into our lives and we can also manifest them for others. Haven't you ever had a horrible, no-good, very bad day and someone says something nice to you and, in the blink of an eye, it turns around? The gesture probably wasn't much to them, but it may have changed your whole outlook.

What miracles can you create for others today?

June 7

It's easy to get bogged down with work and responsibilities. I take on more than I can handle and instead of managing it all with grace I get frustrated and annoyed—and try to blame someone else for my difficulties. I get grumpy when my plate is too full because all I want to do is sit down somewhere with a good book.

One of the touchstones of my sobriety is the philosophy of service. If you're in a fellowship, this is something that comes up in every meeting, and there's a very good reason for it. People are actually happier when they are putting others' needs in front of their own, despite what the modern media would have us believe. By putting yourself into service to others you get out of your own head and into a space where you are creating an entire world of well being—even if it is just bringing the donuts.

When I get angry with a client for making me work so hard, first I grab a bite to eat. While I am chewing my food, I think about how lucky I am to be of service to this person or this business that employs so many people. When I take myself out of the mindset that I am being bothered and put myself into the place where I see myself as a humble servant, I am much happier to get back to work. Plus, the work itself is better because it is no longer about me and more about the big picture.

Happiness blooms from being of service to others. What's interesting is that by giving something away, it almost always comes back to us.

June 8

Some days don't go the way we want them to. The plans get changed, you're not motivated to do anything or you screwed something up and are feeling terrible about it. When I have days like that it's hard for me to feel grateful, offer service, think about miracles or do anything other than curl up on the couch with a blanket over my head.

The fact that we can't control everything is something that alcoholics have a difficult time processing. In our sobriety we have had to admit that we have no control over alcohol and that was hard enough, wasn't it? Why must we give up control over every little thing?

The simple answer is that we really can't control anything anyway. You can't control whether you're going to feel like crap on a Monday and have no interest in creating that boring spreadsheet. When you're in that mood you'd be hard-pressed to find anyone who blames you for making a mistake. If someone else revises the meeting schedule or you were late because of a traffic jam, there wasn't anything you could do about that.

It's good to remember that everyone in the world has days like this. When you screw up, be honest about why. I've often had to explain to co-workers that I was sick or feeling crummy or the meeting time threw off my schedule. Most of them give me that knowing nod like they've been there, too. A bad day is not the end of the world, and there's no reason to drink over it.

If your day is bad, reflect on how much better it was for you than for countless others. Remind yourself that you aren't the only one to ever make a mistake or get flustered when the schedule changes. Remember that no one is thinking about your mistake because they're so wrapped up in their own world. Then go to bed and try again tomorrow.

June 9

I love being sober and all the joys, friendships and creative projects that have resulted from it. Not having to worry about hangovers or what I may have done or said the night before is not only a relief, but it also frees up brain space for me to think of other stuff. Any stuff. Sobriety is miraculous, and I highly recommend it for everyone.

The other thing I have enjoyed in my sobriety is meeting a whole cadre of sober friends. I adore my sober companions because they are full of that sobriety energy. They have entertaining stories to tell and they are the types of folks who will help out in almost any kind of emergency.

All that is true, and a gift, but sometimes I don't want to just hang out with sober people. There are quite a few people in my life who still drink and I still hang out with them because they are lovely, charming and interesting. Some of them are high-functioning alcoholics, some are medium-functioning alcoholics and some are those types who can have a glass of wine with dinner and then stop. (Bizarre.)

It was a lot harder at first to keep these relationships up because I was still struggling with my obsession with alcohol. Before I quit I would hang out with these drinkers with the express purpose of getting as drunk as possible. This was not necessarily their goal, but it certainly was mine.

After I pulled myself together I found it easier to incorporate drinkers back in. I found reasons for us to meet in places where drinking wasn't done, like a hiking trail (although lots of people do carry a flask on the trail). A place like this makes me less tempted because it's not a trigger for me, and if my companion swigs from flask it only ruins her hike, not mine. I despised going to bars for a long time, but now it's fine to meet up with some drinking friends, have a cranberry cocktail and leave before things get ugly. Oh, and I have definitely gotten to the point where I don't give a shit what the bartender thinks, either. I used to worry about that.

Mostly I do hang out with sober people in sober situations, but I am glad to be able to mix and match a bit more now. When I was drinking I missed out on so much because my reality was altered. Now that I am back, I don't want to miss a thing.

June 10

My mouth sometimes gets the better of me, and it's usually when I am trying to prove how smart I am. For years I believed that if I was able to cleverly point out a problem or craft a hilarious complaint, people would see me as intelligent, insightful and oh-so-witty.

What I have learned in sobriety is that complaints breed contempt. Far from being seen as a brilliant mind, my co-workers, friends and family were all rolling their eyes every time I opened my mouth to offer a critique.

Sobriety has brought so much gratitude to my life that I have learned to look for the reasons why things work as opposed to why things don't. I can see those around me offering positive feedback to others, along with encouraging words, and I try to emulate them as opposed to thinking they're silly Susie Sunshines. I don't always succeed.

Recently I pointed out a flaw in a co-worker that no one else had seen before (he wasn't in the room). Horrified, I apologized to those with whom I was speaking. I didn't say anything to the co-worker only because I didn't want to hurt him. But I did remember my screw up and I tried to pay special attention to him in our next meeting to see how we were similar instead of trying to uncover a flaw that may or may not be there.

How can you use your own smarty-pants ways to help rather than hurt? Can you put your brilliance to work to promote positivity today?

June 11

One of the things we are encouraged to do in sobriety is to continually assess our behavior. We are on the lookout for those small slights we do to others, our selfish responses and all the times we put ourselves first rather than thinking of what would be of benefit to all. This kind of constant evaluation is difficult for anyone, and can be particularly daunting to the alcoholic.

I found that early in my sobriety I was sorry all the time. I was sorry for not smiling at the security guard. I felt sorry for denying my dog the cookie he really wanted even though it wasn't our scheduled cookie time. I apologized to everyone, for everything, to the point where I felt drained, unlovable and hopelessly damaged.

While I think it is deeply important for us to own our role in our problems and to express an apology where it is warranted, I also believe that our daily list can included some plusses along with the minuses.

When you take your daily "inventory" make sure you see your kindness, generosity, selflessness and tenacity. Take a few moments to congratulate yourself for staying sober for one more day. Say "hooray" for your accomplishments. Keep a smart balance in your life by owning your fabulousness as well as your faults.

June 12

The alcoholic mind has a hard time sticking to the words in front of it. When we read an email, for example, we usually don't just read the words, we read *into* the words all kinds of things that aren't there. We try to pick apart what the sender "really" means by that, what's their motive, how will this all turn out, what are they trying to get, why are they trying to trick me, am I in trouble... And on and on.

One of the best pieces of advice I ever received in sobriety is to just read the print. For example, I am a landlord and I have a very difficult time holding my tenants to the rules. I make allowances for them and try to see things from their perspective. As a result, I get late payments, tenants who break things, renters who break the lease or take advantage of my good graces. When they send emails claiming that they can't pay the rent on time, I immediately spin off into all the reasons behind it, why they deserve a break, how I can help, etc. rather than just *reading the print and responding to it accordingly.*

After I received this piece of advice I suddenly became able to read, "the rent will be late," and respond with "that means you will pay a late fee." I don't have to read beyond what they said, have any sort of emotional reaction to it or solve their problem. I read the print and respond. It's that simple. And it works with everything.

What parts of your life could be improved by just reading the print?

June 13

Getting sober automatically makes you a non-conformist. Every level of society supports drinking, and probably most people you know don't see anything wrong with using alcohol. If you're rich you indulged in three-martini lunches. If you're poor you enjoyed a 12-pack after your shift. There is very little difference in these two choices other than the amount you paid to get blasted. And both choices, regardless of your financial situation, put you in a place where you chose to be with people as sick as you were.

You're sober now. You're different from most people you knew. You're a swan. Don't surround yourself with ducks.

You have the right to be with people who lift you up rather than drag you down. You have the right to choose with whom you spend your time. You have the right to spend time alone, getting to know the person you covered up for all of those years. You have the right to find another way to spend Saturday night.

Where are the other swans? Often they're in AA meetings or other sobriety fellowships. Sometimes they are at the gym, in the park, on a walk or strolling through a bookstore. You'll find swans at art class, at a writing symposium or volunteering their time to be of service to others. There are swans at your neighborhood library and there are swans at music lessons, trail runs, book clubs and church groups.

The swans are out there waiting for you with open wings! Forget about the ducks that drag you down and swim with the swans.

June 14

One of my favorite stories is the Taoist tale of farmer with an odd attitude. When his horse ran away, his neighbors said, "Such bad luck..."

"Maybe," he replied.

When the horse returned with three other wild horses, the neighbors exclaimed,"How wonderful!"

"Maybe," he replied.

His son tried to ride one of the untamed horses, was thrown, and broke his leg. The neighbors offered their sympathy on his misfortune.

"Maybe," answered the farmer.

The very next day military officials came to draft young men into the army. Seeing that the son's leg was broken, they passed him by. The neighbors congratulated the farmer on how well things had turned out. "Maybe," he said...

I often think of this story when I believe things aren't going my way. I remember all the things I thought were a disaster that turned out for the best—and all of the things that seemed a blessing that turned out to be a nightmare. I lost my job, but found a new one I liked better. I got married, but became a miserable alcoholic. I got divorced, but in my solitude I found sobriety.

The truth is that we don't know what the universe has planned for us with all of the seemingly wonderful or terrible things that happen. Perhaps it's best to take everything as it comes, and greet it with a heartfelt, "Maybe."

June 15

Perfectionism is another form of procrastination. We believe that if we can't do something perfectly right away then there's no point in even trying. In my experience, this line of thinking comes from the same source that tells me a drink will solve my problem. Perfectionism, like denial, is a device our egos use to keep us stuck in our unhealthy patterns.

Never let the perfect be the enemy of the good. In my sobriety I have failed in every way except drinking again. I have been selfish, self-serving, rude and difficult. I have had pity parties and temper tantrums. I have quit in a huff and stormed off in a rage.

But I have also experienced kindness, grace and understanding. I have recognized the traits I share with other alcoholics, and have dealt with emotional turmoil with rationality and selflessness. It's good. It's not perfect.

No one has ever promised you perfection in sobriety. But every day there's a little more good than the day before. Never let your false belief that you have to be perfect stop you from striving for the good.

June 16

I recently had an experience that made me want to have a drink. I should have seen it coming from a mile away, but I was taken off guard.

My belief in having multiple income streams sometimes results in some very busy workweeks. This particular week found me up before 7 a.m. and home after 8 p.m. for three days. I traveled in and out of areas with varying degrees of Internet coverage, all while being responsible for some very physical tasks. In between the running around I was desperately trying to stay connected to my clients, as I also had some non-negotiable deadlines.

I was exhausted, angry, starving and irritated with my partner, who had been barking orders at me for hours. In the fellowship I attend, the combination of all of these feelings is a major danger zone, and it's illustrated by the acronym H.A.L.T., which stands for Hungry, Angry, Lonely or Tired. Any of these occurrences are enough to send a sober person running for the bottle, but when all four are present we're headed for DEFCON 1.

How did I solve this problem? I suffered. I wasn't in a place where I could reach out to my sober fellows, and I wasn't in a situation where I could reasonably ask for a time out. So I gritted my teeth and I suffered through the craving. It was not pleasant, fun or calming, but I survived it.

When you find yourself in an extreme situation, it's always best to reach out to someone who can talk you off the ledge. If help is available you should always take it.

But if it's not, and your find yourself white-knuckling it, hold on. The suffering, intense though it may be, passes. Eat some food, take a nap... But never, ever drink. Suffer through the craving and then suffer some more while it passes. The discomfort you feel in this moment is worth it to avoid the devastating consequences of giving in.

June 17

When I was heavily into my disease, I was very fortunate to avoid picking up addictions to anything other than alcohol. I loved smoking cigarettes as well, but I never developed an infatuation with pills or hard drugs. However, I do see and recognize how easy it would be to make that leap. In fact, I courted a relationship with pills, but I couldn't find them and couldn't get my doctors to prescribe anything strong enough for my liking.

I had a minor outpatient procedure once, and although it was a very short operation, it is also known for being quite painful. Not only did my doctor refuse to give me anything for the pain and anxiety beforehand—no Tylenol, no Xanax—but she denied me any follow up pills afterward. I was really put out by this, especially since my addiction was wondering if it could switch its allegiance from swill to pills.

In somewhat of a huff, I confronted my doctor. "What exactly do you recommend I do while I recover?" I recall saying. "Just *suffer*?"

She asked me if there was anyone to care for me at home. I said there was and she replied, in her lilting Jamaican accent:

"Then he should make you a blueberry pie. That will make everything better."

This, to say the least, charmed me. Her sweetness disarmed me, and reminded me that there are non-chemical ways to get through pain. A caretaker and pie. Of course!

Plus, I see know that the universe was doing me a huge favor by keeping my grubby, addicted mitts off of pills of any kind.

These days, when I think I need a chemical solution, be it an over the counter pain medication or a cup full of a caffeine boost, I think about blueberry pie and wonder if maybe there's a more wholesome remedy I have not yet considered.

June 18

It's funny how aging doesn't really make us feel any older. I see in the mirror that I am older from those lovely crows feet, dark circles and "laugh lines." I have over 40 years' experience to draw upon that illustrates that I am older. I pay taxes and have a mortgage. I like old people things like birding and theater. I creak when I stand up.

But deep inside, all of these years, I have been wondering where the adults are that are going to tell me how to live my life, give me credit for a job well done and save me from my mistakes. I still feel like I am eighteen years old, so where the heck are these grown ups who are supposed to be running things? Why are they so late?

The despair I felt when I realized that the grown ups were never coming because *I am the grown up* cannot be overstated. I mean, are you kidding me? *I* am responsible for my own life? Preposterous.

I hate to tell you this, but the grown ups aren't coming. We are the grown ups. We are the ones responsible for staying sober and cleaning up our messes. We are the ones who need to pay our debts, both financial and spiritual. We are the ones who congratulate ourselves for a job well done, and we are the ones who recognize that we may be on the wrong track.

By getting sober you've done an incredibly adult thing. Maybe this being a grownup thing will work out. How can you be a better grown up today?

June 19

June 19th, also known as Juneteenth, is a day of celebration, reflection and remembrance. It's a commemoration of June 19th, 1865, the day that slaves were emancipated in the state of Texas. Nowadays, it's recognized nationwide as a day to honor those whose lives were inexorably damaged by the atrocity of slavery and to rejoice in their hard-won freedom. Today's leaders encourage these celebrations to focus on education and achievement, and to provide a platform for all Americans to truthfully acknowledge our history.

Even before I got sober, Juneteenth was one of my favorite holidays. I love the emphasis on facing the reality of our past while turning our hearts and minds to a hopeful future. I am touched by the growing interest in this holiday throughout the world, as we all become more educated about our true cultural heritage. It's a day to spend reading, writing and listening to the revelations of those who have experienced things I may never understand. It's a day to remember that we are all human, and that each and every one of us deserves the chance to thrive in this life.

Now that I am sober, Juneteenth takes on an even deeper meaning for me. I am free, and I relish this freedom every single day. With a clear mind and an open heart, I have the ability to further appreciate the struggles of others and work every day to ensure that I work toward the good of all of us, not just one group. My alcoholism has awakened me to the truth that we are all connected, we are all so very fragile and we each get but one chance in this life to make things right.

June 20

Do you ever miss the drama of drinking? I hate to admit this, but sometimes I do. While I love my sober, orderly, calm life, there's a part of me that gets so bored with clean kitchens, a good night's sleep and folded laundry.

When these feelings of ennui would creep up early in my sobriety, I had no idea what to do. Usually I would apply myself to some sort of household task to keep my mind off the boredom. I would still feel fidgety and purposeless, but at least the bathtub was clean.

As I progressed through sobriety and learned to see the underlying reason for many of my emotions, I realized that I was bored because I was being boring. I missed the drama of drinking because I hadn't put any effort into creating healthy drama.

There's nothing wrong with wanting drama in our lives. The trick is to transform what we thought was drama (petty fights, lover's spats, gossip sessions, wild nights) into drama that's truly exciting, overwhelming and awe-inspiring on a soul level.

Spend a few minutes lying on your back and looking at the stars when you need a beauty boost. Want to be in the mix where there are struggles and difficulties? Volunteer your time, your experience and your listening skills at a senior center, alcohol rehab or wildlife rescue. Looking for a wild time? Perform that song you wrote at open mic night, speak at your church or audition for the community play. Need an adventure? Go zip lining, take a long hike or swim in the ocean.

We didn't have drama when we were drinking. We had drinking when we were drinking. The real excitement starts when you're sober enough choose to have healthy, constructive experiences.

June 21

Happy summer solstice! It's the longest day of the year, and the perfect day to spend precious extra hours celebrating your new sober life.

Throughout the world, people gather to rejoice on this day. Latvians run through the streets naked. The Swedish dance around a decorated maypole. Visit Croatia, and you'll find folks in traditional costumes paying homage to the birth of John the Baptist. In Denmark, you can be sure there's a party around a bonfire. Everywhere (in the Northern Hemisphere, anyway), the summer solstice is a chance to take stock mid-year and reflect on how you've spent the last six months, and decide how you plan to spend the next.

The summer solstice is like an un-birthday or a new New Year. Use today's extra light to shine a spotlight on your hopes and goals for the rest of the year. Plant the seeds of desire and nurture them in the coming months so that you have harvest full of grace.

June 22

When I got sober, so did my partner. He is not an alcoholic, and he's one of those lucky blokes who has a take-it-or-leave-it opinion on drinking. Since I have officially cleaned up, he has had the equivalent of exactly one glass of wine. He doesn't ever miss it, nor does he ever struggle with needing a drink after a hard day, when he's tired or when he's hungry. He sees the advantages of sobriety from a health perspective. His ability to focus on work, be truly present with the kids and calm himself down have all improved.

I am very fortunate that I have his support, and I am also fortunate that I have someone else's experience to witness. When I am struggling with wanting a drink, he never preaches or condescends. He just listens. By being the other sober person in the room, he gives me an example to look toward. I can see all of the benefits of his sobriety at work in his life and I can aspire to have those things, too. And the truth is I do have all of those things. It's just harder for me to see them when I am having a tough time.

Not all of us are so lucky. Perhaps those closest to you have not quit drinking. Perhaps they make you feel weird or maybe they jokingly try to tempt you into drinking with them. My best advice is to seek out those who are sober and connect with them immediately.

You will never be able to erase all of the drinkers from your life. However, there are thousands of sober people out there who would be delighted to meet you, to offer a helping hand and to serve as your example when you see absolutely nothing good about being sober. AA meetings are great places to start. So is your church. You can also call helplines and find recovering people online. Ask the universe for the support you need and it will arrive.

June 23

Summer is the loudest season. Birds tweet and shriek as they revel in the warmer weather. Swimming holes and local pools are the last places to find quiet, as they are filled with children who for some inexplicable reason start screaming the instant they hit water. As the sun sets, frogs, cicadas and hundreds of other singing insects rev up a happy tune.

Embrace the sounds of summer and join in. It's the season for bursting into bloom, for expressing yourself fully, for turning the volume up to 11. It's a completely different attitude than, say, fall, where everything turns inward and we are naturally inclined to be more introspective. Summer is the time to express yourself.

You're sober. You're proud. Let's hear it for sobriety!

What can you shout from the rooftops? Where can you laugh out loud? When can you burst into song and join in the sensational symphony of summer?

June 24

Have you ever noticed how some people have all the luck? They get the guy (or gal), the job, the house and the trip around the world. They always seem to fall in to the right job or find the perfect sale.

The unifying thing I've noticed about all of the lucky people in my life is their attitude. They assume things are always going to work out, and guess what? They do! They don't assume everything is going to work out because everything they do falls perfectly into place, but because they are happy with what they *do* have, and what they *actually get*, rather than wishing things were better or different.

Not only do they focus on the things that are good in their lives, they also are willing to adapt as things unfold rather than getting caught up in trying to make everything fit into their preconceived notion of how life should be.

Some people are naturals at being able to go with the flow, and following that flow into a life of abundance. Others of us have to work at it a bit more. When I find myself struggling against what I do have versus what I want to have, I have a few quotes to rely on to get me back on track:

"We Indians have a saying: 'In the end, everything will be fine. If everything is not fine, then it is not yet the end.'"—The Best Exotic Marigold Hotel

"I am a great believer in luck. I find that the harder I work, the more I seem to have."—Thomas Jefferson

"Remember that sometimes not getting what you want is a wonderful stroke of luck."—
Dalai Lama XIV

Are you feeling lucky today? If you're sober, that may be all the luck you need right now.

June 25

I've recently become aware of some of the little traits, patterns and opinions that have dictated the outcome of my entire life. These barely noticeable ways of thinking not only led me to alcoholism, divorce and some very unhappy events, but they also resulted in some success, happiness and joy, too.

When we examine our lives to try to understand how we "got here," it's usually the big things that take our attention: the job interview we botched when we were hungover, the choice to not finish college, the bad partner we married... But all of these decidedly big things were possibly the result of small patterns of thinking that we probably aren't even aware of.

My own pattern includes the belief that I am not "allowed" to do certain things. I don't believe I am allowed to be angry (which has created a deep resentment, in some cases). I don't believe that I should be allowed to be in charge of a group. I don't believe that I am allowed to experience an array of rituals that are common to the human experience. Things like a big, beautiful wedding, a fabulous fortieth birthday party or an adventurous trip to celebrate a milestone are all things I don't think I am allowed to do.

Now that I have identified this subtle pattern I am able to address it as it occurs and change it. I don't exactly fly off the handle, I have no plans to get married, I missed my fortieth already and I am so frugal that an adventure is not financially possible, but I am definitely working on the idea that I am allowed these things. These limits were self-imposed. No one ever told me I wasn't allowed, just like no one said I wasn't allowed to get sober.

Turns out I was allowed to get sober. Now that I have found this small pattern that has dictated the outcome of my life to this point, I am looking forward to being allowed to let it go.

June 26

Like learning to play an instrument, sobriety requires daily practice. I recently read a story about actor, writer and musician Steve Martin, who is a virtuoso banjo player. By all accounts, learning the banjo is a very complicated endeavor, and becoming good at it is rare. When asked why he decided to take on such a difficult challenge he answered that if he practiced every day, in 40 years he would be someone who has been playing the banjo for 40 years.

Martin had the vision to play the long game with his banjo playing, and it was a long game with a daily commitment. Alcoholics Anonymous wisely recommends that we take our sobriety one day at a time. Keep in mind that if you keep practicing your sobriety every single day, by the end of a year, you'll have a year of sobriety. By the end of ten years, you'll have a decade of sobriety. And by the end of 40 years of practicing every single day, you'll be an expert with 40 years of sobriety.

That's a long game I'm willing to play. Aren't you?

June 27

Alcoholics are self-absorbed. Don't take that personally—it's just true. It's true of me, too. My alcoholism grew out of my obsession with getting what I wanted when I wanted it, all of the time, no matter the consequences to anyone else.

I still suffer from a complete preoccupation with myself, even though now I actively work on it. I remind myself that humility, caring and serving others are the cornerstones of my sobriety. I work very hard to actively listen and be present when I am with others. I attempt to infuse all of my work with the idea that I work for the sole purpose of helping people, and not for my own aggrandizement. It takes time and practice, but I am fully committed to shifting my thoughts away from myself.

It helps me to take a moment each day to think about other addicts who have not gotten sober. During my meditation, my evening prayers or on a long drive, I'll take a few breaths to remind myself that I was once part of a very different club—a club full of drunks, addicts and egoists who were unwilling and unable to change. There are still people in my life who suffer daily from the affects of alcohol and drugs. There are millions of people around the world who will never get sober, who don't know that sobriety is an option and who will die of this disease.

Any time you're feeling wrapped up in your own thoughts, take a few moments to send some love to the addict who still suffers. If it's the only thing you do for someone else today, it's enough.

June 28

One of the most powerful things you can do in this life is to own your own screw-ups. Don't blame the dog for eating your homework. Don't throw your co-workers under the bus for the project being late. Don't blame your mother for your alcohol problem. Own your role in every mess and pretty soon you'll find that you're in far fewer messes.

By taking responsibility for your mess-ups, failures, oversights or mistakes, you have the opportunity to assess why it happened and how you can change things in the future so that it doesn't happen again. It's the powerful position to take in life. By blaming others we become a perpetual victim and our situation never, ever improves.

Case in point: I have a rental unit and my current tenants broke their lease. They moved out without paying the final month's rent, which is to be expected. But what I didn't realize is that they did not pay their water bill, resulting in dry faucets when I went to clean and prep the place for re-renting. (I don't know if you've ever tried to clean a house without running water, but I can tell you that it doesn't work.) I was perturbed and spent several moments lambasting the tenants for being irresponsible, selfish and rude.

But then I had the grace to realize that I should have called all of the utilities as soon as they moved out anyway. The fact is that I did not call the water company to have the billing switched over into my name, as I am required by law to do. If I had done what I was supposed to do, it wouldn't have mattered that they didn't pay their bill.

What power I felt in that moment! It was my fault. I owned it. I was instantly rid of negative feelings. Plus, I made a mental note that as soon as anyone else moves out, the first thing I will do is call the utilities. By owning my part in this snafu, I can ensure that it will never, ever happen again.

If you think you're weak when you admit a mistake, you are dead wrong. It's the exact opposite. In the face of a mistake, the ONLY way to get your power back is to own your part in it.

June 29

It's summer, and we've spent much of the month of June tuning up our sobriety. Let's take the month out by doing something straight up delightful.

I had a school friend named Michelle, and she was the kind of person who was always up to something fun. If she wasn't learning how to read tarot cards, she was taking a knitting class. One day, she showed up in a convertible and took me to brunch with the top down even though it was 40 degrees outside! We were freezing, but it was exhilarating. That was the kind of thing Michelle did, and I loved her for it.

She once decided that she was going to memorize Edgar Allen Poe's famous poem, "The Raven." It's a long poem by any standards, but she was determined to get the whole thing—and she did. She could rattle off the entire thing. This captivated me, and I realized even then that this was a skill that nearly everyone could master. I set out to memorize a few things of my own, most notably a poem by Lord Byron called "She Walks in Beauty."

Anyone can memorize something that they love. In my sobriety I've found that memorizing certain quotes or sayings helps me to remember why I decided to set out on this journey. In life, I've found that setting out to memorize a little something gets me out of my head and into the world of a passage, a poem or a song, offering me a few hours of relaxation as well as a fun parlor trick that people love.

Let's memorize something! It can be a your favorite poem, *The Cat in the Hat*, a meditation that inspires you... Or, how about something you use every day like the bus schedule? Maybe you could memorize everyone's birthday at your job or in your favorite class. Perhaps there's a prayer you'd like to have down pat.

Give your sober brain a bit of a workout by memorizing something today. You'll be surprised how much fun it is.

June 30

"We must be willing to let go of the life we've planned, so as to have the life that is waiting for us." —Joseph Campbell

Those of us that have experienced the desperation that comes along with alcoholism—
and the decision to get sober—are experts at not getting the life we envisioned.

I remember proclaiming, in my early years of drinking, that I would never let myself become an alcoholic because I loved drinking so much. I envisioned a life of tipsy celebrations, elegant wine drinking events and glamorous, wine-soaked get-togethers with friends. My life was going to get better and better, I was going to be richer and richer, and alcohol was going to be my constant companion.

But it didn't work out that way. The gentle giddiness that came along with early drinking transformed into slurring, tripping and blacking out. The lighthearted girl that came out to play after a few drinks was pushed aside by a bitter woman who white-knuckled her way through blinding daily hangovers. To get sober I had to let go of the life I planned, be brutally honest that it wasn't working, and embrace the life that was waiting for me.

My life is not glamorous. I do not have rich friends or throw glitzy parties. I travel on a budget (when I can afford it at all), and I work several jobs at a time in order to meet my financial goals. I read. I run. I write.

My life did not turn out at all like I had hoped. Instead, I became a reprehensible drunk and had to throw aside my ideas of a luxurious lifestyle *so I could save my own life.*

I am sober, and I work hard at sobriety every single day. My goals are reachable. My sleep is sound. My body is healthy. But this is not what I planned.

What life is waiting for you now that you're sober?

July
Embracing Independence

July 1

The freedom from alcohol is one of the greatest gifts you'll ever receive. We got it wrong for so long, didn't we? When I uncorked a bottle and poured a glass, I often did it with a bit of a chip on my shoulder. *No one can tell me what to do*, I would think. *I'm an adult and I am FREE to live my life however I choose.*

Oh, how mistaken I was.

Far from being free to live my life, I was beholden to the bottle. When I was drinking I would lose my freedom to make good decisions. When I was drinking, I wasn't free to do anything else but obsess about alcohol, plan to drink alcohol and spend a whole day recovering from drinking alcohol. Freedom? Hardly.

If we are adults with jobs, children, community obligations, mortgages and responsibilities, we will never be "free" to do whatever we want when we want. In sobriety, we have learned that—far from being a burden—our commitment to these grownup demands will actually keep us grounded.

But every day, every moment, every hour and every minute we have freedom from alcohol. And that means we have the freedom to feel, think, decide with a clear mind and an open heart.

July 2

The truth does set us free. As kids, most of us learned to lie. We would fib about our homework being done or where we were on Saturday afternoon. Sometimes we would take on really tall tales that would eventually get discovered before any major harm was done. If we were lucky enough to have been born into a social structure that valued honesty, chances are we would grow out of the lying stage to discover that a life lived with as few secrets as possible is much more fulfilling.

But those of us who weren't so lucky, or who were narcissistic, self-conscious and fearful, might not have learned this lesson. If we eventually became alcoholic, chances are we took lying to a whole new level of complexity.

A life lived sober requires thorough honesty. And I am not talking about the little assertions that your friend does look great in that dress when she doesn't or that you loved the meal when you didn't—those are small kindnesses and not at all what we're talking about here.

I'm talking about that big moment, the one where you looked in the mirror and realized you couldn't do this anymore. That moment, that decision, is the touchstone of your honest life. And if you can recall that instant in times when you're wobbly, it is a truth that will set you free from alcohol time and again.

July 3

On this eve of America's Independence, let's visit the past for a few moments. Although I don't like to spend too much time digging around in my past because I try to stay present in the here and now, I do find it useful to recollect those final few days before my sobriety date.

I do this not because I want to make myself feel bad or dredge up old embarrassments, but because I want to recall the reeling, raw experience that left me so devastated that the only thing that would help was to quit drinking. These terrible feelings, these awful remembrances, are profoundly useful.

Remembering those few days keeps me centered in my sobriety. Any time I feel like a drink would settle things, or that I am somehow "missing out" on life, I take hold of those memories and grasp them like I would a talisman in my pocket. All of this hard work, soul searching, facing my demons and sacrifices are because I never want to feel that way again. I have scratched, clawed, breathed, cried, raged, slept, wandered and worried to get to this place of sobriety. I have earned my own independence from alcohol, and the memories of those final few days are all I need to remind me to hold firm to what I've fought for and won.

July 4

Happy Independence Day to those of you who live in the United States! And Happy Independence Day to everyone who is free from the tethers of alcohol.

This is a day to reflect on the true meaning of independence. For me, being independent is the essential belief that I can do what is necessary to take care of my family and myself. That doesn't mean I don't ask for help or that I don't rely on others when I am out of my depth. My independence is wholly predicated on being flexible, continuing to learn intellectually, to grow spiritually, to keep up with technology, to remain physically active and emotionally mature, and to do as much for myself as possible.

I have a rental house that is always in a state of disrepair. It has been a financial, emotional and physical burden, and a great source of stress over the years. It's like having a 1300 square foot hungry baby that demands constant feeding and attention. When I was drinking, this house was the "cause" of many a bender, so great was my anxiety over my predicament. Poor, poor, pour me a drink, as they say.

In my sobriety, I found myself in the midst of a major overhaul of this rental. Every surface needed to be repaired, every appliance was falling apart, every wall needed painting—you get the picture. It was ten weekends of eight-hour days where I was covered head to toe in paint, filth, detritus and dirt.

The difference was that this time I appreciated the skills I was developing. I learned how to take apart my oven to fix a stain on the inside of the window. I learned to repair the washing machine (which I thought I was going to have to replace) by viewing an online video. I bought, built and operated a gas-powered pressure washer. I discovered how to prune the bushes so they look more like trees than weeds.

I realized that this seismic shift in attitude was a part of my growing confidence in sobriety. I was tired, worried and a bit stressed out while working on the house, but I was and still am *no longer a victim*. If there is a problem, I know that I can solve it. If there is a skill required, there's no doubt I can learn it. This is independence. This is pride. This is sobriety.

July 5

What can you teach yourself? A magnificent byproduct of my sobriety is the realization that I can learn to do anything on my own. I had no idea that this would happen, or that I would transform into this learning machine, but I did and I am having a wonderful time honing my new skills (even if I never perfect them).

I like yoga. I like yoga because it's sort of like dance, but you're not performing or trying to please people. I like it because anyone of any skill level can participate. I like that it's like learning a new language, and that all the positions (or *asanas*) symbolize something. One of the other reasons I like yoga is that after you learn the basic asanas, you can practice any time, anywhere, with very little space and with no teacher or instructor.

I recently attended an all-day yoga retreat for a little tune-up and I ran into an old friend. We were delighted to see each other and were trying to make plans to get together again. She thought another yoga class would be great and she asked me about several different studios, none of which I had visited. "Where do you practice?" she asked. "At home," I responded. "I practice on my own with the help of online videos."

"I could never do that," she said. "I need someone telling me what to do."

Do you think that's true for yourself? Do you feel like you need instruction in order to stay focused on or to participate in learning? If so, I challenge you to learn something on your own as soon as possible. Yoga's great, but it might not be your thing, and that's fine. There are infinite resources for teaching yourself how to solve math problems, how to use a graphics program on your computer, how to cook something special or a few words in American Sign Language (or Italian, or French...). In the spirit of independence, give yourself a chance to do a little independent study.

July 6

Vikram Gandhi is a filmmaker who set out to prove to people that they do not need the teachings of a guru to embrace fulfillment, joy and contentment—everything they need resides inside them. He impersonated an Indian guru with the name "Kumare" and took his "teachings" (which were mostly hilariously ironic) to yoga studios, meditation spaces and groups of gatherers in Arizona.

What transpires is riveting. These kind people, most of whom wanted answers (like all of us), fell into blind devotion to this fake Kumare, who eventually revealed his charade. I won't spoil the ending for you, but I will say that the message impressed upon me so deeply the idea that we all have a guru, a higher power and a spiritual leader *within us.* We can access the space where we are truly fulfilled completely on our own, simply by listening to the messages we are receiving from our own hearts and minds.

Be your own guru! Create your own meditations and your own sacred readings and spaces. Write your own prayers. Play your own music.

If you have people in your life to whom you go for advice, for wisdom or for a friendly reminder, that's a wonderful part of a rich life. But never hand over your power to someone who claims to have all the answers. You are the only one with the answers that will guide you on your journey.

July 7

"You don't have to worry about burning bridges if you're building your own."—Kerry E. Wagner

When I read this quote for the first time I didn't quite know what to make of it. I had been told my whole life that you never want to burn bridges, burning bridges is the worst possible thing and if you burn a bridge you darn well better start trying to repair it or the sky will rain frogs and the earth will implode.

Wagner's words have stuck with me not only because they are absolutely counter to everything I grew up believing, but also because I found so much truth there.

During my drinking days, my bridge burning was of the staggering around, dropping matches in gasoline, flaming my way to the sea sort of burning. I was an alcoholic and if you got in my way, come hell or high water, I would cut you off, cut you out or cut you to pieces behind your back.

In my early sobriety I worked diligently to mend as much damage as I could, with varying results. Now, I try not to do damage in the first place. But a recent event had me dropping a nuclear bomb on a family bridge, and I did it because it was the moral thing to do. This quote pulled me through that difficult time because its truth rang like a bell. I had to demolish this bridge because people were being lied to, stolen from and misled. There are members of my family who may never speak to me again because I revealed their misdeeds. But I will be fine because I have a network of strong bridges I have erected in my sobriety, like a strong career, loyal friends, financial stability and an unshakable confidence. I would like for these family members to be in my life. But if they aren't, I can live with it because my own bridges are failsafe.

July 8

One of the most exciting times in anyone's adult life is the transition to living in your own home. Whether it's an apartment with roommates or a space with your spouse, most adults get to relish that first moment where all we survey is our own.

I've accumulated a lot of stuff, and subsequently had to let a lot of stuff go, both literally and figuratively. When I was drinking I wouldn't think twice about loading up a car full of purchases, bringing it all home and then forgetting all about it. Cheap things broke. I bought items I "might need," stored them somewhere and never looked at them again. Impulse shopping was common, and I would often spend way more than I could afford because I "deserved it."

To claim my sobriety I had to walk away from a lot of stuff, and in rebuilding my life I have severely edited my possessions. I never go shopping for fun. I rarely purchase anything "expensive" without thoroughly researching my options. I take meticulous care of what little I do have because I want things to last. Much like my sobriety, I maintain my possessions carefully to ensure I have them for a long, long time.

This attention to caretaking serves as a metaphor for my sobriety, but it's also an action-based way for me to exercise my independence. By caring for my things, I learn how to fix them when they break, tune up items that need it and ensure that the items I buy last a long time. In addition, caring for my things is very much an expression of caring for myself. By maintaining things I ensure that they work properly and look good, thereby removing unnecessary sources of stress.

Everything I survey is mine. But through my sobriety I value my things in a completely different way. I care for my things because sobriety has taught me the importance of daily maintenance.

July 9

In this month of discovering our independence, it's time to face a cold, hard fact. Most of us are outsourcers. What this means is that we pay others money to do things we either can't do or don't want to do rather than learning how to do them. This affects our ability to be truly independent because we need others to do certain things for us.

There are always going to be tasks where you'll prefer professional assistance. I recently hired some guys with a truck to haul some yard waste away because it was cheaper and easier than renting the truck, loading it myself and driving it to the compost. However, there are probably also things you're outsourcing on a regular basis that you could do for yourself.

How often do you go out to dinner? You're outsourcing your cooking. Do you pay someone to maintain your yard? You're outsourcing your gardening (and forgoing some great exercise). Doe you hire someone else to do your taxes? You're outsourcing your finances.

Sobriety can be the gateway to complete competency. Those hours you're not spending chugging down booze can be the hours you use to trim your shrubs into topiaries, make a meal or manage your money. With the Internet at our fingertips there is virtually nothing we can't learn how to do, becoming more and more independent in the process.

July 10

The Declaration of Independence is a unique historical document in that it is one of the first to mention the pursuit of happiness. It's an interesting concept, that we have an unalienable right not to *be* happy, but to *pursue happiness.*

The word *pursue* indicates striving, clamoring or running after something that remains *just out of reach*. The word choice is particularly notable in that I think it influences something about our American way of life—a way of life that is predicated on work, competition and striving for the American Dream, a dream that promises happiness (if we ever actually arrive there).

In our drinking days we were continually swept up in this crazy-making pursuit of happiness. One more drink would always do the trick wouldn't it? We were willing to pursue bottled happiness to the ends of the earth.

What if, in our newfound independent state, we stop pursuing happiness and start accepting it? Let's think of happiness not as something to be tracked and hunted, but rather something that thrives within us. Let's opt out of the chase, and develop our own inner resources, stoke the internal fires of contentment and stop running after that elusive "happiness" that's always around the corner. If we sit still long enough, the happiness will pursue *us.*

July 11

"As long as you keep a person down, some part of you has to be there to hold him down, so it means you cannot soar as you otherwise might." —Marian Anderson

How do you feel when others around you are successful? When you hear news of friends making a big splash in their chosen field, or winning some kind of award, do you snarl or do you celebrate? Are you in a position like being a manager, teacher or leader where you can directly influence people? Do you use that power to promote others' talents or to hold them back because they might threaten you?

What I love about Marian Anderson's quote is that it reminds me, in those moments when I am inclined to thwart someone's goal or get in the way of their idea, that in order for me to truly keep them from achieving I have to be there to keep them down. Any time you limit someone else's potential you are also limiting your own.

In sobriety we have been given another chance to create the life of our dreams. Next time you feel yourself acting out toward someone else's success with spite, malice or jealousy remember that in order to keep that person down, you are focusing on them, and not focusing on your own goals.

July 12

It seems counterintuitive, but in my search for independence in my sobriety I often depended on others for ideas. I learned two things. 1) There are always others out there who want the same things you do, and are actively working toward getting them. It is crucial to connect with them to get their wisdom and advice. 2) No one achieves anything completely alone.

The first part is twisted only because one would think that a life of independence can only be achieved in solitude. I realized that, like sobriety, I couldn't work toward independence without the ideas and help of others. That realization led me to the discovery that no matter how independent we become, we will always rely on others for certain things.

It's as basic as understanding that I couldn't write this book without the computer someone else invented and the word processing program others created. Someone else built the roads I drive on, someone else makes sure my electricity works every day and someone else is in charge of making sure the water comes out of the faucet every single morning.

Instead of thinking that I could never achieve total independence from anything, I simply realized that I must be grateful for the interdependent systems that allow me to accomplish the things that are important to me. Plus, it makes me realize that my words, work and behavior may contribute to someone else's success.

In our quest for independence, let's be sure to gratefully remember those upon whom we rely, and to remember to hold ourselves tight to all of the things for which we are truly responsible.

July 13

Don't you love those people who are always full of great stories, useful information, wise advice and handy how-to? I do. There's something very generous about people who share what they know.

I tend to be the opposite. I certainly like to read and learn and make myself better. But I tend to waste what I know only on myself. I think this speaks to two things. 1) That I am insecure about my own talents and, 2) There's something self-centered in my thinking that keeps me from sharing the stuff I have found out.

I'm still working on this one. I can write about the things I know all day long, but I am terrible at sharing my knowledge with people in person. If I find myself in a situation where I am required to "teach" anyone anything, I am more wrapped up in how I sound, if I am making sense or if they think I am smart rather than whether or not they are getting the lesson. This is a defect of my character, and I am tackling it day by day.

So I ask you—are you wasting what you know? What, in your lifetime of experience, in your journey through addiction and back again, are you not sharing with the world?

What amazing things have you learned that others could benefit from?

July 14

"The worst thing you can do for someone you care about is something they can do on their own." —Abraham Lincoln

When I first joined a sobriety fellowship, I volunteered to be responsible for handing out the literature, most of which was free. Our guidebook, however, cost $10. A newcomer asked me for a free book because she couldn't afford it. I responded by telling her I could give it to her, and made a mental note to give the treasurer $10 so the meeting wouldn't go into debt.

That's when Judy jumped in and said, "The book costs $10 and we don't give them out for free." The new person was astonished (as was I, since I had promised a free one), and she claimed again she couldn't afford it. Judy then said something I'll never forget. She asked the woman how much she had spent on her last night drinking. "I bet you didn't think twice about spending more than $10 then," she said.

I think it's obvious that the newcomer left without a book, but I left with a very important lesson: that showing love often requires letting people figure out how to accomplish something on their own. We trick ourselves into thinking that true generosity means giving and giving and giving again. But Judy pointed out to me that in order for people to feel truly accomplished, for them to grow and mature, they have to find their own way to do things.

If that newcomer didn't think it was worth $10 for the guidebook to her sobriety, she probably wasn't ready to tackle the tasks ahead of her. She won't get sober until she can make it happen for herself.

I forget this with my kids, too, and I jump in to complete things for them when they struggle. But I must remember that in order for them to grow they must learn to make the sandwich, do the laundry, write the paper or finish the math problem all on their own. It feels strange, incorrect even, but when you think about it, expecting anything less is actually unloving.

Are there areas where you can step back and let others learn for themselves? Are there things others are doing for you that you can take on yourself?

July 15

In stories that focus on a hero's journey, stories like *Star Wars* for example, there is nearly always a moment that makes it impossible for the hero to go home. In *Star Wars*, Luke wants to join the rebel forces, but until his farm burns down and his caretakers die, he has no compelling reason to make the journey. Once the farm is gone Luke has no choice but to go out and seize his destiny. He becomes independent of the system that kept him stuck and is forced (apologies for the pun) to make the steps toward becoming the man who saves the galaxy.

In your sobriety, are you still holding on to your fall back position? Are there enablers who still encourage you to drink? Are there people who will pick you up from jail, pay for your plane ticket home from rehab or drive you to the store to get more booze?

If your sobriety is at the forefront of your life, it may be time to destroy the farm. Luke Skywalker found that the only way the force could thrive in his life was to have no other option.

What things can you leave behind in order for your real journey to begin?

July 16

Self-esteem is a feeling of competence and worthiness. Self-esteem is not the arrogance of thinking you are better than anyone or your ability to brag, nor is it really based on how you look or dress, what you drive or the opulence of your estate. Hundreds of thousands of people who look like they are oozing self-esteem are actually insecure, frightened little children inside.

That's because the only way to develop self-esteem is through accomplishment.

Dressing yourself a certain way is not accomplishment. Surrounding yourself with fine furnishings is not accomplishment. Bragging to others about what you saw or whom you know is not accomplishment.

If you've been told in your sobriety that you lack self-esteem, then it's time to start building it, day by day. And the only possible way to do it is to set goals and achieve them.

Let's not start with something like a 50-mile marathon. Let's start with taking out the garbage. Don't raise the bar so high that you can't accomplish it, start with something small and attainable. Instead of ordering a cheeseburger for lunch, get a salad. Instead of watching TV for a half hour, take that time to read the book you've always wanted to tackle. When you feel the urge to shove that unpaid bill in the back of the drawer, take it out and look at it. Create a day-by-day plan to pay it.

Self-esteem comes incrementally, over time. It is developed small step by small step, by making better decisions, even if they are tiny, until you start to create a whole that reflects accountability, trust, competence and motivation.

July 17

There is a marked difference between rebellion and revolution. Rebellion is more closely akin to the feelings we had while we were still drinking. Rebellion is the "you can't tell me what to do" frame of mind that led us down dark pathways.

Revolution is a shift from within. Rather than resisting the rules imposed on us externally, revolution is a turning toward something. Revolution embraces new ideas and philosophies; rebellion rejects external ideas. Revolution is a radical, holistic change in how we see the world and our place in it; rebellion grows out of our terror of being asked to change.

Sobriety, in order for it to be successful, requires a revolution. Don't point your natural rebelliousness in a different direction and expect your sobriety to stick. If you're now rebelling against drinking, there is no real evolution in your mindset. You're using the same weapons in a different battle.

But if you embrace the revolution, the total top-down transformation in how you are in the world, you will succeed more effortlessly than you ever imagined. Step out of the rebellion and allow yourself to be swept up in the revolution. It's where you'll find your peace.

July 18

My studies about independence happily led me to the writings of Tom Hodgkinson and his cohorts at *The Idler*. This bright group of philosophers, writers, teachers and layabouts taught me so much about letting go of my preconceived ideas of a successful life. I continually turn to their pages for reassurance that a life outside of the socially accepted systems is not only aspirational, but also attainable. Certainly sobriety, more than any other weird idea I've taken up, is the most controversial, and the one that puts my dot outside of the circle more often than any other philosophy.

From *The Idler*, I was introduced to the idea that true anarchists never break the law. (As a person who votes regularly and stays involved in local politics, I don't consider myself an anarchist in the slightest, but in my whole life I had never read a defense of anarchy. Naturally this got my attention.)

How can this be? My vision of anarchists is the Molotov-cocktail-throwing, safety-pin-in-chin, leather-clad, Mohawk-coiffed rabble-rouser. In fact, this is not what defines them whatsoever.

The true anarchist is someone who tries to stay out of the government system they so heartily disagree with. If they broke the law, they would be submitting themselves to the system. This means that the true anarchist pays their taxes, stops at red lights, registers their car...

They understand that the minute you break the law, you give someone else power over you.

Invite a little true anarchy into your sobriety. Be revolutionary in your unwillingness to submit to its authority. Remind yourself that the second you have that drink, you are handing your power over to something much more sinister than a local cop or district attorney. You are handing power to your disease. And your disease will do way worse to you than give you a fine or lock you up. Your disease wants you dead. That's a good enough reason for me to follow the rules, how about you?

July 19

Sarah Turner and Lucy Rocca, authors of *The Sober Revolution*, have discovered that more and more women are embracing sobriety. Men are, too, of course, and they explore the cultural movement of sobriety on their terrific website, soberistas.com.

If you are a sober person, now more than any other time in history, you are part of a powerful movement toward independence from destructive outside forces. You are not alone. You are contributing to a groundswell movement of people who have realized that a life lived in a perpetual fog is not a life worth living.

When you tap into this community, whether it is online, in a local fellowship or through reading and study, you'll find that there is massive support for what you have chosen to do on every level. Not only will you find the revolutionaries who have stepped away from alcohol, but you'll find people who regained their lives when they quit smoking, changed their diets, downsized their living space, lost weight, took up exercise, built a business, started a band or pursued creative interests.

The sober revolution is one of many radical shifts taking place in the world. So many of us, after being tossed around by financial devastation, illness, trickery in the marketplace or government corruption are editing the things from our lives that have no value and grasping on to things of true depth and meaning. Eliminating alcohol is a monumental step, and lucky for us, there is a community of like-minded souls out there waiting for us to join them in our journey toward self-reliance, rational behavior and profound meaning.

July 20

There's a little organizational tip I picked up along the way that seems so silly and simple, that I was surprised that it ended up transforming my whole life.

That seems like an overstatement, but it's not. Here's the tip: if it takes less than one minute, do it now.

Are your keys in your pocket and not in the key bowl by the door? It takes less than a minute to put them where they go, so do it now.

Does that stack of junk mail need to be thrown out? It takes less than a minute, so do it now.

Do you need to email a thank you note to your aunt? That can take about a minute, so do it now.

What I have discovered through this method is what my partner refers to as, "Past you taking care of future you." I always know where my keys are. My desk is clutter-free so that I can spend time on things that matter rather than searching for stuff under piles of junk. My family hears from me on a regular basis so there are no hard feelings.

When we put things off in the present we set ourselves up for frustration in the future. Sometimes this idea boils down to really elemental things like making your bed in the morning so you have a fresh, clean place to sleep that night. Sometimes these decisions are profound, but still simple: stay sober for the next minute. Then the next. Then the next.

Get things done in the present, so when you look at the past you can see how each positive step has led you to a life of simple order, small accomplishments and daily sobriety.

July 21

It's impossible to talk about independence and freedom without at some point exploring the concept of surrender.

Surrender has the unfortunate reputation of being a negative. If your favorite sports team surrenders, that's not good. If you're fighting a war and you surrender to the enemy, I think most people look upon that with a frown. No one ever wants to surrender the point, surrender the election or surrender his or her guns.

But the type of surrender I am talking about is spiritual surrender. It's a handing over of control to something outside yourself, and an acceptance of what IS rather than what you WANT THINGS TO BE.

Author Anne Lamott once said that everything she's let go of "has claw marks on it." She's a true seeker of spiritual fulfillment, a recovering addict and a deeply thoughtful human—and even she has trouble surrendering! It's not easy, but all of the world's greatest minds agree that learning to surrender is one of the key reasons we are put here on this planet.

You can practice surrender by writing your worries down on a piece of paper and then throwing it away. You can practice surrender by not harping on your partner when they didn't do the dishes the way you wanted. You can practice surrender by allowing someone to pull in front of you on the highway rather then edging up and making sure there's no room.

As you practice these small, daily surrenders letting go of the bigger stuff will get easier and easier. You'll find yourself able to surrender your past, your regret and your grief. You'll find yourself surrendering to your total sobriety and whatever losses or gains that come along with it. You'll one day wake up in the spaciousness that your surrendering has created and realize that your control has been replaced with courage, serenity and love.

July 22

"The great man is he who in the midst of the crowd keeps with perfect sweetness the independence of solitude."—Ralph Waldo Emerson

I could rewrite this quote to read, "The great man is he who in the midst of the crowd keeps with perfect sweetness the independence of sobriety."

As your faith in your sobriety grows, and as you learn to surrender to your path, you will find yourself in *solitude* because of your *sobriety.*

You will also find that if you develop a healthy solitude your sobriety will be that much stronger.

Early on in my sobriety I began to notice how many references people made to drinking. I do realize that my work in the wine business required talking about how to sell and market wine, but what I am talking about is the casual comment, the light joke, and the suggestion of drinking. There were so many throw away comments about the need for a drink, the want of a drink and how funny drinking is that you could fill a journal with them.

At first I felt like I had to join in, laugh or toss in my own one-liner because I did not yet feel secure in my sobriety. Only after I dug into the work and surrendered to my disease did I see these moments as opportunities to practice my sweet independent solitude, my sweet independent sobriety.

I have a good sense of humor and, after what I've seen and done, very little offends me. But I realized that I could no longer take part in drinking repartee because my disease was no longer funny to me.

Joking about being hungover or too drunk to drive was no longer an appropriate topic. In these moments, when the jokes start flying, I simply sit in my solitude and my sobriety and realize that my new life requires that I foster my own independent way of thinking.

My way of thinking is going to save my life. My ability to be centered in my solitude at moments where I am excluded will keep me sober and sane. I relish my sweet independence in solitude and sobriety, and I now know that every time I am alone in a group my independent way of thinking becomes stronger and more lasting than ever before.

July 23

It's time to unpack some myths about freedom, mostly the kinds of myths perpetuated by our brilliant and gleaming advertising culture. If we were to believe the marketers, our true freedom can only be attained when we have the right car, the biggest house, the most exotic vacation, the best clothes and cosmetics, and of course, the right cocktail.

All of these things are lies. The only path to true freedom is to free yourself from wanting or needing any of it. Let's look at the practical realities:

The right car = Expensive monthly payments and insurance.

The biggest house = A lifetime of mortgage payments, maintenance, cleaning and worse, interest payments.

The most exotic vacation = If you can't afford it, you can look forward to paying for this on your credit card statement for years to come.

The best clothes and cosmetics = Time wasted on shopping and money spent on things that are essentially disposable.

The right cocktail = A life of slavish devotion to an addictive substance that robs you of your money, your time and your self worth.

Your journey to sobriety has enlightened you to the idea that an external solution is not the path to happiness you once thought it was. Similarly, tying yourself to the desire for any of these material things will not lead you to freedom. They will possibly lead you to a life of debt, which is essentially handing over your freedom to a bank or credit card company.

The idea that we must have *things* to be *free* is the great myth perpetuated by our society, and one that has already trapped you into an alcoholic life. If you were like me, you were convinced that your freedom was at the bottom of a bottle and that your happiness depended on having all the right stuff and as much of it as possible.

Remember: Nothing anyone sells you will ever make you free.

July 24

During one of my massive house purges one of my family members asked me if I ever miss anything I throw out or give away. Of course I said no because I usually don't (although there is one pair of pajamas I would love to get back), and the reason is that moving my possessions along frees up space in my house and clears the clutter so I can have more free time instead of constantly cleaning. Clearing the clutter also re-calibrates my thinking so that I ensure that I make purchases that are good values, better for the environment and are long-lasting.

Her question got me thinking about missing things. If we fear that we will miss things in life perhaps it's a good idea to cultivate a few things that no one can ever take away from us.

Sobriety is one such example. No one can ever steal this from me. (I can hand it over, heaven forbid, but no one can take it.) If I've read a classic novel, no one can ever undo what I learned from it. If I study a foreign language, my ability to speak it will forever be mine. Once I figure out how to fix a broken washing machine, there's not a reason in the world that I won't have that ability forever.

True freedom requires the ability to separate the things that can be taken and things that will always be ours. Anyone can steal my car. Not a person on this planet can take away my sobriety, my knowledge or my skills. In letting go of my attachment to my stuff, my baggage and my addiction, I make so much more room for the peace that comes from nurturing the things in life no one can ever take from me.

July 25

You are free to make mistakes. You are free to not know the answer. You are free to question. You are free to speak your mind. You are free to remain silent. You are free to cause a ruckus. You are free to walk away. You are free to make a mess. You are free to clean it up. You are free to be kind. You are free to be grateful. You are free to choose health. You are free to stay sober.

One of the ways we experience freedom is through having lots of choices. Nowhere is this more evident than at the grocery store, where you can choose from 14 different brands of canned tomatoes.

We believe it is a good thing to have thousands of choices, but studies have shown that too much choice can be stultifying for some of us. Many of us get overwhelmed when there are too many selections, and instead of being invigorated we shut down.

I am definitely one of those people. I see that list of freedoms that I wrote and I get the shivers. I've created too many options! Any of those actions could be the right way to handle a situation, and how would I know what the right one is? Just thinking about all of the different choices makes me anxious.

With great freedom comes great responsibility. The one thing I realize is that I am also free to do the next right thing. (And that next right thing is nearly always the choice that will help bolster my sobriety.)

July 26

When we think about freedom and independence, we often go to that place where we envision escaping from it all. A friend of mine calls this mindset "going to Jamaica," and what she is describing is that moment when we are so frustrated with our lives that we not only envision escaping, but we have to go all the way to Jamaica in our minds in order to feel that we've gotten far enough away from what's troubling us.

I experience this way of thinking as well, but my Jamaica tends to be a tiny, well-appointed apartment in some charming town. And I live ALL ALONE. No kids leaving their towels on the floor. No man barking out orders in the morning. No dog constantly begging for treats. I'm alone with my books, my writing, my yoga mat... *Ahhhh, Jamaica*.

Very slowly, over much time and through much effort, I have found myself escaping to my Jamaica much less frequently. Although I am free to leave and regroup any time I want, my sobriety has helped me to create a life that I don't want to leave. My home is not fancy, but it's comfy. My family is much calmer and more serene than ever before, largely due to the fact that I am not continually recovering from a hangover. My renewed energy levels help me to enjoy my work. With all its imperfections, minor frustrations and daily difficulties, I actually like my life now. I'd rather be here than anywhere else in the world.

Now that you're free from the oppression of alcohol, do you think you could create a life that you don't want to escape from?

July 27

I am a news addict. I have regularly forced myself to step away from the Internet so that I don't get swept up in the daily drama of wars, corruption, greed and other things that get my goat. I like to think that I am an independent thinker, but my strong emotional responses to manipulative headlines, one-sided arguments that blatantly support the opinion I already had, and columns written by people who kowtow to my way of seeing the world do nothing to help me think for myself.

Regardless of how passionate or inflammatory a persuasive argument is we must remember to get our own facts. One of the strongest examples in my life of needing to do my own research is my journey to sobriety. The people I drank with all shared my behavior patterns and opinions about drinking. They thought it was great, that I was fine and that all this boo-hooing about my terrible guilt and hangovers was par for the course of a life well lived.

I listened to them, much like I seek out like-minded folks in the news media, to help build support for my own thought processes. *I must be right,* I think. *This column by so-and-so reaffirms my opinion!* Or, *I must not be an alcoholic. My friend so-and-so says I don't seem drunk at all.*

You know that making the choice to get sober was a huge leap forward in learning to think independently. Where else might you be following the crowd to your detriment?

July 28

As independent, sober people, we are free to prioritize our time any way we would like. Saying you don't have time for something or someone means that you have prioritized other things in its place.

I'm not saying this is a bad thing. I say I don't have time to go to Sunday brunch with my girlfriends because I have prioritized working on this book instead. That's a positive choice.

But there are times I throw around the "I don't have time" excuse when I'd rather be doing something else. I have recently said, "I don't have time" to attend a fundraiser. That's because the season finale of my favorite show was on that night. I prioritized TV over helping raise money for our local parks. Not my finest moment.

I used to say I didn't have time to be in the local play, work on my writing or volunteer at the bake sale because I prioritized drinking over everything else. I couldn't even plan to do things in the mornings because I never knew how I'd feel when I woke up. Chances are I'd be so wrecked you wouldn't want my help with anything anyway.

Now that you're sober, think about how you use the phrase "I don't have time." The fact is that we all have the same exact hours in the day, and we have more choice in the ways we use them than we think. When I told people I didn't have time for the things they asked me to do, I was telling them that I didn't think they were more important than my drinking or my hangover. Now, when I tell people I don't have time, it's a little signal that I am either being self-caring (by choosing to work on my creative projects) or self-centered (by plopping myself in front of the TV).

In our sobriety we will discover a treasure trove of free time, and we are free to choose how to use it. Just check in occasionally to make sure you're using it wisely. It's what any independent adult would do.

July 29

I love listening to people complain. Not because I think that complaining is a good use of time, energy or spirit, but because you can tell everything about a person by what they complain about.

For example, my friend Em is a world-class independent thinker. She earns her own keep, manages her home, takes care of her kid (and other people's kids!), oversees a small farm of animals and makes her own sculptures and quince jelly. She is an ideal example of a sober, free person who takes care of herself. Her complaints include things like: "You don't call me enough," (she wants closeness with her friends) or, "It's hot today," (and then she invites me swimming.) I maybe heard her complain once about her boss being a bit difficult, but then she traipsed off to go meditate about it to calm her nerves. Her complaints are few and far between because, as an independent person, she is quick to find a solution and then execute it. She takes responsibility for herself and is willing to do the work to make herself better.

Then there's Erin. Erin has been complaining about the exact same things in different clothes for the past 20 years. Her husband is an insensitive jerk. Her publisher is an idiot who makes her rewrite everything. Her father died and left a mess of the will, so she will get nothing. Her mother won't die fast enough (she wants the inheritance). Her aunt is a busybody who either isn't around to help enough or is always around bugging her to "spend time" with her. She doesn't make enough money and her husband won't help her. I've never heard a solution. I've only see Erin become more and more of a victim over the years.

As you gain more independence in sobriety, listen to the tone and manner of your complaints. Are you putting yourself in the role of the victim, like Erin? Or are you becoming more of a problem-solver, like Em? Are you waiting for someone else to fix your issues or do you see that you can fix them yourself? (Or if you can't fix them can you manage how you respond?)

You are free to complain as much as you want. But you are also free to pay attention to the tone and topic of your complaints and then solve them. You are free to become the hero of your story, rather than the victim.

July 30

Until I got sober I didn't realize how shackled I was. I thought I was a shining example of independence. I worked, had two homes, a savings account and the freedom to pursue my favorite pastime— drinking. Drinking promised me a life well lived. Drinking was a glittering social activity. Drinking is what the adults in my life did after a long day at the office, a long week on the road or on long Sunday afternoons.

The truth of it was that I had drunk myself into a kind of prison. I was severely limited in the things I could do because I either wanted to be drinking or I was recovering from drinking. Far from the glamorous, independent woman people saw, I was actually a terrified, insecure, anxious person who would have no idea how to take care of myself if the bottom really dropped out of my life.

The Big Book of Alcoholics Anonymous promises that once we are sober we will "intuitively know how to solve problems that used to baffle us." What a beautiful idea! And it has proven to be true in my life time and time again. Now that I am no longer in a chemical haze, I not only know how to approach my life maturely and thoughtfully. I also know that I can take care of myself no matter what happens because my mind is clear.

I can truly claim my independence now. Of course I still rely on others for support, wisdom, kindness and the odd favor. But I have learned that part of the getting is giving back too. We take a little, we give a little. We learn a little, we share a little. Now that I am free from alcohol I am free to give more of myself. And the more I give, the more I grow.

August
Accepting Challenge

August 1

"What would you attempt to do if you knew you could not fail?" —
Annoying Job Interview Question

This is a classic question meant to get at the heart of your true passion in life. Maintaining my sobriety is certainly at the top of my list. However, I believe this line of questioning does more harm than good.

Here's why. The "couldn't fail" part peaks the interest because it's nearly the same as having a wish granted. You can't fail, so there's no reason in the world why you can't skate on out there in the next Olympics and take home the gold medal. That must be your true passion!

The question is also misleading in its use of "attempt." If you cannot fail, there is no "attempt" there is only "do." "Attempt" implies that there is a possibility you won't make it, even with that weird little promise of success at the end.

Maybe we should ask ourselves: "How much are you willing to sacrifice in order to achieve [insert dream here]?" Because the truth is, even with this magical guarantee that you cannot "fail," most things that are high on our list of things we daydream about doing take hours and hours of lonely work. In the real world, the only guarantee against failing is a steadfast determination to do whatever it takes to succeed. Most of that requires solitude, labor, commitment, willingness and discipline. And you still might fail!

Most of the things I currently spend my time doing have no real measure of success or failure. I take figure skating lessons, and I will continue to do that for as long as I am physically able. I focus on my sobriety through reading, writing and working with other addicts. I like to run, but it's yet another thing I do that has no real end goal other than making it home without a lung collapsing.

We shouldn't determine what challenges we want to accept based on a projected or promised outcome. I skate because it makes me happy and I get a little better each time. I practice sobriety because it makes me happy and I get a little better each day. I run because it makes me happy and I go a little farther each month.

Pick your challenges by the journey you'll have, not the destination, and you'll always have the energy and enthusiasm to pursue them.

August 2

Math was always my most challenging subject. There was no math problem I couldn't royally screw up, no formula I couldn't forget and no test I couldn't fail. I struggled mightily with math in high school, and there wasn't a teacher or tutor alive who could help. I thought it was hopeless and so did everyone else.

In college I was forced to take a year of algebra as part of my core curriculum, and a strange thing happened. All of a sudden, math just "clicked" for me. It was as if I finally understood a foreign language. I learned to love my algebra class. I viewed every problem as a puzzle to be solved, and I excelled. I earned an A+ in that class! It's still one of my proudest achievements, but I have no idea how it came to be. A little "click," and everything changed.

I keep waiting for that "click" with my sobriety. I keep hoping there will be a moment when I no longer have to struggle so hard, screw up, fail and rely on my teachers to pull me through. In fact, the deeper I move into my sobriety the less I feel a click coming on. I am able to solve problems, but the more I solve, the more questions are revealed.

Sobriety isn't something I can check off my to-do list. It's not an equation to be solved. And although everything would be easier for me if it were those things, I'm learning to be patient on this wondrous journey.

August 3

I have learned more about embracing challenge from watching my kids give up than just about anything else.

My boys are the kind of people who give up on something the moment it gets difficult. Occasionally there's pouting involved. Sometimes, if they do decide to stick it out, they put the bare-minimum effort, time and creativity into the final output.

I have tried everything I can think of to motivate them. I've tried the carrot. I've tried the stick. I've yelled. I've cajoled. I've encouraged. I've praised. I've done things for them to demonstrate how easy it is. But now they are teenagers and basically they refuse to do anything that requires effort.

I have been dealing with feelings of disappointment, failure and frustration because of this for quite a while. Now that I am sober I can't blot out my daily disappointment. I can't pull a veil down over my eyes and pretend that everything is okay. Like every parent, I want the best for my kids. I want them to be excited about life and rise to every challenge. But they don't. And it drives me crazy.

So how do I manage this? I can't control this situation, so I have settled in to a nice, healthy acceptance of this reality. I love my kids, and I don't want this to ruin our relationship.

I use their apathy to motivate myself. Any time I see them giving less than their best I take up one of my own projects and do a little extra. In those moments when they pout or withdraw, I honor their emotion, allow them a chance to talk about it if they want to, and then go check one more accomplishment off my daily to-do list. I have had to transform my disappointment in how they are behaving into motivation for my own actions.

The cornerstone of a solid sobriety is the understanding that the only thing I can control is how I behave. When I get overwrought over my stepkids making bad choices, I re-affirm that I will make more good choices. Ideally they'll see my example and, when they mature, they'll rise to the occasion.

August 4

Sobriety offers all of us the opportunity to approach challenges, work or projects with a fresh attitude and a new perspective. When I was drinking my work life was a long, uninteresting slog that I had to get through in order to get back to my bottles of wine. I was either sick, making myself sick, or recovering from being sick, and the result was an inability to bring anything but the bare minimum to any challenge.

Now that I am sober, feeling great and full of energy, I approach everything I promise to do with a willingness to do more than the minimum.

I do this not only because I have the increased vigor of sobriety, but also because I view all projects and challenges as opportunities to learn. I give my best effort because I am making up for a lot of years where it took nearly all of my capital to hoist myself out of bed every morning.

Doing more than the bare minimum looks like this:

- If my skating coach asks me to "do one more," of anything, I do at least three more.
- If I am hired to rewrite a website for a client, I also provide them with key messages or a few extra examples to choose from.
- When I am close to the end of a project at work, I let my superiors know when I will be available so that they can assign me additional projects.
- When I make my to-do list, I always add a few extras that are "nice to have" rather than "need to have" so that I can attack a few extra projects that will make my life better.
- If I have a deadline, I strive to meet it early.

Simply taking on the challenge of getting sober is a huge step toward not settling for the bare minimum. For me, being sober has been the most challenging, most rewarding thing I have ever done. Think about it—now that you've taken on sobriety, is there anything you can't do? And then do a little extra?

August 5

Was my drinking "failure-related" or were my failures "drinking-related?" If you had asked me this while I was drinking my answer would have been that I drink because I can't seem to get anything right. Poor me!

Now, I realize that all of my past failures were predicated on the fact that I was drunk or hungover 100% of the time. How can anyone succeed when the only focus is where the next drink is coming from?

What would logically follow is that, now that I am sober, I am a huge success! Everything works the first time! My thinking is flawless and all of my projects are Nobel-worthy!

I wish.

I still fail. In fact, I recently made a very stupid financial decision that made me $1000 poorer. I also said something hurtful to someone in my family. Oh, and then I slept through an important work deadline. I also failed to release this book on time. So, fail-free I am not.

The difference is that I accept responsibility now. I own my failures and I make a conscious effort to learn from them. Rather than feeling like the world is out to get me, I know now that I need to read the fine print in contracts. Rather than trying to find the reasons why my family member deserved to be called out, I humbly apologized. Rather than assuming that the deadline was unfair, I learned that I need to keep better track of my responsibilities.

My failures now are no longer related to anything other than my ability to learn from them. Rather than absorbing these mistakes as further reason to punish myself, I see them for what they are:

things that I cannot change, but that I can keep from happening again. There's power in that.

August 6

I never cease to be amazed at this one true fact: you only get out of something what you put into it.

What this means is that the amount of reward of any activity is directly proportional to the amount of enthusiasm and effort you bring. In my experience, this is never not true. One obvious example is the thoughtfulness, interest and study we bring to our sobriety. If we approach our sobriety with all the curiosity, willingness to learn and enthusiasm to become a better person without alcohol, then a delightful sober life will follow. But this principle works on just about everything else as well.

I joined the board of a local non-profit. I genuinely wanted to help, but when I began attending the meetings I realized that this group was a disaster—disorganized, dispassionate and disconnected from their true mission. I was a good trooper, attending meetings, volunteering for fundraisers and generally doing exactly what was asked and not much more. I considered quitting because I wasn't getting anything out of it.

I decided to try something a little different. Rather than quitting and leaving the group to figure things out on their own, I doubled my effort. I created a task force to write a solid strategic plan, increased our social media presence and drafted a common-sense marketing plan. When I started out I was on my own, but as my enthusiasm has grown so has the energy of the whole team. We still have a long way to go, but this focus has made the process a lot more fun for everyone and we've grown closer.

Next time you're faced with a challenge that leaves you feeling like you want to cut and run, consider whether it might be more interesting to amp up your effort. There's a good chance you'll end up with a much more valuable experience.

August 7

One of my favorite lessons in recovery is seeing the similarities in myself and others, rather than the differences. As an alcoholic my natural tendency is to think of myself as separate, different and *special*. This lesson reminds me to admit where I am just like everyone else, and forces me to feel a connection—a unity—with those around me. It's not always easy, but it is always rewarding.

Similarly, my alcoholic thinking resulted in a thought process that convinced me that I was "too good" to do certain kinds of work. I couldn't see how the work benefitted me, only how these certain tasks weren't befitting a refined, sensitive unicorn like myself.

My how things have changed! Any time I feel that I am above a certain task or responsibility I take a moment to consider what I am learning. A great example of this is my work with the non-profit I almost gave up on. As I sat alone at planning meetings no one cared to show up to, or manned a booth at a festival all alone, I could have easily slipped into an indignant huff. (Full disclosure: there may have been a little huff or two.) But instead, I choose to look for opportunities to do better. I have learned how to draft a strategic plan for a non-profit and now I am learning to write grants. I don't know how these skills will benefit me in the long run, but they certainly won't hurt!

When you are feeling challenged, unappreciated, or overworked do you think you can find the learning opportunity? If there are none, how can you create your own?

August 8

I remember seeing a woman on television who had experienced terrible losses. Her family was ripped from her through unspeakable violence, and she was often overcome with grief and depression.

The hostess asked her how she continued to cope. The woman responded, "I just keep getting up. No matter how bad the pain is, I put my two feet on the floor every morning and get up. Then I get on with living."

I found her answer equal parts chilling and inspiring. During my darkest days, days I when I was tempted to hide my hangover, my desperation and my sadness from the world, I would remember her words and just get up. Then the day would unfold as it would. Sometimes the feelings would improve, sometimes they wouldn't, but I kept getting up. I got up so much that it made sense to get sober so I could actually enjoy myself.

Just keep getting up. Keep going in. Keep being there. Keep moving. Whatever it is that you need to do to *get through it*, keep doing it.

August 9

My goodness, work can be dull. Some days, no matter how hard we try, the day stretches out before us with nothing but boredom on the horizon.

Boredom stresses me out like almost nothing else. When I first got sober I was B-O-R-E-D. No matter how much I tried to fill my drinking time with healthy activities, I would find myself prostrate on the couch with nothing to do that interested me. When I worked in an office and didn't have the freedom to come and go as I liked, it was the boring days that just murdered me. I didn't mind the run-around mornings or the last-minute evenings, but some days there wasn't much to do and I would feel like I was going to lose it.

I have learned two great approaches for boredom. The first is to let myself be bored and pay attention to the fear, irritation, anger and longing that inevitably come up. Since I often have no choice about being bored at work or elsewhere I find that if I soften into the experience, the boredom takes on a new kind of serenity. I'm always glad when the boring situation comes to a close, but at least I don't feel homicidal afterward.

The other is to try to find ways to keep my mind or hands challenged. If it's a boring work project I try to time myself to see how fast, or, depending on how much time I have to fill, how slowly I can complete it. If I am stuck at the airport with nothing to do and no interest in the latest fashion magazines, I play word games with the signs. I read the words and try to see how many other words I can make. Or, I test myself to see how fast I can alphabetize things. If I am with the kids and we are all teetering on boredom, I make up games like "spot the pink pants" or something else completely random in order to keep us all from freaking out.

Boredom is a huge irritation in sobriety—and in life in general. I challenge you to find a new way to tackle your boredom. Whether you decide to submerge yourself in bored bliss or make up your own silly fun, you'll feel more in control.

August 10

I have noticed something that many alcoholics have in common: they don't like to be alone.

For some, part of the allure of daily drinking is that it makes easy work of finding other people to hang around with. There are bars everywhere and people in them. Those people are usually tipsy when you get there so striking up a conversation is oh-so-easy. Sometimes, we drink and dial with friends who aren't here but will be more than happy to share a glass or two while we're on the line. We invite our friends over for drinks and gossip every night of the week.

Being alone, especially when sober or newly sober, can be terrifying. Not only did we become accustomed to dulling our feelings and memories with alcohol, but we also chatted our heads off while drunk in order to stop thinking so much. When we were alone we couldn't turn off the memories. When we were silent, our addiction, regret and pain screamed at us.

In this month of challenges, take on the challenge of silence. Create a space for silence in your home. Sit there. Let the silence absorb you. Learn how it makes you feel. Take this silence on the road with you. Any time you feel tempted to blurt out an opinion, savage someone with gossip or give that advice, choose silence instead.

Learn to be comfortable in the spaces between your words and your thoughts. You'll find magic in the silence if you take the time to listen.

August 11

My friends and acquaintances watched me transform from Party Girl to Sober Susie. They certainly weren't there for every gut-wrenching moment, but you tend to notice that the girl who usually swings from chandeliers has been sitting in the corner nursing a sparkling water. People noticed. They asked me about it.

One friend in particular called me a few days after a party where I was noticeably sober. She was going through a difficult experience that involved a teenager whose mother had been imprisoned. The teenager needed a place to live, and my friend was kind enough to offer her shelter.

The problem was that my friend was a daily drinker, sometimes to excess, and she did not want the teenager to find out. She felt that the child had been through enough and didn't need to deal with a tipsy caretaker, too. She wanted to taper off, but she had no interest in AA or any other recovery program. Basically, she called me looking for a magic bullet. She wanted to know what I had done to "get over it."

I think anyone reading this knows that it's not quite that simple. I didn't know what to say, so I took a deep breath and out came:

"I've never regretted not drinking."

Apparently this was enough because my friend was able to abstain from alcohol for the few months her houseguest was there. She later told me she never regretted not drinking either (although she did pick up drinking again, later).

I use this as a mantra for all kinds of challenges. I have never regretted not drinking. But I also have never regretted not making the snide comment. I have never regretted not eating the bacon-covered donut. I have never regretted not pointing out someone's flaws. I have never regretted not staying up past my bedtime.

The point is that you can identify the things you don't want to do and then never regret not doing them again. That's all the magic bullet you need.

August 12

I recently read an article that explained that cyclical thinking is better than linear thinking for achieving long-term goals. While you try to wrap your head around that idea, I'll see if I can explain what this means for rising to new challenges while sober.

The article was specifically geared toward people saving money, but let's see if it works for those of us who are working to achieve long-term sobriety. The idea is that linear thinkers believe they can always get sober "down the road." They believe there is plenty of length left in life's long highway so that when they decide to dry up they can easily do it later on, when the mood strikes. What inevitably happens is that the linear thinkers keep putting it off until later—and later never comes.

Cyclical thinkers see time not as a line, but as linking circles of recurring events. That means they value their sobriety *now* and understand that building up a life of sobriety day by day means that they can have more sobriety under their belt in the future. By focusing developing daily habits, we can make the recurring events in our lives much more pleasant as they keep happening (if we stay sober).

As far as money goes, researchers said that cyclical thinkers in their studies saved 82% more than linear thinkers. I have no proof to back this up, but I bet cyclical thinking leads to more successful sobriety as well.

August 13

"Failure is an event, not a person."—Zig Ziglar

Everyone fails at something. The only way to ensure that you're never going to have some colossal failure on your list is to never attempt anything at all.

As Ziglar's words suggest, it's vital for us to separate the failure from the person. Failure describes something that happens to a person—usually someone who is trying very hard to succeed. In order to protect our delicate, sober being I suggest we remove the word "failure" from our vocabulary entirely. That way we can ensure that we never incorrectly apply it to ourselves.

I have failed in getting sober. My fall from the wagon was spectacular. And that's just one failure. If I really start listing them all (divorce, fired, wrecked the car, set the house on fire) we'll be here all night. It's possible that I have more failures in my life than successes. But I never view myself as a failure. No one, no matter how far down the scales they have gone, is a failure if they are working on sobriety. It is the most difficult journey most humans will ever undertake. And if all you ever do is this, you're a huge success.

August 14

My stepson came up to me holding a key chain in one hand and a handful of keys in the other. "The key chain broke," he whined. "It's broken. Where should I put it?"

I could tell he was annoyed and he wanted to drop the mess on me and run back up to his video games.

"Fix it." I said.

"I don't know how." He seemed equal parts annoyed and astonished that I would suggest such a thing.

"Neither do I," I said. "Figure it out."

And he did. He went away for about five minutes and came back holding a repaired key chain.

"I think if I bend it a bit here, I can make it even stronger than before." He was now fully engaged in this puzzle, and he was trying to improve upon the original design!

This short interlude got me thinking about how we rise to meet challenges in our lives. If we see something that's broken, do we drop it and run, hoping that someone else will jump in to make the repairs? Or do we challenge ourselves to get involved, look at the problem and try to improve it?

What broken key chains might you fix today?

August 15

Avoidance is a method I use to protect myself from challenges. Avoidance includes flat-out avoiding things, like crossing the street when I see the folks with religious pamphlets coming my way. Avoidance also includes procrastination, like when I check my favorite blogs just one more time before I start my writing for the day. Avoidance at its worst is psychological, like when I simply refuse to believe a painful truth. I avoided admitting I was an alcoholic for years.

Decades of daily practice have made me a skilled avoider. Learning to face my responsibilities, engaging in activities that seem unpleasant at first and having the discipline to jget to work are some of my greatest challenges.

My friend Cathy had been avoiding sending an unpleasant letter for nearly thirty(!) years. She finally got up the gumption to write it and send it, and when she did, she said she felt lighter and happier than she had in a long time.

Her story made me realize that we don't ever truly avoid anything. If the universe puts something in our path or on our to-do list, it's best to take care of it as quickly and directly as possible. Otherwise you'll be held under a weight, followed by a shadow or unable to relieve a vexing pain.

Next time you feel like you want to avoid something, run screaming toward it instead. You might as well have some fun scaring the shit out of it before you tackle it head-on.

August 16

"To make a deep physical path, we walk again and again. To make a deep mental path, we must think over and over the kind of thoughts we wish to dominate our lives."—Henry David Thoreau

I have a sober friend Monica who, by all accounts, has a fascinating life. She travels the world for work and is able to build ample vacation time into her schedule. She most recently returned from a two-week meditation retreat at Thich Nhat Hanh's Plum Village in France.

She told me that while she was away on this last trip that she would call her mother and complain of loneliness, or boredom, or that things weren't going exactly the way she had envisioned. When she returned and showed her mother the photos of her trip (all of which were full of smiles, people, parties and experiences), her mom pointed out that Monica's "life looked pretty good to her!"

Monica realized that her feelings of loneliness, self-pity or frustration might not be a result of anything that's actually happening, but could actually be a habit. She's simply taught herself over the years to find the one thing that makes her feel rotten and focus on it.

Lucky for Monica, she is not only aware of this nasty little habit, she is also aware that she can change her thought patterns with practice. She has challenged herself, when ruminating on her perceived problems, to replace these thoughts with gratitude. If she keeps this up she'll replace her negative thought patterns as effortlessly as she created them—and she'll finally be able to appreciate the amazing life she has created for herself.

August 17

Not all of our problems are perceived. Some of them are very real and very challenging. Getting and remaining sober has been one of my real life challenges. It's something that requires daily maintenance, work, study, reflection and commitment. Everything else—my divorce, losing jobs, my struggles with anxiety and depression—is a cakewalk compared to the challenge of sobriety.

I consider myself lucky in that regard. I am surrounded by sober people who put their sobriety first, and who are also dealing with overwhelming crises that would be terrible with or without alcoholism. Jenna has an inoperable brain tumor. Donna is facing the removal of all of her teeth due to an autoimmune disorder. Ann's husband died. Katherine's daughter is in rehab again.

I hear their stories and am filled with worry and compassion. What I don't have is an answer—nor do they expect me to. But I wonder how I would deal with these things. I never come up with an answer. My musings on overcoming challenges and facing failure in sobriety don't measure up.

I don't know how I would handle any of these terrible events. And maybe it's okay not to know. Maybe admitting you don't know lets the universe know your cup is empty so it can get busy filling it with the strength you need to face what's next.

August 18

I'd like to think that I am the kind of person who flourishes outside her comfort zone. No challenge is too great, no pressure too intense. I've got my big girl pants on and I can rise to any occasion!

What's funny is that for the big things this is mostly true. I don't shy away from "big" challenges anymore because I know how to break down tasks into smaller bits and take them on one piece at a time. Where I get frazzled is the little things that unexpectedly arise throughout the day.

For example, I was running a meeting recently and one of my co-workers asked me to plug my computer in to the overhead display so everyone could see what I was talking about. I don't know if I showed it, but for some reason this had me completely put out. I was right in the middle of presenting, I had sent the info before to everyone and I didn't want to project my computer desktop onto a screen where everyone could see it.

I was out of my comfort zone, and though I think I handled it okay, inside I was seething.

But why? It seems so stupid, but writing about it now gets me all riled up.

I did not like being asked to do something out of my control. Plus, I felt foolish for not thinking of it, AND I didn't want everyone to see into the "secret" world of my computer desktop. Apparently I still don't like relinquishing control. I also don't like looking foolish. Plus my ego is obviously still wrapped up creating the image of an organized person. Wow.

Just when I thought I had my comfort zone issues handled, it turns out that I still have quite a bit of work to do.

August 19

Vision boards. Goal setting. Time-management tools. To-do lists. Inspirational quotes. Affirmations. All of these things are useful when taking on a challenge. It's wonderful to decide what you want and then follow the path toward achievement. In fact, I have used all of these methods at one time or another and I can vouch for their efficacy.

But sobriety has made me readjust my reliance on these things. Since sobriety isn't something I can check off as "done" I have learned to savor the journey.

When I first started figure skating the goal was to take the tests, earn the medals, win the title and really "become" a skater. Since getting sober I have started to see my practice as something that unfolds naturally. I show up on the ice. I practice. Some days I get noticeably better at something, some days I take a painful tumble (or both).

These days I'll accept a challenge for the joy of doing it, and I worry about the outcome later. I have a general idea that I want to publish something on Amazon, create a plan for a non-profit or run up that big hill, but I have completely let go of any expectation (other than doing my best on the tasks at hand) or desire to influence the outcome.

It feels a little loosey-goosey sometimes, all of this letting go. Sometimes my projects take longer than before, but it doesn't matter because I am having much more fun right here and now.

August 20

Gretchen Rubin, Author of *The Happiness Project* puts herself in a room and doesn't leave until she has completed a challenge. She built her own website that way. Cal Newport, Author of *How to be a Straight-A Student* and *So Good They Can't Ignore You*, suggests making an "event" of a scary task. One of his examples is writing that paper at a coffee shop far from your house. Have someone drop you off and pick you up so you can't escape early. I have used both of these terrific suggestions for taking on a challenge, and they work like a charm. But mostly I use what I call "The Power of One Hour."

I can't take credit for the concept (although I did come up with the catchy, rhyming name). It's a tip I picked up from the Red Room Writer's Society. The theory is that in order to complete a novel you have to focus on it one hour at a time. Amazingly, this process works for just about everything. One hour is the perfect length because you have plenty of time to get engaged, work deeply and then rest when your mind and body are naturally ready.

If I can devote one hour to the things that are important to me I can make a huge amount of progress. The meetings of my recovery group are one hour. I devote one hour, three days a week, to my non-profit group. When I have a deadline to meet, I set the alarm for one hour, get the fidgets out and work away. I can always commit to an hour. If an hour feels like too much at first (I couldn't sit for an hour of meditation when I first started) you can commit to ten minutes, six days a week. You will be surprised at your progress, and dedicating an hour will seem like nothing in no time.

August 21

Although I bristle at the motivation gurus who espouse the "great attitude" theory about the way to achieve your goals, having a good attitude can't hurt. I have a hard time expecting cancer patients to never have a down day. I don't think encouraging someone in mourning to "cheer up" and "try to see the good" is helpful. It's flat-out insulting to expect someone to smile through excruciating pain. Fortunately that's not the kind of positive attitude I am suggesting here.

What I am talking about goes more like this: I read a monthly astrology column. Every now and again, the column reveals that Mercury is in retrograde. When this occurs, so do problems. Messages are confused. Electronics don't work. Appliances explode. Computers crash. Basically the whole world breaks and there's nothing you can do to fix it.

The kind lady who writes the astrology column looks at it this way: Mercury in retrograde gives us a chance to see what's being miscommunicated, what's broken or where we need to slow down. What a great attitude! Until I read her viewpoint I always looked at Mercury in retrograde as a batten-down-the-hatches scenario. Now I see it as an opportunity to make repairs.

Coincidentally, my sobriety date fell in a Mercury retrograde period. It was true that this occurrence allowed me to shine a spotlight on what wasn't working and fix it. If it can be true for appliances, I'm pretty sure it can be true for hearts, minds and souls.

What "broken" thing can you see in a new light today?

August 22

Let's reflect on the negatives of always having a positive attitude. Let me clarify by expressing that, for the most part, I do believe that looking at the sunny side of things makes daily life more pleasant. When I lose a board game (which is beginning to happen more frequently as my stepkids grow), the boys will say they "feel sorry" for me. I don't! It was fun, and we had a great time hanging out. That's a positive attitude that is right-sized and makes sense to the matter at hand.

Barbara Ehrenreich, author of *Bright-Sided: How Positive Thinking is Undermining America*, argues that too much positive thinking can be detrimental. She suggests that an abundance of positive-only thinking leads to an almost maniacal unwillingness to see anything but positive outcomes. Too much positive thinking actually threatens our ability to see things for what they really are, and becomes dangerous when we positive-think ourselves into outright denial.

A great example of wrong-sized positive thinking was my insistence that my alcoholism would sort itself out "one day." I was a big believer in the idea that things only get better, so it makes sense that one day I would wake up and be effortlessly sober and feel great about it. Other examples of "negative" positive thinking include believing your debt will somehow be paid off without any sacrifice on your part, the belief that your illness will go away without any medical intervention or that it's a good idea to get a mortgage you can't afford because you plan on making more money in the future.

By all means, be happy, joyous and free. But take a look at those areas in your life where too much positive thinking may be keeping you from a richer, deeper, healthier reality.

August 23

Sobriety ushers in a whole new set of feelings—good feelings! It may not happen right away, but at some point you're going to feel like you're on that "pink cloud" that AA talks about. I've watched people on their pink cloud challenge themselves to run a marathon, go skydiving, join a Zumba group and join a choir. It's natural, when you feel exuberant, to want to push yourself to try something new.

Do it and worry about the outcome later. If you've always had a yen to take up surfing, but then you find that bobbing around in salt water all day isn't your thing, that's fine. Maybe you have always wanted to run a marathon, but in your training you discover that your knees aren't what they used to be. Oh well.

But then you'll try the thing (and it might be a think you never in a million years thought you'd like) and it's THE thing. Whatever it is, it's the perfect intersection of challenging, fun and new. And you love it. I swore that I would never take up biking. It's hot. It's dangerous. You have to wear weird clothes. Helmet hair. But then I tried it, and now I can't get on my bike enough.

Use your good feelings to get up some gumption to challenge yourself to a few new activities. If you don't find your favorite right away, keep trying. You know what they say about having to kiss a lot of frogs...

August 24

Sometimes when I'm in the middle of a challenge I start to feel sorry for myself. It's hot/raining/too cold to run. This hill is much steeper than I thought. I'm thirsty/tired/sore/achy. I can't think of anything new to write today.

It's time to call the *waaah*-mbulance.

Alcoholics are notorious for indulging in self-pity. It's one of the main reasons we get ourselves into a pickled state to begin with. However, I try not to let myself get too carried away. (I admit that occasionally I will call timeout and go hide under the bedcovers...) When I am really drowning in a sea of "I-can't-do-this," I take a moment and think of all the people who really can't do things, but do them anyway.

I am inspired by Surfer Bethany Hamilton who, despite losing her arm in shark attack, continues to win competitions. I am in awe of Bob Coomber who hikes some of the world's toughest trails—in his wheelchair. When I struggle to write, I think of Jean-Dominique Bauby who suffered from locked-in syndrome. He dictated his entire book *The Diving Bell and the Butterfly* by blinking one eye.

There are people in the world who would love to have the health, wellness, sobriety and determination you have at your disposal. Next time you think of giving up, think of someone who has every right to quit, yet doesn't.

August 25

"A successful man is one who can lay a firm foundation with the bricks others have thrown at him."—David Brinkley

As recovering alcoholics, we spend a lot of time trying to release others from blame. It's true that there's zero value in blaming others for our problems. This only leads to anger, bitterness and resentment, which lead to drinking.

However, this quote reminds me of the transformative experience of sobriety. We can release others from blame, but that doesn't mean that painful events perpetuated by people who hurt us didn't happen. Instead of using those pains inflicted upon us by parents, teachers, friends, enemies or frenemies as excuses to tear ourselves down with addiction, let's transform that energy into an indestructible foundation of self-awareness, compassion and drive.

One of my favorite teachers called me stupid in front of a class. This event occurred 23 years ago, but you'd better believe I brought that up to every person I could, every time I was drinking. Basically, by drinking the way I did, I set out to prove her right.

Since getting sober I can reflect on the actual context of the words and the situation where it happened. I can now see that her choice of words was bad, it was more of a joke that flopped. It's my fault that I let this nasty thing live for as long as it did. Not only have I changed how I see this issue, I can now quickly forgive people who inadvertently say the wrong thing to me. Plus, I work very hard to make sure no one ever has occasion to call me stupid again!

As those bricks come flying toward you, don't let them smack you in the head. Catch them and stack them to build your foundation of strength.

August 27

Throughout my childhood, I believed I was destined to be a star. I was in every community theater production, dance classes, singing groups... If there was a show to be performed, I was there.

I was fortunate to be able to transfer to a high school in Atlanta that had a world-class theater study track. Academy Award® winners had studied with the director of the program! I *knew* that I was on my way to the stardom I so desperately craved. I was the best of the best in my town of 10,000 people, so heaven knows I was ready to storm the stage in Atlanta.

It didn't quite go that way. I was in all of the productions at my new school, generally well liked and whatnot, but I never got a lead role. I was never asked to perform in any little side productions or special events. Basically, when I was thrown into the big pond I was overlooked. And boy, was I indignant. I saw parts that were *perfect* for me going to people with *half* the talent. When I was placed into the beginner dance troupe, I quit instead of taking the class and improving my skills so that I could move up.

When I whined to a teacher in the arts program about being shafted, she explained to me that I wasn't getting the recognition I so richly deserved because I simply didn't work hard enough. I didn't volunteer my time to build sets. When groups of singers would get together at lunch to work out a tricky section of the music, I wouldn't show. I would forget rehearsals altogether sometimes and then make up whopping lies to cover my tracks. My teacher was right, but I still didn't get it. I didn't get it until many years later, after I sobered up.

One of my greatest life lessons was staring me right in the face, and I used it as an excuse to be angry rather than to confront the reality about my personality: I was a person who was unwilling to rise to a challenge. I was a person who thought I was owed something without working for it. I was a person who thought I was better than everyone, although I had done nothing to distinguish myself from the pack.

As a sober adult, any time I don't want to show up to the meeting, or meet the deadline, I think of this conversation. If I had understood what she was talking about then, rather than 20 years later, I could have avoided so many disappointments.

Are there areas in your life where you see others getting the kudos you think you deserve? Are you bringing your best self to the challenge?

August 28

One of the biggest smokescreens I faced before getting sober was the belief that I deserved to "be somebody." By virtue of being on the planet, and having these oh-so-special qualities of cleverness, wit and general adorableness, I should be bestowed with all of the treasures, accolades and honors reserved for exceptional people.

When this VIP treatment failed to materialize I drank to manage my disappointment. I blamed others. It was never my fault I was passed over for the promotion (or laid off). My marriage was a disaster because my husband failed to realize how magical I was (as I snored in bed until noon with a hangover). I wasn't invited to speak at the conference because the organizers were too stupid to acknowledge my vision. (I could go on, but I think I've made the point.)

That's why I think it's so important for my own sobriety to focus less on "being somebody," and focus more on "doing something." I have thrown myself into challenges because I feel so much better when I am serving, working and achieving rather than sitting around wondering why no one has appointed me queen of everything.

The challenges I accept will probably never get me any recognition or accolades, but with every small act of "doing" I feel myself becoming something so much better than I ever imagined.

August 29

Many alcoholics stay mired in their disease because they don't realize there is another option. Many of us grew up in homes where our immediate and extended family members were alcoholic, so we believe that's "what people do." If generations of our family and friends all manage their problems by drinking, using and otherwise avoiding life, then how are we supposed to know there's another way?

I honestly don't have a great answer for this, and I am always astonished at the sober people in my life that got it on their own, despite the fact that they are yet another person in a long line of alcoholics. My guess is that somewhere, deep inside, their true self (or higher power?) worked very hard to get their attention. To their credit, they listened and then the path became clear.

One very wise teacher once explained to me that once we start following our hearts, the universe finds ways to accommodate us. Perhaps that's happens to people who, against all odds, find a way out of their disease. They hear a small voice and they listen.

What is your inner voice challenging you to see differently?

August 30

What do we do when one of life's challenges knocks us for a loop? What happens when we don't have the answer? How should we respond when we have nowhere else to turn?

In the words of Winston Churchill: *"Never, never, never give up."*

Don't give up. Never quit. Get up and keep going. This is all galvanizing advice, and words that build a fire in my belly every time I read them.

In the face of gravest circumstances I suggest you never give up. But you can always *give it up.*

Here's how you do that:

Step 1: Get on your knees.
Step 2: Ask for help.
Step 3: Hand it over.

Whether you believe in God, Allah, the Universal Now, The X-Men, the Great Spaghetti Monster or nothing at all, there is great freedom in giving up our pain to whatever may be out there listening. Then, when you rise, never, never, never give up. We're all pulling for you.

August 31

"Look at a day when you are supremely satisfied at the end. It's not a day when you lounge around doing nothing; it's a day you've had everything to do and you've done it." —Margaret Thatcher

I grumble on the mornings when I have to wake up early. I pout when I see my to-do list. I experience numbing anxiety when I consider how I am going to accomplish it all, have time to exercise, work on my own projects AND stay sober. Some days I throw in the towel completely and I "give myself a break" by sitting on the sofa and binge-watching *Gossip Girl*.

One hundred percent of the time I take that break I feel disappointed in myself. I experience restlessness, not relaxation. One hundred percent of the time I face my fears and confront the challenge of my list I feel proud, satisfied and that "good kind of tired."

Similarly, there are days when I long to let go of the whole sobriety thing. Not start drinking, I don't mean that. But a day where I don't have to read, meditate or make a gratitude list about what it means to be sober. Those days are fine, but the committed days are the ones where I fall asleep happy.

Take the challenge. Face the fear. Tackle the list. These are the things that add up to a life of satisfaction, self-reliance and sobriety.

September
The Divine

September 1

I had a hint that my alcoholism was a spiritual malady—although when I first started seeking solace in the ephemeral I would never have admitted I was either an alcoholic or spiritual.

I grew up in a religious southern town with non-religious parents. We didn't go to church because my mother didn't like being asked to help in the nursery. My dad was anti-religion because of his upbringing in a strict Catholic home. I wanted to fit in with my peers, though, so I would ask to go to church on Sundays. My dad would drive me in his pajamas, drop me off at the front door, and I went to services alone.

When I was older, married, deeply depressed and being crushed by a raging drinking problem, I once again turned to the church—the Catholic church to be more specific. I converted to Catholicism at age 28 expecting to be relieved of my pain. I was not. In fact, the idea that I was working so hard to belong to the church, attending mass and STILL feeling like I wanted to throw myself under a bus was too much to bear. I stopped attending. Got divorced. Continued drinking.

So imagine my surprise several years later when I got sober, started meditating and found the spiritual fulfillment I had been seeking. No one bothered to mention to me that a relationship with the divine starts inside me, not in something "out there."

A connection to spirit can make your sobriety so much richer. It doesn't mean that you'll always get the parking space, that the test results will always be negative or that you'll always win the argument, but it does offer you a built-in compass to determine whether you're in alignment with your soul's true desires. Who wouldn't want that?

September 2

Any discussion of spirit seeking requires a mention of meditation. Oh, how this used to vex me! Before I got sober there was no way in hell I was going to be able to sit still for thirty seconds, much less thirty minutes. I was a perpetual motion machine, and frankly the thought of being alone with my thoughts made me want to drink more.

So many people share this experience with meditation. It seems so *hard*. Well, it is and it isn't. It's hard because we make it hard. All that's really required is that we sit there. Thoughts are going to happen, emotions are going to bubble to the surface and we're going to feel some little aches and pains. Sit there anyway. And then sit a little while longer. Maybe add a few more seconds.

There. You've meditated. Don't attach anything to it. Don't expect to experience rapturous visions of our creator (although you might.) Don't sit there waiting for a voice from beyond to guide your next move (although this could happen, too.) Sit there. Sit for one minute at first. The following week, add another minute and so forth. No big whoop. Meditation isn't like most other things. It's one of the only activities in your life that requires almost no effort whatsoever.

So sit. Sit some more. Eventually it will all make sense, and you won't have had to lift a finger.

September 3

"Zen does not confuse spirituality with thinking about God while one is peeling potatoes. Zen spirituality is just to peel the potatoes." — Alan Watts

I'm not even sure I fully understand what Zen is. I imagine it's a sense of peace in all things, or that "I'm-a-boulder-in-the-middle-of-a-rushing-river" feeling. Maybe it's total detachment from outcomes, ego striving and painful desires. I think I want that.

That's why I love this quote so much. My limited brain may never grasp the concept of Zen or achieve enlightenment, but I do know how to peel potatoes. I can peel *the hell* out of some potatoes. Carrots, too.

Sobriety inevitably throws the veil off of our more troubling memories and emotions. You can expect the first few years to be a rollercoaster, with major mood swings punctuated by calm moments on that lovely pink cloud. When I find myself being overwhelmed with guilt, regret, sadness or some other decidedly non-Zen emotion, I go peel some potatoes. If I don't have any potatoes, I peel some carrots. I also chop salad, fold the laundry or vacuum the carpet. That's it. Just do the thing at hand.

The point is to focus your awareness on the weight of the potato in your hand, and the way the peeler settles into your grip. Notice how the flesh of the potato feels when you strip off its skin. Is there resistance? Pay attention to the sounds of the peels hitting the sink. Is your sink metal or porcelain? How does the water feel on your hands? What shapes to the peels arrange themselves into as they wash down the drain?

This awareness can be applied to everything you do throughout the day. Keep peeling those potatoes and one day you might become a Zen master without really trying.

September 4

"If the only prayer you ever say in your entire life is thank you, it will be enough." —Meister Eckhart

Prayer is such a sticky wicket.

Not only do many of us come to our sobriety with tons of religious baggage that needs to be sorted out, but most of us are never really taught to pray properly. The prayers we learned growing up might feel outdated, hypocritical, patriarchal or exclusive. Perhaps our childhood prayers weren't answered and we harbor resentments about that. There's something so indescribably *off-putting* about people who say they are "going to pray on it" or that they were led to some decision through prayer. Besides, praying can feel really embarrassing, especially when we have no idea to go about it.

It took me a while in sobriety to come around about prayer. But since I was willing to go to any lengths to stay sober (just as I was willing to go to any lengths to get loaded), I knew I had to give prayer a chance.

I started with a simple, "Thank you." I would say thank you when I woke up and when I went to bed. I would say thank you before I ate lunch. I would say thank you when my boys arrived home safely. I wasn't even sure who I was saying it to, but it was easy, it seemed to be a nice thing to do and it made me feel good.

Eventually my thank you's got more specific or I would offer a lead-in before I dropped the thank you into the conversation. Over time I found myself chatting away about gratitude in my head to whoever was listening. I got over my embarrassment about prayer and began to include blessings of peace, gratitude and lovingkindness into my meditations, not only for people I know and love, but for all beings.

Thank you will always and forever be absolutely enough. But I am glad that those two simple words became the gateway for me to find ease with sharing my sincere wishes with the power that is listening. Thank you for that.

September 5

As I write this I am feeling very irritated that I have to go to an event tomorrow afternoon. Tomorrow is Sunday, and I reserve Sundays for reading, relaxing, exercising, meditation and otherwise immersing myself in activities that make me feel connected to spirit. Essentially, I try to keep a Sabbath, and now that I have committed myself to something I am feeling off-kilter.

When I was drinking, Sundays were spent recovering. Now, Sundays are spent *in recovery*. I use the time to further my study of spirituality and sobriety, and to be quiet and still.

I'm still getting used to the idea of protecting my Sabbath as sacred, so when this event presented itself (it was very important to a friend of mine that I go) I of course said I would attend. I'm regretting it wholeheartedly now.

Those religions that keep a Sabbath do so to offer a day to God. It is a day of rest from the pressures of material society. For me, this day is Sunday because that's what works in my schedule. You could choose to make Monday your day, or Friday. But if you can set aside one day a week—even one day a *month*—you will find that this downtime becomes sacred to you.

That's why I am feeling so off. Sunday is the one day a week I can focus my attention on mental relaxation and spiritual rejuvenation. Instead I will be spending my day in my car driving to and from an event. I am happy to be there for my friend, but in the future I am going to guard my Sabbath with biblical force. It's that important to me.

September 6

My sobriety fellowship ends each meeting with the Lord's Prayer. We hold hands and say the Lord's Prayer together before trotting out into the world again, sober for one more day.

There are a lot of opinions about this practice among group members. Some people don't know the Lord's Prayer. Some people believe it represents a repressive patriarchy. Some people have terrible memories of this prayer being used to terrorize them into behaving a certain way. Often I find myself holding hands with someone who simply does not say the Lord's Prayer along with us. That's their choice.

I have practiced yoga for about 15 years, and in that time I have attended nearly every kind of class you can think of. Many of them include a chant at the beginning or the end, typically in Sanskrit and often wrapped up with a hearty "Om." Although I have been practicing yoga for a long time, I usually have no idea what we're saying when we're chanting. It's in Sanskrit, for heaven's sake. We could be pledging all of our future earnings to Justin Bieber for all I know.

I gladly participate in these chants, though, because I believe that joining voices with my companions creates a vibration that seals in our practice and our intention. Similarly, I say the Lord's Prayer, not because I need to demand my daily bread, but because I want to share my voice with the others who are on the path to sobriety with me. Our voices become one for those brief moments and there is an indescribable connection. The words are totally irrelevant at that point.

September 7

Alcoholics overcomplicate everything. When the topic of religion comes up, we can really go off the rails. Not only are we often reminded of how religion has failed us, but we're also really full of ourselves so if we don't see magical results right away it *all* must be total bunk. Some of the stories we hear in religious traditions, whether it's Christ walking on water or Buddha sitting there under the Bodhi tree, require a willing suspension of disbelief that many of us aren't capable of.

I was lucky in my catechism to meet Father Frank. During one of our classes, he rolled in on his wheelchair and took his place at the head of the class. None of us had met him yet, and we were quite keen to hear his wise counsel. He started with these words:

"The thing to remember in all your study," he said, "Is that all of the stories in the Bible are true."

This resulted in quite a bit of murmuring amongst the students. We were all in, make no mistake, but it was asking quite a lot of us to accept ALL of the stories as true!

"All of the stories in the Bible are true," he continued. "And some of them actually happened."

What a relief! What a unique perspective! Father Frank made it very clear to me that evening that to focus on the events in a religious mythology is to truly miss the point. What's more important, that Jesus magically increased three loaves and three fishes into enough to feed a crowd, or that he inspired people to *share their food*? What truly happened wasn't a magic trick; it was a transformation of people's souls. In that moment, everyone shared. Isn't that more important?

All of the stories in all of the world's religions are true. They point us to a world of compassion, letting go, sharing, kindness and connection. Just because most of them probably never happened doesn't make them any less truthful.

September 8

My conversion to Catholicism required weekly classes, a retreat, some foot washing (no joke), and a massive baptismal service to take place at one of California's most beautiful missions on the evening of Easter vigil.

Now this was how to do a ceremony! The church was packed to the gills. Hundreds of candles glittered, the smell of incense created a reflective mood and the choir sang soul-stirring music. I was very impressed.

When time came for the homily, I braced myself for a long-winded speech about resurrection, renewal and the importance of this day in the creation of Christianity. Father Frank wheeled his wheelchair onto the stage, looking quite sharp in his fancy Easter vestments.

He said: "Jesus died. He rose from the dead. Nothing I say can possibly compete with that."

And he wheeled himself right out of the building.

As you can imagine, the congregation erupted into laughter and applause. The sound was overwhelming. Tears of joy streamed down the congregants' faces.

Although I no longer practice Catholicism I think of that moment any time I am trying to overcomplicate my spiritual practice. Father Frank showed a room full of believers just how simple our gospel can be, and how our beliefs are much more powerful when we don't overdo it.

September 9

I'm one of those people who avoided Twelve Step programs because I didn't want to face the higher power question. I did go to some AA meetings the first time I tried to dry out, and found them tremendously helpful, but I also had a therapist at the time and I thought that was enough. (Or so I told myself. Basically I couldn't get on board with prayer, meditation or anything else that required me to be alone with my thoughts.)

I have recently taken up the Twelve Steps and joined a thriving local twelve-step recovery community. My sobriety has never been stronger. My faith has never been more profound. My connection to divinity is palpable. I have the Twelve Steps to thank for this, even though that's not originally what I sought when I first went back.

I like to look at the Twelve Steps as a master class in living like an adult. We are required to submit humbly to a power greater than ourselves. We are expected to take responsibility for our actions. We are encouraged to serve. We are shown the way to be disciplined. We clean up our own messes.

By walking through the steps one at a time I have developed a spiritual practice that is based on the desire for humility, opportunities to serve and inner quiet. In those simple changes I have found a deeper understanding of my place in the universe and my connection to all beings. If you're hesitant to try a Twelve Step program, I understand. Try it anyway. You never know where it might lead.

September 10

In his book *One Breath at a Time: Buddhism and the Twelve Steps*, Kevin Griffin tells the story of his first conversation with an addict named Lee who was interested in the Twelve Steps, but wants nothing to do with all the "God crap."

Griffin assured him that the Twelve Steps don't require any specific belief or faith in a higher power. He suggested that Lee simply acknowledge that *he* (Lee) wasn't God, and start from there.

I think that's a brilliant beginning. We may not be able to ever get comfortable with the concept of a higher power. (Griffin writes: "Frankly, there are all kinds of reasons *not* to believe in God, scientific or otherwise.") One thing I think we can all agree on is that, whether there is a God our not, *we* certainly aren't it.

Let go of the belief that you can affect the outcome of anything. I find this idea extremely comforting. If I am not God, I guess I can stop worrying so much. If I am not God, I can admit I don't always have the answer. If I am not God, I can stop trying to move everyone around my life like players on a chessboard.

Take a deep breath and rest easy in the idea that you are not God. You're just one sober person learning to live this new life one day at a time. Isn't that better?

September 11

One of the things I have enjoyed about developing my spirituality is finding what works for me. I have created a practice that fits into my schedule, my lifestyle and my goals. I meditate at weird times during unusual activities, like when I'm running. I try to keep a Sabbath. I read the spirituality books that are of interest to me. I participate in activities that keep my body healthy, my mind clear and my hands in service. I do lots of yoga. I stay sober.

When embarking on a spiritual path it's important to find the things that feel natural to you, otherwise you'll probably step off sooner rather than later. I find that running can catapult me into a meditative state. But maybe you are transported when you are in your garden or working on your car. Actor and musician Jack Black once said, "I don't have any real spirituality in my life—I'm kind of an atheist. But when music can take me to the highest heights, it's almost like a spiritual feeling. It fills that void for me."

Create your own spiritual practice. Fill it with the activities, study and thoughts that *fill you*. Whether you believe in God or not, I'm pretty sure she would approve.

September 12

If and when you take off on a spiritual journey (and I highly recommend you do) you'll find lots of different philosophies and activities to spark your interest.

The Twelve Steps are a fantastic place to start. What's great about the Twelve Steps as a spiritual practice is that it gives you lots of things to do, and that's important for the newly sober.

You could also read about Buddhism or attend a Buddhist gathering. The Sufis have healing circles. Native Americans can offer sweat lodges and a variety of other meaningful rituals. Right now, you could probably find a drum circle to join, a meditation labyrinth to walk or a Quaker meeting group to visit. I like *The Course in Miracles*, as well. This is a Christ-based spiritual practice that helps you release the pull of your ego. Maybe one of those big churches with a rock band tickles your fancy.

Have you heard of Laughter Yoga? I've never tried it, but it's impossible to watch an online video of Laughter Yoga and not break into giggles. Why not give it a go? Spirituality doesn't have to be all silent and sourpuss.

The point is that there are thousands of ways for you to explore spirituality. There is no one path, for you or anyone else. Find what you like and go after it one step at a time.

September 13

Early in sobriety, on a day when I was feeling particularly annoyed with the world, I also had the added bonus of being stuck in traffic. So there I was, angry, disconnected and gearing up to justify a tall, cold glass of wine when I got home.

As four lanes were merging into three, I let a beat-up old car in front of me. Imagine my surprise when I saw the bumper sticker that read "Do It Sober."

Have you ever seen a bumper sticker that said such a thing? Neither had I. And that car stayed *right in front of me* for the rest of the drive home. I haven't seen that bumper sticker since.

This is an example of synchronicity, or "the helping hands," phenomenon as Joseph Campbell calls it in his book *The Power of Myth.*

Synchronicity is that almost imperceptible occurrence of little coincidences that lead us down the path to our destiny. In that particular moment, I needed a dose of assurance that staying sober was a good idea (man, I wanted that drink!), and there it was, on a tacky old car.

Spirituality calls upon us to pay attention. It's quite possible that all of these synchronistic things have been happening all along, but we were too drunk to notice. Now that you're sober and you're looking for a spiritual connection, try to see all of the little ways life lines up to hand you your bliss.

September 14

No one ever taught me how to pray properly. My family never said grace before a meal, and we weren't encouraged to "pray the Lord my soul to keep" before going to bed. I memorized the Lord's Prayer at some point, although I am not really sure when that happened, or why. There were a few little sayings I memorized during my conversion to Catholicism, but nothing that could be used as a prayer in times of need.

When I started to pray for help with sobriety, I was pretty stumped. I would basically start rambling. Thanks here, help there, bless this person over yonder... It was an unfocused mess, just like my formerly alcohol-riddled brain.

I picked up Anne Lamott's brilliant book, *Help, Thanks, Wow: The Three Essential Prayers*, not a minute too soon. The book provides exactly what it promises: a simple way to pray for the prayer-challenged.

Lamott encourages people to be honest in their prayer. Step away from the showy, "plastic sushi," TV-style prayers and say something that's true.

She says: "If you told me you had said to God, 'It's all hopeless, and I don't have a clue if you exist, but I could use a hand,' it would almost bring tears to my eyes, tears of pride in you, for the courage it takes to get real—really real."

Say what you really mean to say. And if it's simply "Help, thanks, wow," that's plenty. Oh, and get her book. Right now.

September 15

I know something about ritual. I worshipped at the altar of cork and bottle for over two decades. My day simply had not begun until I pulled the cork, poured myself a glass and drank deeply. I liked this ritual so much I repeated it several times a day.

With sobriety, my ritual disappeared. It would be a stretch of the truth to say that I have found a replacement as steady, as daily, as that one, but I do want one. I make my bed every day, but I'd actually like to have a few special rituals to look forward to.
At this point, I don't even put much effort into birthdays, holidays or other events. I think I am missing out.

The purpose of ritual, in my mind, is to pull us out of the dreary day-to-day struggle to work, feed ourselves and go to the bathroom. Rituals remind us that life is more than our endless to-do list.

One small effort I am making this year is to celebrate my sobriety birthday with a hike and a seed-bombing (seed bombs are little balls of native seeds; you toss them into a muddy patch and they grow). Maybe this ritual will spark some creativity in this area for me.

I've always liked the Jewish ritual of touching the Mezuzah when entering or leaving home. A Mezuzah is a small decoration that holds a piece of parchment with a sacred prayer. Acknowledging this prayer when coming and going reminds the faithful of their unity with G-d. What a sweet, simple and profound way to connect every single day.

I'm hardly a religious scholar, but I feel confident that creating our own rituals to remind us of our divinity is quite alright. Do what feels right in your own spirit. Maybe it's 32 jumping jacks every morning. Perhaps it's bowing to the rising sun. Let your ritual be the thing that makes you connect to spirit in your own, unique way.

September 16

The Twelve Steps ask us to believe that a power greater than ourselves can relieve us of our alcoholism. I had to believe this to get sober because absolutely nothing else worked. It was either accept my higher power or look forward to a life of blurry memories, deteriorating health, ruined relationships and probably jail at some point.

My higher power continues to take shape. She's ever changing, morphing from a giddy Santa Claus-type to some sort of wise, super-serene yoga gal. Sometimes she's on my back, urging me to get my lazy butt out of bed or pointing out that I could put more effort into an important project.

I can't help but wonder, if my higher power is the only thing that can save me from alcoholism, why couldn't she save me from getting wasted to begin with? Where was she all these years?

The only way I can answer this is that she must have been there all along. I just refused to see her. I was so convinced that I had everything under control that I told my higher power to shove off on a daily basis. "I got this," I said. "I don't need anybody." So, per my request, she stepped into the shadows and waited for me to come to my senses.

The funny thing about higher powers is that they don't hold a grudge. The second I became willing to work with her, to truly connect and to let her will, not mine, be done, she showed up with bells on.

The Course in Miracles explains that God misses us when we're not around. Not in the "Gee I wonder where Meredith has been all this time," sort of way, but on a crazy, cosmic level our mere human brains can hardly perceive. Without our full participation in the spiritual the universe is incomplete. Whether you want it or not, your higher power is holding your space for you. Why not claim it?

September 17

Can you even remember all of the mornings you woke up and said, "God, if I ever get over this hangover I am never drinking again"? Maybe you had a moment where you made a bargain with the universe like, "God, if you help me make it home tonight without running anyone over I will never drink and drive again."

I wouldn't even try to tabulate all of the promises, requests and flat-out begging I burdened the universe with while I was drinking. There are thousands, no doubt. For someone who didn't believe in God or any kind of higher power, I sure did a hell of a lot of praying.

This is not special. Drunks have been doing this for centuries. The difference between sober people and those still actively drinking is that one morning we woke up, told God (or our mirror, our cat or the tree outside our window) that we were never drinking again, *and we meant it.*

In that moment, our higher power, divinity, the late JC or whatever it was, took over for us. It was that easy. We received nothing more than a swift, light and graceful replacement of our will with theirs, and our lives were forever changed.

Never underestimate the power of a sincere request. Higher powers simply can't resist them.

September 18

So much of my pre-sobriety life was about chasing down external experiences. I was near manic about the need to be somewhere, doing something, and it had to be *life changing, magical and inspiring.* Then, when it was all done, I'd get drunk and pass out.

I was always on the lookout for the remotest of hikes that lead to seasonal waterfalls that only four other people have ever seen. I signed up for treasure hunts where I'd spend hours zipping through San Francisco trying to find the clues. I would stand outside for hours in 100+ degree heat (or torrential rain) to spot a rare bird. Then, as I mentioned before, I would celebrate by getting drunk and passing out.

When I fully gave myself over to sobriety and the spiritual emphasis that comes along with it, a radical shift occurred. I didn't notice it, but over time my interests became internal. Although I never put words to it, it's clear that my focus has readjusted to my inner life.

This is going to make me sound like a huge bore, but it's true. These days I would rather stay home and read a novel than power hike to the top of a mountain. This evening some friends invited me to San Francisco to see a play I have been dying to see, but I declined. I would prefer to spend my evenings in meditation, doing some light yoga, writing this book or sketching out some ideas for my next creative project. In short, I am curious to see how my thoughts and feelings are developing, rather than distracting myself with watching other people do stuff, or creating a false sense of accomplishment.

Aren't you curious, too, to see what's really going on inside you? I bet it's fascinating.

September 19

I don't always feel very spiritual. I am easily agitated, especially when I'm hungry. I lose patience with my family when they don't do what I say the minute I say it. I have a sharp tongue and a smart mouth and, unfortunately, I am not afraid to use them.

However, I have discovered that if I behave as if I am spiritual, spiritual acts will come forth, and my mindset will naturally reset itself.

By "spiritual acts" I don't mean parting the waters or healing the sick. I simply mean turning off the spite spigot and treating other people the way I would want to be treated.

Isn't this the cornerstone of all spiritual philosophies, though? The meditating creates connection and the Sunday services are uplifting, but if we aren't treating other people nicely, then what's the point?

If I have meditated all day, and then emerge from my room swearing a blue streak because someone forgot to put the dishes away (again), my spirit hasn't made any forward progress. I may have had a nice time in the quiet, but spiritual feelings without spiritual acts are nothing.

If you're new to the spirituality trip and are looking for a great place to start, treat others nicely today. Then do it again tomorrow, even if you're feeling rotten. You may be surprised to see your mood change, your step get lighter and (dare I say it?) your spirit soar just by following the classic Golden Rule.

September 20

I believe that a solid spiritual practice is built on good sense.

I live in Northern California, so let me tell you that I have been subjected to all sorts of airy-fairy spiritual nonsense. I can tell when a load of hoo-hah is coming my way because the practitioner, writer, guru or what have you, does not live their life with any common sense whatsoever.

One of my more "spiritual" acquaintances lives in a home that is stuffed with religious iconography. There is a Buddha statue over here and a painting of Isis over there. Watch out or you'll topple her stone Ganesha collection. The air is thick with sandalwood incense. If you didn't know who lived there, you'd walk in and think, "Wow, here is someone on a real spiritual journey."

The problem is that this dear person does not choose to live her life with good sense, so all of her spiritual intentions fall flat. Her relationships are a disaster. Her drinking is out of control. Her mood swings are often unbearable. She is pathologically unable to think of anyone but herself.

I would like to suggest that it is far more important for you to keep your promises, pay your bills, delay gratification, stay sober and clean up your own messes than to have the right "Om" T-shirt. A strong spiritual life also includes maintaining boundaries, which means that you can provide service to others, but don't let them trample all over you. A strong spiritual life means that you no when and how to say no, when and how to say yes and when and how to say nothing at all.

If you want to take stock of your spiritual progress in your sobriety, don't look to your dreamcatcher, St. Francis medallion or stained glass window. Maintain a checklist of common sense behavior and your spiritual life with flourish in its wake.

September 21

The word "Namaste" (pronounced nah-mah-STAY) offered a gateway into my spirituality.

I, like many sober people, struggled with the idea of a higher power, of surrender and of taking time out of my oh-so-important schedule to meditate. However, at the end of each of my yoga classes the instructor would say to us, "Namaste," and we would reply, "Namaste."

Namaste is a Sanskrit word that, loosely translated, means, "the divinity in me salutes the divinity in you."

For years I couldn't see the divine if it smacked me in the head, much less honor any sort of divinity inside me. But in class, I could see the divine in others, and I deeply loved the moment when I could honor them for their connection to spirit.

It took many, many years for this practice to open my heart, humbly, to my own divinity. Now, still, when I feel myself slipping away from this life-affirming truth, I look for hints of the divine in those around me and am reminded that we are indeed all connected.

Namaste.

September 22

Getting sober opened my eyes to a wondrous (dare I say *miraculous*?) realization: I am not the center of the universe.

I may have paid lip service to this idea while I was still drinking, but I did not understand this on a deep, cellular level until I had been sober for quite a while. In fact, the drinking me would never have allowed this blasphemy to occur. Of course I was the center of the universe!

The problem with believing that you are the precious orb around which all other human, animal and celestial activities must revolve is that it's a whole lotta pressure. It means that your every thought is of supreme importance. Every action has life-changing consequences. Others are closely watching everything you say or do.

I remember a co-worker from years ago who lived one block away from work, but still drove her car to the office every day. She didn't want people looking at her while she walked.

That's what believing you are the center of the universe does to you. It creates this neurotic belief that everything is about you, that people are always looking and that you must control everything.

You are a precious and essential part of the universe. Bringing calm to your being and celebrating your spirit are absolutely necessary to the serenity and peace of us all. But you're not the center of it. You're not in charge. And none of it is specifically about you. Not in the way you think, anyway.

September 23

How do you imagine a spiritual experience feels? It's hard to resist the idea that it's the radiant flash of light, followed by a vision of preternatural beauty and the effortless appearance of some formerly missing wisdom into your mind and soul.

Eckhart Tolle, Author of *The Power of Now* and *A New Earth*, describes an experience during a bout of severe depression that found him awakening in great peace and without the sense of the "self" that had made him so miserable. He spent the next few years wandering around London in a state of euphoria. St. Joan had visions, Mary was visited by angels (and we all know what happened next) and Buddha experienced some significant spiritual turmoil on his way to enlightenment.

I have yet to experience anything nearly this dramatic. I've had a couple of pretty intense dreams and a slew of coincidences that seemed like anything but, but that's about it. The drama would be nice, and certainly memorable, but for now my daily spiritual experiences look like this: staying sober, helping others, keeping my promises.

Like most people on a spiritual journey, I would welcome the lights, vision and wisdom. Sounds fun! But if it never happens, it's quite enough for me to keep moving, keep helping, keep praying...

September 24

I'm nobody! Who are you?
Are you nobody, too?
Then there's a pair of us, don't tell.
They'd banish us, you know.
How dreary to be somebody!
How public, like a frog.
To tell your name the livelong day
To an admiring bog!
—Emily Dickinson

Are you a member of the Super-Special Unicorn Club? I am the Founder, CEO, Executive Director and Ultimate Dear Leader of just such a club. So precious, so sensitive and so easily victimized am I that I had to spend over two decades drinking myself nearly to death in order to function.

I was a Super-Special Unicorn when I was drinking. My problems were the center of my world and if you didn't care as much about me as I did, you were out with yesterday's news. I became a Super-Special Unicorn for a while in sobriety, too. Now that I was sober, I was soooo much better than everyone else. I didn't really say anything directly to anyone, but I could be quite judgmental and superior on the inside.

I didn't revoke my Super-Special Unicorn status until much later, until my spiritual study pointed out to me, time and again, that this creation of "self," this ever-eager ego, was not only not real but probably conspiring to keep me miserable.

I am still working with this one, but I can't even begin to tell you how nice it is to NOT have to express my opinion. Sometimes I don't have an opinion at all! That I no longer insert myself into conversations, force all the attention on to me or perform to make people like me is miraculous—and so liberating. I don't always succeed, but in every situation I try very hard to be mindful of speaking only when it is in service to the project, idea or situation, never to make myself look good.

It's taken the realization that I am an integral part of the universe to let go of the idea that I had to be "somebody" all the time. Being a sober nobody with a deepening relationship to the spiritual nature of the world is better for me than making a big splash at a party no one will even remember the next day.

September 25

My alcoholism developed in service to my ego's need to escape. My ego is an adept story-spinner, and when my reality wasn't matching what I imagined I deserved from life, I drank to dull down the disillusionment.

To this day, I occasionally indulge in escapist fantasies. When I am feeling particularly in need of spiritual rejuvenation (usually because I have let myself lapse in my meditation practice), I envision myself becoming a monk. I like to think about myself walking peacefully through a flourishing garden, sitting atop my zafu cushion or quietly reflecting on life's mysteries in my simple-yet-comfortable room. I have a shaved head and flowing saffron robes. I effortlessly arise at 4 a.m. and fall into a deep sleep at 8 p.m. every night.

It's ridiculous, but this fantasy is often preferable to picking up the garbage the dog has strewn all over the floor or shouting at the kids to do their homework already.

My spiritual journey will probably not lead me to forsake everything for a monastic existence. I haven't even prioritized a weekend retreat on my schedule, ever. Just seems so indulgent...

The point is that we don't have to turn our backs on the aggravating details of life to find a connection to spirit. Maybe it's more difficult out here than behind the stone walls of a monastery; I really don't know. I only know that escaping my responsibilities is not what my higher power has in mind for my spiritual journey. Though it may be a struggle, it's my job to create space for serenity inside, regardless of what is happening around me.

September 26

Learning to serve others is a great place to start when putting your spirituality into action. For the self-centered alcoholic this can be a lifelong, day-by-day, minute-by-minute process. Throughout the day I find myself having an almost physical struggle to act in accordance with the greater good rather than what serves me personally. I am a grown, adult woman, who is in it to win it with this whole sobriety thing, and I have Herculean inner battles with putting others first. Don't be so hard on yourself if this is something you deal with, too.

It recently came to my attention that part of spiritual growth is not only learning to give of yourself to others, but also to *learn to take what others offer you.*

When I visit my friend Em she falls all over herself to make me more comfortable. There's tea, water and snacks. Sometimes there are gifts. I never leave without fresh eggs from her chickens or lemons from her tree.

It took nearly a year of our friendship for me to get comfortable with this. I was trying to learn to give to others and yet here is this person showering me with affection and fresh produce...? I couldn't reconcile it.

What I realized is that this makes her feel good. She likes giving to people. She wants to be useful. She is naturally loving and giving, and her greatest joy is providing help or a solution for people she cares about.

I can relate because I always feel useful when somebody asks me to pick something up for them, or I lend them a book they've been wanting to read. I like feeling useful, too, once I get over my selfishness and do something nice, for heaven's sake. Sometimes the most selfless thing we can do is to let others do nice things for us, and to sincerely thank them for it.

September 27

Your spiritual practice should not feel like a punishment. There is no need to wear a hair shirt to remind you of your sins. Your higher power would be appalled if you starved yourself, worked out until you threw up or otherwise harmed your body to make up for anything.

Your spiritual practice can and should feel like a cool dip in a divine pool. Your meditation, even if it is only five minutes a day, can be a time when offer your heart to spirit. Your daily walk, evening reflection or weekly visit to a sacred place is the opportunity to reflect on forgiveness—for others and for yourself.

Alcoholics have a lot of demons that can get riled up when we try to give ourselves the peace we deserve. If you are actively seeking contact with your higher power, but are being troubled by dark thoughts toward yourself or others, talk to someone. Find a friend in a recovery group, make an appointment with your clergy or your doctor to find some relief from the spiritual pain that's bothering you.

Your pain is real, and you deserve to find relief. Ask for help, and begin your spiritual practice anew.

September 28

Alcohol keeps us separate from our divinity. There's no way to maintain conscious contact when we are barely conscious.

Sobriety is our opportunity to tear down the wall that separates us from our divine nature. It's the time to learn how to put our ego aside and delve into our true purpose. What joy there is in the hard work before us!

But before we move forward, we must take inventory of the other behaviors, chemicals or thoughts that may be keeping us from optimal connection with spirit. Since you stopped drinking are you overeating? Over exercising? Are you creating drama where there was none? Do you have other addictions, like pills, that need to be addressed? Are you indulging in way too much sugar or caffeine?

I replaced my alcoholic behaviors with over napping, over smoking and overworking. I had all this free time when I stopped drinking and I got very caught up in trying to fill it. I napped when I was bored—and this can also be considered an escapist behavior. I smoked because it was "the only thing I had left." I worked because I was trying to make up for lost time.

What I was really doing was avoiding the stillness that's required for spiritual reflection. I could trick myself into thinking I was meditating as I drifted off to sleep. I could say a prayer of gratitude as I puffed away. I called my work "service" and thought that was enough.

This was all a huge cover up for doing the real work. I still fall victim to some of these behaviors, but I try to resist the urge. If I feel tired, I meditate instead. I haven't completely eliminated the smoking, but it has really cut down and I don't bullshit myself about it anymore. I keep my work and my service separate.

338

Are there areas in your life where alcoholic behaviors are masquerading as spirituality?

September 29

The easiest thing to put on the back burner is your spiritual practice. After all, it's not something anyone sees. Your boss is never going to check in to make sure you meditated. The kids probably won't insist that you go get some time for yourself. It's so much easier to sleep in than go to services or go to a meeting. Reading spiritual materials is fun, but not nearly so much fun as a romance novel or something with vampires.

A good friend pointed out to me that we must make some time for spirituality every day. She explained that the food we ate last week wouldn't nourish our bodies today, just like the spiritual moment we had a month ago won't keep our soul filled today.

This idea makes it so much easier to take even the smallest amount of time to be still and connect. Our souls need this refreshment like our bodies need food and air. Don't starve your soul.

September 30

Let's always remember September as another chance to refresh our spirit. There's that subtle chill in the air, the leaves are turning and we're at the gateway of fall—the perfect time of year to turn inward.

Like the changing of the seasons, our spiritual journey is not linear; it's a cycle of continual change, rebirth and renewal. It may be completely different from one year to the next, or even one moment to the next. Be present always, and look for those subtle shifts in your mindset and in your heart. That's growth. That's redemption. That's spiritual sobriety.

October
Rage, Regret and Resentment

October 1

Regret for the pain we caused while drinking can swallow us up if we let it. I can't begin to tell you all of the thoughtless actions I would take back, the hurtful things I would un-say and the valuable time I would use differently. Some nights, as I am falling asleep, I am so consumed with regret, embarrassment and shame that it's hard for me to settle down.

It's important to remember when regret has you in its clutches that not only can you not change the past, but it's possible no one else remembers what you did. This doesn't excuse your terrible behavior, but I have discovered on more than one occasion that, upon apologizing, the person whom I thought I harmed had no idea what I was talking about.

This is not to let you off the hook. What this means is that we are being self-centered. This kind of regret casts us as the star of our own movie, and it assumes that everyone around us is as deeply invested in our behaviors as we are. I've sat down with people with tears in my eyes, a sincere apology in my heart and deep shame in my soul only to have them respond with, "Huh?"

Don't allow your grandiose, self-centered, alcoholic brain make you wallow in regret for things that may not even matter now. Save your regret and your corrective actions for the handful of things that actually deserve your attention.

October 2

No one is immune to resentment. Most alcoholic drinkers have a steady flow of resentments that keep us in our cups for years and years. I was so bitter over all of the slights I had endured that I was willing to literally kill myself over them.

My parents didn't love me enough. My husband ignored me. My boss never realized my brilliance. I didn't get the part in the play, the job I deserved or the award I thought I had earned. I had no problem identifying things for which I was entitled and was denied. If someone pointed out to me why my resentment was unnecessary, I would find another one to replace it. I lived for resentments, and my resentments fueled all of my decisions.

What I discovered was that not only were my resentments my excuse for drinking, but they were also my excuse for absolutely everything. I used my resentments as an excuse for not even trying to become a better person. I certainly couldn't challenge myself to succeed because I was still so angry about that "thing someone said" about me all those years ago—or whatever.

In order to stay sober I have had to drop 100% of my resentments. I cannot afford to nurse those negative feelings for any length of time, no matter how powerful the pull. In many ways, not allowing the first resentment has become more important than not allowing the first drink.

As a result of clearing out my resentments, I not only feel more secure in my sobriety, but I feel more confident in every aspect of my life. It's amazing all the positive things that flow into the space you leave when you cut out the cancer of resentment.

October 3

It's very tempting to loll around in our regret while we're moving through the first months of sobriety. We may be confronting feelings of regret for the first time in our lives. We may also feel that our regrets mean that we don't deserve to be happy, at peace or serene. We feel that we deserve to be punished for all the terrible things we did, said and thought.

You're allowed a day or so of regret sads. I'll even give you three days, to be totally generous. Get in there and roll around in your regret. Get dirty in it. Make yourself feel terrible. Say all the things you think you deserve to hear.

Then stop. You're not helping anybody.

The only antidote to regret is kindness. If your regret makes you feel like you owe the world a pound of flesh then get out there and do something nice for somebody. Regret that isn't transformed into kind action is completely wasted. And we're done getting wasted, right?

October 4

Did you know that venting your anger actually does more harm than good? I never would have guessed it, but it's true. You think you feel better after, but you really don't.

In fact, according to an article in *Psychology Today*, published on September 25, 2013 by Brad J. Bushman, Ph.D., "...venting anger is like using gasoline to put out a fire: It feeds the flame. Venting keeps arousal levels high and keeps aggressive thoughts and angry feelings alive."

Aggression, even toward people you don't know, is more likely after you've vented your anger. Apparently vigorous exercise is not recommended to deal with anger, either, because it simply perpetuates the aggravated state by increasing your blood pressure and heart rate.

So what do we do with anger when we've got heaping handfuls of it? It's better for everyone if you just "get rid of it." Bushman suggests counting to ten, listening to soothing music or deep breathing. He also says that watching a comedy, petting a puppy or performing a charitable deed can help because these activities are "incompatible with anger and therefore they make the angry state impossible to sustain."

Maybe next time you feel a surge of anger coming on, don't call your best friend to vent. Try giving the dog some attention, picking some flowers for your girlfriend or some deep breathing. Anything's better than hanging on to feelings that make you feel aggressive, agitated and aggravated.

October 5

"Whining is anger through a small opening." —Stuart Smalley

Aside from being annoying and unattractive, whining plain pointless.

We all feel powerless, overlooked and misunderstood throughout our lives. Many of us feel that way several times a day! But when you spend your precious energy whining to your mom, your dad, your friends or your siblings about your life, you're not only alienating them, but you're not making any positive steps toward owning your own experience.

Try to catch yourself whining next time and see if you can dig down to the anger underneath it. This is a far more useful practice than trying to get people on your side or to use their platitudes as a reason to stay stuck. Are you whining about your boyfriend forgetting to call? Maybe you're actually angry because you're in an unbalanced relationship. Are you complaining that your boss doesn't understand you? Maybe you're angry that she points out that you're not really trying your best. What are you really angry about? What do you resent? What can you change or forgive?

You can't be an emotionally sober person and still whine. It's not possible. So let's address what's really going on, make the appropriate change and grow up. It's better that way, you'll see.

October 6

Super-Special Unicorns like us don't like criticism. Even if it's meant and delivered in the kindest, most helpful way possible, we get our hackles raised at the mere mention that we may be doing something wrong.

I can typically judge how correct someone is in their criticism of me by how angry I get. If I get really angry, they're usually spot on. I'm busted and I don't like it. If I launch a campaign to try to get everyone else to see my side (usually behind the critic's back) then I KNOW I have been called out for something that needs to be fixed. Immediately.

Now that I am sober I can use this anger as a tool, rather than a hindrance. I can judge whether I agree with someone by how vehemently my anger makes itself known. This seems crazy, I know, but the fact is that I have been able to tone down the emotional reaction, stop taking the critique personally and really listen to what someone is saying. When it's true, I feel it. I'm uncomfortable, but at least I have something I can work with rather than running around trying to prove why I am right and they are wrong.

This is master-level emotional sobriety, and it's available to all of us. Next time someone says something that makes your blood boil, don't react. Count to ten and think. Are they telling you something you really need to hear? Can your life change for the better if you listen?

October 7

Who are the top two most-resented human beings in the world?

Our parents.

Can you go on and on about all the crummy things your folks did growing up? I can. They didn't listen. They refused to understand me. They failed to provide me with the best opportunities. They were selfish and inconsiderate. They simply grew tired of parenting and gave up. They got everything wrong, and it's all their fault that I have failed at work/marriage/art/life.

Some parents were criminally negligent or put their children in extreme danger. Some were so selfish they forgot they had children to raise at all. A few of us were subjected to parents with addictions, gambling problems or other obsessive behaviors that made them unfit to care for a child.

Some people shouldn't be parents. If you got two of those (or more, what with all of the stepparents that often come in and out), then I am deeply sorry. You have been given a terrible burden to bear, and it's true that you may spend your entire adulthood trying to heal your childhood.

But here we are. We're sober, and we're working so hard to get better. The resentment you have toward the adults you were stuck with as a child may be keeping you stuck *now*. You don't have to stay in that mindset with them anymore. Your life is yours to create and the best revenge is a life well lived.

Try to let the resentment toward your parents go. When it comes up again, let it go again. And again. Then see if you can forgive them. As an adult in recovery, it's not only suggested, it's required.

October 8

Anger comes with the territory with alcoholism. I was angry when I drank and I was angry when I couldn't drink. Then I would get angry about a bunch of other stuff and drink because of that.

Now that I am sober, my anger is completely different. It's not a slow burn like it used to be, revealing itself in slurred words and slammed doors at the end of a very long night. It comes on fast now, it's hot, and then it fizzles. For justified anger I can usually find a solution by using my big-girl words or by walking away and managing it on my own.

Sometimes my anger lingers, though. I'll get peeved about something and it hangs on for dear life, despite all of my heavy breathing, counting or sock folding. If I can get myself to calm down, I usually realize that I haven't eaten in a while.

It's funny to write that because I think in all of our searching we look for spiritual, emotional or philosophical answers. Surely my emotions are tied to the great turning of the spheres, the tides or the alignment of the stars...? Nope. I just haven't stuffed something in my gullet for three hours.

A friend of mine told me of her struggle with postpartum depression. She said she'd be sitting there and it would hit her that she needed to cry, hit someone, hit herself, drive off a bridge... Or maybe she needed a donut. (The donut always worked.)

Don't overblow things or assign depth to them that isn't there. Your emotions are real to you and shouldn't be ignored, but wouldn't it be great if you could feel better by eating a donut?

October 9

I am harboring resentment toward one of my family members, and working through it has been like untying a huge knot. Just when I think I have released it I stumble upon another tight area that needs to be patiently loosened and let go. I'm working it and working it, and no matter what I do it's holding fast.

The way I see it, my family member—who is also an active alcoholic—is getting some financial breaks and praise for something that is, at best, poorly put together and, at worst, a long con. That's all I need to say about the details. What's important here is how I am transforming my resentment into action.

Like I said, this one's got me in its grip. There's emotional energy here, though, and rather than letting myself get frazzled I am using it to bring fresh vitality to my own projects. When I see this person dropping the ball, I go back to my own files to make sure that I have taken care of all of my due diligence. If I hear that this person has lied about progress, I send an email to my clients letting them know where I am on their project. When get burned up about the money that is being wasted, I spend my afternoon organizing my finances to make sure I am taking care of my family and myself. When I get angry that he takes no responsibility for his addictions, I recommit to my own sobriety.

I can't control what's happening with my family member. The only thing I can do is recognize when toxic emotions have me in their grip and take action to relieve the pressure.

October 10

Regret is only useful in how it can change you. One of the side effects of regret can be compassion, if you let it.

I still cringe when I recall some of the stupid, embarrassing and selfish things I did while I was drinking. There are a handful of stores I will no longer shop in because I am too humiliated to run in to the sales clerks who work there. One of the cashiers at the corner store once pulled me aside and told me he thought I drank too much! He was right, of course, but even in sobriety I haven't been able to muster the courage to go back there.

However, my regrets about public disgraces, private behavior and all of the things I would give anything to take back have given me a deep well of compassion for others who make mistakes.

I often see people in stumbling through my town, drunk in the middle of the afternoon (there's an Irish Pub a block away from my house). When I was drinking I would make some smart-ass comment in an attempt to draw attention away from the fact that I wanted to join them! Now, I feel for their suffering. I can no longer judge anyone harshly for acting silly in public, making a poor judgment call or failing. I just can't. I have compassion for the range of human experience in a way that I never could have if I didn't experience my own profound regrets.

Let your regrets go. And then let them transform your heart.

October 11

Does social media make you resentful? It's designed to.

Sometimes Facebook posts send me to crazy town. There are all of my acquaintances, with their perfect families and their perfect teeth in their perfect picket-fence homes. Oh they're in Hawaii this week? How nice. Look! This one won an important prize. Oh my goodness, these folks are in Paris again? And her nose job looks terrific! These two are celebrating 20 years of marriage, prosperity and bliss, bliss, bliss...

The logical suggestion would be for me to get off Facebook altogether. But since that's not going to happen, I have to remind myself that Facebook's main purpose is to make me feel dissatisfied. Facebook exists solely to make us unhappy with our own lives so that we will buy things from their advertisers.

Pinterest, Instagram, Snapchat—all of these things came into being to sell us stuff to make us happy. And they start by making us very, very unhappy.

Get off the e-juice if you can. However, if you decide to stay connected, never forget that your dissatisfaction is their number one goal.

October 12

"Mistakes are always forgivable, if one has the courage to admit them."—Bruce Lee

In order for me to get sober, I had to learn how to accept responsibility in a healthy way.

Before, I would put the blame on my self as a defense mechanism, virtually insisting that everything is my fault so that the offended party couldn't stay mad at me. This was an unhealthy use of blame that was not borne from a place of sincerity, but from a place of manipulation. By turning blame on myself I did not make proper amends, fix my messes or deal with the aftermath of my behavior in a useful way. I threw myself on my sword so completely no one could stay angry with me for long. I also continued to act like a little shit because I learned nothing.

I no longer deal in blame. I don't blame others for their actions, nor do I blame myself for mistakes. I do hold others *accountable* for their actions and I take full *responsibility* for the mistakes I've made and the misunderstandings I have caused.

I remember making minor mistakes at work and developing elaborate fictions, finger pointing and falsehoods to cover my tracks. When I was a kid not only would I run at the first sign of trouble, but if I was caught I could detail all of the reasons why someone else was at fault.

It's so much easier, and certainly less time-consuming, to admit that you've gone awry. If I miss a deadline, I tell my boss why, even if it's painful. I released this book several months after promised, and I'll tell you it's because I was procrastinating. I'm human. I am fallible. And so is everyone else.

Let go of blaming yourself and others. Next time something goes wrong when you're responsible, 'fess up and move on. The minute you find yourself concocting an elaborate blame game to save your ass, stop and tell yourself the truth. Then tell someone else. You can't lie to everyone and stay sober. I'm not sure why, but for some reason these two things cancel each other out.

October 13

I'm not sure if this is true for you, but many of the regrets I wallow in are ego-based.

That means that I am less likely to tear my hair out over how I treated my ex-husband and more likely to shudder when I remember that I fell off a barstool in front of a new client (they fired my firm a few weeks later).

This is why I have to let these regrets go. My regrets tend to center on ego damage or embarrassments over times when my "image" was at stake.

When I wallow in that empty, fluttery feeling of humiliation-based regret I know that my ego is gearing up to get me drunk. I look back on that girl and I think she's worthless, stupid, shallow... *Poor, poor, pour me a drink.*

I have to transform this regret and humiliation into compassion for the wasted girl falling off the stool in front of clients. She was 22, living alone for the first time, desperately lonely and in the grips of a disease that would take a massive toll on her for the next 15+ years. I feel sorry for her because I know what mistakes she's about to make. This night is nothing. Plus, she's probably the only one who remembers it now.

What is the nature of your regret? If you are feeling regret over something real—a ruined relationship with a family member or a life-altering occurrence you can't undo—then reach out for help from professionals who can assist you through these painful feelings. You can take action to make amends for these types of regrets.

But if you're freaking out about looking bad, dip in to your compassion, and try to find some softness for the sad, drunk person you used to be. Your time is much better spent trying to help someone else than it is reflecting on your past idiotic behavior.

October 14

The farther along you get in your sobriety, the more likely you are to recognize how alcohol affected your whole life, not just those drunk moments when things went nutty. You may begin to think wistfully about past wine-soaked relationships or dredge up nostalgia for jobs you lost or friends you miss.

In my case, I get caught up in the idea that maybe my marriage wouldn't have been so horrible if I had been sober. Knowing what I know now about the joys of sobriety it's impossible not to see that things would have gone much more smoothly if I wasn't swimming in wine the whole time. I wonder if we would have actually gotten divorced at all? Did my alcoholism make me unable to discover new pathways to reconciliation? Was my brain so addled that I made things worse than they actually were?

Well, the answer is a resounding "yes." When you drink every day, your system is continually bombarded with mind- and body-altering chemicals. There is no doubt in my mind that my drinking had a direct effect on how I processed everything in those years. Alcohol made it possible for me to reside in a continuum of victimhood. My hangovers gave me a distraction from my real issues—it's hard to open your heart to a loving solution when you are seriously going to puke. right. now. All the time.

I feel all three R's when I realize how I let alcohol quite literally ruin my life. I feel rage over the idea that I realized all of this too late. I feel resentment that I had to figure all this out myself. I feel regret that no matter how sorry I am there is nothing I can do to change the past.

I must continue to learn from my past, but not dwell on it. Now, at least I have the comfort of knowing that my assessment of any

357

situation and my participation in any relationship comes from a clear mind and open heart. Some days that's the best I've got.

October 15

One of the first things I encountered in AA was something they call the "son of a bitch prayer."

The general idea is that if you are clinging to resentment around someone in particular, you should pray for them every day for two weeks. And they don't just recommend sending them a few good vibes. They suggest that you pray for that person to receive everything you want for yourself, and that includes health, riches, curlier hair and a great job.

Depending the depth of your vitriol toward this person you will hate this at varying levels. I find that when I say the son of a bitch prayer for folks it takes me about three to five days of full bore praying before I'm no longer steamed. By day seven I am making up creative things to grant them, like a cat that doesn't shed or to be relieved of their car payment. By day fourteen, I've usually forgotten what I was so mad about in the first place, and if I can't greet them with a smile and a hug, I can usually forget about it and be polite.

It's a little magic, and it really does work. Next time someone's got you worked up, say a little prayer for the son of a bitch and you'll feel a lot better.

October 16

Sobriety is not a magic fix for rage, resentment and regret, but it does open the door to encourage those pesky feelings to move on. I am rarely paralyzed by these feelings anymore, but I have found that I am still capable of feeling hostility toward certain people, places and things.

The most pernicious thought I have is that someone or something is a "pain in the ass." I don't ever say this out loud, but when I am asked to pick something up for a friend at the store, my initial thought is "what a pain in the ass." When my kids (my kids!) ask me to look over their homework, there it is: "What a pain in the ass." I have to run out to meet a client? "Pain in the ass."

It's totally involuntary, but now that I am aware of it I am trying to find a replacement. Have you ever caught yourself in a habitual hostile thought?

October 17

Do you know what it means to be passive aggressive? This is behavior that is the expression of negative feelings indirectly through non-cooperation or manipulation. Dealing with passive aggressive people is *the worst.*

The problem is that you never really know if they meant to behave so badly toward you or if you misread the situation. The passive aggressive person may continually "forget" to do a simple task you repeatedly request of them. The passive aggressive person may show up late to all of your scheduled meetings in order to gain the upper hand or to frustrate you. The passive aggressive person "accidentally" burns dinner so that you never ask them to cook again.

The most outrageous example of passive aggressive behavior I ever witnessed happened recently (and I thank heavens it wasn't directed toward me because I think I would have committed a homicide.) My dear friend, who shall remain totally nameless, recently had a baby. It is her third child; her second baby died in childbirth. It's logical that throughout her pregnancy and for the first few weeks after the birth she would be emotional and anxious.

Her husband, a sweet and humorous guy for the most part, is not very helpful around the house. He forgets things, or gets caught up in his own dream world. My friend has felt abandoned during these first months of raising the new baby. She's holding it together, but isn't receiving the kind of support she really needs.

When the baby was four weeks old, the husband brought home a new puppy.

I am going to let that sink in for a minute. *He brought home an eight-week old puppy while his family was still adjusting to a brand new baby.*

Our mutual friends shrugged this off like it's "just his way." *He's a box of rocks*, they say, *hardy har-har*. I disagree. I think bringing this bundle of chaos into an already difficult situation is his way of expressing mountains of repressed hostility.

My point is to be aware of this behavior in yourself and others. If you catch yourself plotting to "get someone" or trying to arouse an emotional reaction in another person through some weird behavior, check yourself to see if you need to address your pain directly instead. And don't ever bring home a puppy without checking with people first.

October 18

Don't take anything personally, even if it's meant to be. The fact is that the person who insults you is expressing more about who they are than who you are.

I once spent two hours on a cruise ship helping a friend locate her online boarding pass for the trip home. She couldn't remember what airline she was on, what company she had booked through or any other details. Through nothing more than persistence and my knowledge of online travel booking, I was able to find it, print it and send her on her way. She never once thanked me.

I spent a couple of days stewing about this lack of gratitude. How could she not even thank me? What did I do wrong? I gave up two hours of hot tub time and I couldn't get a thank you? I took this very personally.

I came to find out that she was trying to lose her boarding pass so that her wealthy sister would pay for her to fly home first class with her. She did really lose it, but she wasn't nearly so interested in retrieving it as I was for reasons that had nothing to do with me. Her lack of a thank you was all about her. Fortunately, I didn't drink over it, and, believe me, this person has driven me to drink before.

Think about the last time you actually set out to be insulting or ungrateful. In most cases people don't decide to attack you personally, and would be mortified to find out that you're hurt, angry or resentful. Next time you're feeling personally attacked, try to remind yourself that it's not about you; it's about another person making their own insecurities, agenda or resentments known.

October 19

"Always forgive your enemies. Nothing annoys them so much."—
Oscar Wilde

Forgiveness is the oil that keeps the sobriety machine running smoothly. It is absolutely required that we learn to forgive others—and ourselves—in order to live a life of blissful sobriety.

Forgiveness is also a mystery. How do we forgive, exactly? I can show you how to meditate. I can teach you how to dance a two-step. I can provide examples of how to cook noodles, execute a three-point turn or map the way to San Jose.

I don't think forgiveness can be taught. It can be suggested, but never taught. Forgiveness comes from a place within us that is deep, elemental and ethereal. Forgiveness is a primal urge that only arises when we consciously decide to be forgiving.

The beautiful thing is that once we access this place of forgiveness, the benefits are all ours. After sobriety, forgiveness is the most valuable gift we can give ourselves.

Tap into this mystery and watch your life miraculously transform. You can start slowly by forgiving the driver who stole your parking space, or start at the top by forgiving your mother for abandoning you. Forgive every trespass, big and small, all day every day, and watch your resentment, rage and regret disappear. A heart full of forgiveness leaves little room for anything else.

October 20

I invited a small group of close friends on a hike to celebrate my first year of sobriety and no one showed up. Eight people RSVP'd, but not one of them came.

Predictably, I had a meltdown. I was just one year in and still a little shaky on concepts of letting go of resentment, dealing with regret and the dangers of pity parties.

To my friends and family who forgot my important day I played it off like it was fine, no big deal. But the truth was that my heart was broken and I wasn't sure how to handle it.

My first impulse was to grab my fuck-it bucket and fill it with booze. I am an alcoholic, after all, and this is how I solve my problems. Instead I cried for about an hour, took a nap and then went to lunch. It was a gloomy day, but not totally ruined.

By allowing myself to feel the sadness and experience it without drinking I was able to keep the resentments from forming. It sucked, sure, but people are busy and I am not the center of the universe. They didn't wake up that morning with a desire to hurt my feelings. Besides, dumping my sadness all over them wouldn't have made me any less sad. Why ruin their day, too? Making them feel guilty would not have alleviated my hurt feelings, so I processed it all myself in the best way I could.

When I look back on that day, I still feel sad. Not angry, vengeful or bitter. Just sad. It still hurts, actually, but it's a thousand times better than any of the pain I felt when drinking. Plus, I'll be sure in the future to always appear at events that I promise to attend.

October 21

"One man's remorse is another man's reminiscence." —Ogden Nash

Like most drunks I have a long list of evenings I'd like to forget. I feel bad on so many levels: for the time wasted getting wasted, for the gossip I spread, for the inability to be truly present for my family and friends and for the shenanigans that ranged from immature to flat-out dangerous.

But even though this continual remorse, degradation and embarrassment is what eventually prompted me to get sober, I have friends who still remember these events as a really good time. They are honestly baffled as to why I would think our drunken escapades were anything but amusing anecdotes.

The only answer I can find is that they didn't have the same experience of sickness, guilt and shame. I don't know why I did (maybe I was that much drunker), but I did. And the only way for me to never feel those things again was to sober up.

I'm happy my former drinking buddies have fond memories of me and our times together, but I can't use their pleasant memories as an excuse to lie to myself about how negatively my disease affected me.

October 22

Any conversation about anger must include a discussion of road rage. I have watched the kindest, most thoughtful and considerate people transform into terrifying beasts once they get behind the wheel of a car.

The car can feel like a safe place to explore anger, I suppose. Usually we're responding in the moment to something that upsets us and then it passes with no real harm done. No one can hear us screaming. Giving someone the finger at 50 miles-per-hour rarely results in fist throwing. We're cocooned in metal, and we feel protected, not to mention totally justified.

But what's it all for, and for whom? When you lay on the horn or scream a four-letter word, do feel better about yourself, or worse? Next time you find yourself getting worked up while driving, try to get ahold of yourself to see if this negativity is worth it. When we react in anger our bodies are shot through with adrenaline and cortisol, our hearts race and our blood pressure rises. It's true what they say about anger being like taking a poison and expecting the other person to die. Plus, as an alcoholic, this emotion can put you in a vulnerable state that prompts you to drink.

Next time you get ready to drive, sit for a moment and take a few deep breaths. Send out some positive energy to your fellow drivers. It's dangerous out there! Try to react with humor, compassion and understanding rather than rage to see if you arrive at your destination feeling peaceful and composed.

October 23

Human beings become resentful when they feel they have been denied something to which they are entitled. It doesn't matter how "big" this entitlement is. I know someone who has nursed a painful resentment into her 70s because her sister got braces as a teenager and she didn't. People can be just as resentful over braces as they are over a theft, betrayal or any other number of offenses.

You didn't get the family you deserved, the job you should have had or the lifestyle you felt you were born for. You can sit and drink, blaming everyone and everything for this terrible slight. Or, you can identify the things you feel you lack and set out to create them for yourself.

Your family is terrible? Join the club. No really, join a club and create a network of people that provides you with the support you need. Didn't get that job? Can you identify the skills you lack and go and get them? Is your lifestyle not what you dreamed? Maybe it's time to tackle your debt, one dollar at a time; or go on that vacation you've always wanted to take.

When resentment over entitlement presents itself to you, it's a sign that you now have the opportunity to give yourself all the things that no one else did.

October 24

As a sober person, you've probably encountered resentment over the fact that others in your circle still drink.

No doubt there are people you know who have a worse problem than you. That's probably why you picked them to drink with in the first place. Maybe they've had multiple DUIs, terrible relationships and resentments of their own that perpetuate their problem—yet they continue to drink. It's hard not to notice these defects in others after you've spent so much time and effort addressing your own missteps.

You can't change them. The only thing you can do is look at their lives as a learning lesson and continue on your path to sobriety. The spiritually connected person that you are now probably wants to share with them the peace and serenity of your sobriety. It's understandable that you want to save others from the path of destruction, but the best thing for you to do is to see, observe, take note and continue to do the hard work of staying sober. If they decide to follow your example then help them in every way you can. If not, send them peace and love, and then let your resentment go so that you can maintain your own health.

October 25

Once you've identified the actions for which you feel regret, you have an enormous power. You have the power to never behave that way again.

Try to assess your regrets analytically, rather than emotionally. It's understandable that hashing over regret will be painful, but when you feel those terrible feelings, try to find the lesson in them and make a positive action plan to keep yourself from doing them again.

Since many of your regrets are drinking related, you have already addressed one of your major pitfalls. Maybe you regret saying terrible things to people. Next time, think before you speak to determine whether you're helping or hurting. You could feel regret over money you "borrowed" or stole. Pay it back. Then determine actions to create more financial security for yourself. If you regret cheating on your partner, definitely don't do that again. And if the relationship ended, make sure you find a new partner who is more suitable and then treat them the way you want to be treated.

All of this seems pretty simplistic, but it's actually great common sense. We do have the power to change, and this will be reflected not in our feelings of regret, but in our actions moving forward.

October 26

Anger is all around. We live in a world full of outrage, road rage, righteous indignation, frustration and annoyance. No matter how hard we work on our own anger issues, we're bound to be in the presence of someone else's blowup, bitterness or biting comments.

It's crucial for your sobriety to be able to recognize that you are in the presence of anger and to avoid getting drawn in. If the situation seems to be escalating toward violence, by all means get yourself out of there. Otherwise, rely on your skills of compassion to understand that the vast majority of all anger is borne from fear.

If you're feeling personally attacked try to understand that the other person is afraid. They are afraid of not getting their way, of not being heard or of losing something they think is important. They are afraid of not being the smartest person in the room.

There is no need to engage the other person in this behavior. You only need to understand that it is not about you personally, even if it is directed toward you. No matter what the situation, you do not have to stand for being verbally attacked, or being around a group of people who are behaving vengefully, gossipy or mean.

And if it's you who is acting out in anger, take a moment to uncover what it is you're afraid of. The more you address your own fears and anger triggers, the greater understanding you'll gain about how to stay sane and sober.

October 27

"You must go into the dark in order to bring forth your light."—
Debbie Ford

Debbie Ford's bestselling book, *The Dark Side of the Light Chasers*, is
an exploration of how suppressing our dark side keeps us from fully
activating our potential. Her assertion is how without one, there is
no other. She also explains that sometimes the things we repress as
"negatives" can be embraced as positive catalysts in our lives.

By diving into our regret and moving through it, rather than
justifying it or drinking over it, we allow ourselves to discover our
kindness. When we accept our resentments and discover our
contribution to them, we are able to transform those feelings into
compassion. The moment we acknowledge that we're angry with
someone because they are behaving in a way we find distasteful in
ourselves, the easier it becomes to overcome our weaknesses.

That's why these emotions are so important in our growth. Without
understanding these impulses and reactions, we cannot create
positive pathways toward a life filled with light.

Let your rage, resentment and regret go, but not before you
sincerely move through them, making every effort to understand
their importance, and using them to adjust your thoughts and
actions toward positive results.

October 28

I launched a plan to read the top 100 classic novels of all time, and discovered that they are all basically about the same thing. Each one is the story of good people trying to stay good despite being thrown into extreme circumstances. Every single one.

And isn't that what we all are every single day? We're just sober people trying to be sober despite extreme circumstances. This requires us to commit to eliminating all of our resentments. We must continually evaluate our anger to determine whether it's justified, and whether we should act on it. We become overwhelmed with regret and are forced to grieve again and again. And all of this without the aid of any mind- or emotion-altering substances.

There are going to be days when we succeed wildly at all of these requirements. There will be times when we fail miserably. Either way, we're staying sober and this fact alone means that we are the heroes—and not the victims—in our own classic story.

October 29

Life is full of pain brought on us by circumstances beyond our control. There's the frustration caused by traffic, despair that arises from losing something we love and the terror we feel when we can't stop something bad from happening. Pain is everywhere and is unavoidable as long as we stay human. No one suffers the exact same circumstances, but most of us have had a tour of the pain spectrum from one end to the other whether we wanted to or not.

Rage, regret and resentment are at least three types of pain that are possible to overcome. Through focus, quiet reflection, heartfelt conversations and action, we can transform these three wounding emotions into a life rich with compassion, empathy and understanding. Though the rage, regret and resentment can feel very justified (and as addictive as alcohol and drugs) you'll discover that showing them the door makes so much more room for peace to settle in.

October 30

"True forgiveness is when you can say, 'Thank you for that experience.'"
— Oprah Winfrey

What are we here for if not to have experiences? Would you really prefer to have been hermetically sealed somewhere, cut off from the pain that brought you to where you are now? Or would you have rather suffered through it all to grow into the magnificent person you have become?

I spent a lot of time beating myself up for being an alcoholic. My mortification was complete. How could I have wasted all of those years and all of that opportunity? How could I have done THAT in front of THOSE PEOPLE? *What was I thinking?*

I also frittered away a lot of years holding onto resentments over small things that people said, big things that people did, chronic things that folks continue to do... Now that I have done the work of addressing these resentments, seeing my part in them and accepting them, I often wonder what all that fuss was about. It's so bizarre, when you really think about it, that we hold onto this "stuff" that's over now. Why do we do that to ourselves? Well, we no longer have to.

You know that you have properly processed your negative feelings about anything when you can thank others for opening your eyes to a new situation. One day you may find yourself quietly thanking your boss for firing you because it forced you to improve your skills and increase your network. Maybe you will thank someone who was abusive to you because that experience helped you identify a problem with someone else—and you were able to help. You get a gold star on your chart the moment you can look at *yourself* in the mirror and give yourself thanks for the harrowing years of alcoholism because they led you to this newfound experience of untroubled bliss, a desire for service and the ability to keep yourself centered and sober no matter what because now you know how bad it can be.

Thank people for the experiences they gave you. Perhaps don't let them move back into the house, work for you again or invest your money. Forgiveness does not mean allowing yourself to be taken advantage of. Ideally, you're thanking these folks for showing you what you need never do again.

October 31

We've spent a month delving into the darker sides of our personalities: regret, resentment and rage. We've discovered that our dark side provides us with a catalyst for change. Without our dark side to compare, we wouldn't know how far we have progressed into the light.

When we put down the drinks, pretending to be something we're not becomes so much more difficult. Without the continual numbing down and dumbing down of my mind, it becomes impossible to believe that I play no part in my resentments. I can't shove my regrets under the mat. And I can't accept that living in rage is normal or healthy.

Processing rage, resentment and regret is a lifelong practice that requires deep attention and unwavering commitment. I have learned that any one of us can choose to address these destructive emotions in healthy ways, never allowing them to take over our hearts or our minds. In sobriety, we have found a better way to live.

November

Gratitude, Giving and Gracious Living

November 1

It's so easy to forget to be grateful. When the boss is on our back, the kids are climbing the walls and the weather is dreary, it is desperately difficult to feel grateful all the livelong day.

Of course we are aware that if we have running water, shelter, a few friends and are moderately healthy that we are better off than literally billions of other people. We know this, yet it's still so easy to feel frustrated, angry and hopeless when times are tough.

No one expects you to be an angel. You are allowed to feel ungrateful when the baby spits up on you again, your significant other is picking a fight or when you're behind on your bills. I get it. But I do have a suggestion that makes the transition from glowering to gratitude, if not perfect, then at least a bit smoother.

Memorize a short prayer or poem about gratitude and repeat it to yourself. That's all. It might be enough to trigger a new mindset—a mindset that keeps you sober for one more day.

November 2

Gratitude lists are often full of the things we are grateful for receiving. We take special note of the person who stopped for us when we were in the crosswalk or those who let us go to the front of the line when we had one small item to purchase. I am often grateful for the meals that were made for me, or the small bonus I was given for doing a good job. At the top of every gratitude list I have ever made is my sobriety, which to date is the best gift I have ever received!

So we're grateful for what we get, but often to we take the time to be grateful for what we are able to give?

Did you take on some extra work today so that a co-worker could attend to their sick child? Be grateful that you had the capacity to make someone else's life a little easier. Have you ever paid the toll for the person behind you? Be grateful that you have the resources to offer someone a smile-inducing kindness. Perhaps you took in a stray or rescued an animal from a shelter. Be grateful that you were able to offer a safe, healthy home for a vulnerable creature.

It's true that the more we show gratitude for things we get, the more good stuff comes our way. It's also true that the more grateful we are for the things we are able to give, the more opportunities to share our gifts present themselves.

November 3

When I was working a Twelve Step program I was riddled with worry that I "wasn't doing it right." I didn't *feel* like I was suffering enough or giving enough or...*something.* There were no grades or tests or ways to evaluate, so basically I had no idea if I was any "good" at it.

For clarity I sought out an Old-Timer, a woman who had worked the Steps for nearly 50 years. She said that you know you're doing it right when "you become a joy to be around."

In your sobriety have you become a joy to be around? Now that you're not drinking you have the opportunity to bring vitality to every interaction and happiness to every encounter. If you haven't been a joy to be around, become a joy today. Don't wait another minute to bring this gift to the world.

Tim, the man who runs the counter at my local Post Office, is the perfect example of this principle in action. For years I looked forward to going to the local P.O. because he was so pleasant, funny and kind that, no matter what, I always left feeling better than when I went in. I'd known him for years, and then ran into him at a sober gathering where he told me that he had been drink-free for over two decades. Well, that explained it! Tim is a sober soul who is a joy to be around.

Are you a joy to be around?

November 4

It's easy to become resentful when we don't feel the way we think we deserve to feel. When we feel tired, overworked, taken advantage of or taken for granted, it's an invitation for resentment to come on in and offer us a drink.

Those of us who want to stay sober don't have the luxury of basking in the feelings that are gateways to resentment. It can be a lot of grueling work to keep those feelings at bay, but it is our job if we are to maintain the emotional balance required for complete sobriety.

One of the best ways to create the feelings of serenity, peace, pride, and confidence we want to feel is to help someone else create those feelings in themselves.

Help a family member relieve some stress about a difficult situation to create serenity. Follow through on your promises to your kids and to friends to give them the peace of mind that you can be counted on. Praise people for a job well done to foster pride. Encourage others to achieve their goals to build confidence.

Identify the ways you really want to feel each day and then set your intention to make *others* feel the way you want to feel. Get ready to have an experience you never expected, and to finally feel the positive emotions you deserve.

November 5

Practicing daily gratitude is a small step that is proven to be life changing. No matter what your circumstances, focusing on gratitude for what you *do* have rather than fretting over what you don't have changes your outlook. Plus, it seems to lead to more of the good stuff coming your way.

However, I'd like play devil's advocate because I have watched others become so grateful that they diminish their own accomplishments.

It is right, proper and preferred that you express gratitude when those around you have helped you achieve something important to you. It is soul-affirming to acknowledge the talented and helpful people on your team. But be sure that you show gratitude for your own willingness to put the work in, your own motivation to keep going when things got hard and your own strength of character. Others have helped you and deserve props, but you're the one who has done the lion's share of the work. And that's a fact.

No one succeeds alone. No one gets sober alone. Be careful that your gratitude stays right-sized and that you allow yourself to feel proud for the extremely difficult work you've done.

November 6

Ahhh, gracious living. In my drinking days I thought I had this dialed in. My homemade lemon drops were in demand at every afternoon soirée. If I was invited to an elegant evening I knew the perfect bottle of bubbles to bring along, as well as what rare wine from an obscure region would be sure to impress my host.

In addition to my charming ability to pick the perfect pours, I also pored over fancy home magazines and expensive catalogs to try to imitate the look and feel of each professional photo. Anything less than the ultimate would not do, and I drank myself senseless trying to attain what was an unattainable ideal.

In sobriety I have been forced to shift my idea of gracious living a bit. I still love looking at pretty pictures of well-appointed homes, but I no longer strive to make my life imitate the images. Occasionally I will indulge in a bouquet for the coffee table or some fresh towels for the guest room, but I know now that trying to achieve greatness in gracious living through materialism is like spending my days chasing after Sasquatch.

Go ahead and entertain yourself with the fine living blogs, magazines and books. Throw together a recipe from a woman who has given herself a royal title. Remember that truly gracious living does not come from killing yourself to populate your life with Pinterest posts. It is your sobriety, your generous heart, your kind thoughts and the keeping of promises that bring a gracious life into our grasp.

November 7

"If we do not feel grateful for what we have, what makes us think we would be happy with more?"—John A. Passaro

One of the most challenging parts of sobriety for me is the idea that I can't check "sober" off my list and move on to another project. Sobriety is a daily practice. Some days it's a struggle; others days it feels effortless. No matter what is happening in my life, in my work or on my sober journey, I remind myself—several times a day if necessary—to be grateful for my sobriety. This is my way of announcing to the universe: "I am grateful for this struggle. I am grateful for this blessing. I am grateful for this lifelong journey. More sobriety, please."

November 8

One side effect of gratitude is humility. It's somehow impossible to feel deep gratitude and maintain an outsized ego at the same time. Humility is a blessing. When you let humility into your heart it also invites its friends peace, serenity and kindness.

Early in my sobriety I was confused about the difference between "humility" and "humiliation." Turns out they are nearly opposites. Humility embraces empathy for others, promotes respect and understanding and maintains our equality with others. Humiliation is the feeling that results from engaging in behaviors that are degrading.

It's easy to see how an alcoholic can confuse these two concepts. We become accustomed to humiliation, usually through our own actions, so when someone suggests that humility is a good thing it might take us some time to let this register. I didn't get it for a long time, although I could tell that I was feeling different about certain things.

I was in a volunteer group where I was responsible for a specific report each week. The leader of the group continually asked me to add different things or run little errands to support the report, even though it wasn't part of the agreed-upon job. One of my friends pulled me aside one day and said, "You can tell that woman to go fuck herself, you know. You signed up for a specific job and she has no right to boss you around."

After my sensitive ears recovered from the blunt language I realized that I didn't really mind that this person was "bossing me around." The way I saw it was that she was an older lady with a painful, chronic illness who lived alone, used food stamps and didn't have a car. If she wanted me to do a little extra or help her out in an unusual way, what did I care? I had time. No biggie. That's when my friend said: "THAT is humility." And I got it.

Nowadays I am proud to embrace humility in the rare moments it occurs (I am still learning, after all). Are there places in your life where you are exercising humility and may not even know it?

November 9

So many of us are about to be surrounded by family in a few weeks. No matter whether you just got sober or if you've been sober for a while you are going to be faced with a whole lot of people who don't get it.

Not only will they not understand the Sisyphean struggle that is daily sobriety, but they may think that since you've been sober for so long you're obviously not an alcoholic and you can have a glass of Syrah, right? My relatives still don't get it, and they insist that I buy all the wine for family vacations because I worked in the wine industry, live in wine country and know about wine. I'm out several hundred bucks every time we get together but my suggestion that someone else be responsible for stocking the bar is met with blank stares and the sound of crickets. So I shut up and buy the wine.

It's probable that no one in your holiday party circle will have any appreciation for your sobriety. Get used to the idea before you enter in to any situations that may compromise your decisions. Have a friend on speed dial and craft an escape plan. Know that the holidays are tough for everyone, not just sober people, and try to find a way to help someone else out. Remember to breathe, meditate and take time for yourself.

Do whatever you must to stay sober throughout the holidays. If you're lucky enough to be surrounded by empathetic souls who support you, then soak up all the love you can! If not, lower your expectations and remember that no one is going to keep you sober but you.

November 10

To live graciously we needn't have a home in the Hamptons, daily floral deliveries or expensive furnishings. Nor must we host flawless gatherings or be invited to the social events of the season. These are lovely things to have, of course, but gracious living comes from within. Your calm, serene sobriety can be the center point for your gracious life.

Here are five ways you can live more graciously today.

1) **Compliment someone**. Offering a sincere compliment elevates everyone.
2) **Take on a task someone else doesn't want to do**. Offer to make the phone call for the overworked co-worker. Do the dishes for your spouse. Run to the store for a sick friend. Its how we act, not how we look, that defines our gracious life.
3) **Show an interest in someone else**. Sometimes we simply forget to ask about someone else. Alcoholics are notoriously self-centered. Ask about someone else and then listen for the answer. Listening is a very gracious skill.
4) **Don't say it**. You have an opinion you need to express. It's likely negative. Keep it to yourself. When you turn out to be right, don't say anything either.
5) **Beautify.** Whether you pick up a piece of trash on the street, repaint an entire room or make your bed for the first time in a month, making the spaces you inhabit more beautiful leads to gracious living.

You don't have to spend any money to invite the spoils of gracious living into your life. Now that you're sober, you deserve a life filled with kindness, interest in others and inspiring beauty.

November 11

We could fill a library with examples of alcoholics overdoing it. We tend to go all in whether its drinking, overworking, over-exercising or any other number of things that can be done to the enth degree.

Since most programs, books and essays about overcoming alcoholism recommend doing things for others as part of your recovery, many of us fall into the trap of overdoing service.

Be of service to others. Help them. Think of their needs above your own when it's right to do so. Try to do the next right thing in regards to your relationships with others. But be careful that your willingness to serve doesn't transform you into someone else's hired help.

Offering your kindness and support to others is crucial to your recovery, and for living a wholesome, fulfilled life. Touch base with yourself occasionally to ensure that your relationships are filled with *mutual* support and help.

November 12

"Happiness cannot be traveled to, owned, earned, worn or consumed. Happiness is the spiritual experience of living every minute with love, grace and gratitude."—Dennis Waitley

As someone who is a student of sobriety, you have learned that your happiness cannot be consumed. It's a small philosophical jump for you to also realize that happiness cannot be found in *anything* outside of us. If you're waiting for the right job, right girlfriend, right shoes or right house to be happy, you're going to be waiting a long time—even if you find all of those things. You must adjust what is inside yourself to access your true and well-deserved happiness.

One of the things I've heard mentioned repeatedly in my sobriety studies is the "geographic." This is the idea that relocating yourself to a different environment will get you sober/make you happy/help you lose weight...One fellow went as far as to suggest that at every state line there should be a sign that reads, "This state doesn't work either."

I can say absolutely that I have done geographics to try to combat my alcohol problem. The problem is that the cliché is true: no matter where you go, there you are.

Before you go jetting off to a foreign country, moving out of your apartment, buying a new car or bringing home any other external fix, find the daily love, grace and gratitude within yourself in order to get closer to the happiness you seek.

November 13

Thanksgiving is approaching, and in addition to the stress we will feel about staying sober, it's logical that we would also feel apprehensive about spending time with family members who aggravate us.

Author Marianne Williamson once described how stressful traveling with her mother could be. Her solution to dealing with the little irritations and annoyances caused by being alone with her mother was to imagine how God sees her. God does not see her mother as vexing, loud-mouthed or opinionated. God sees her as a kind-hearted, fearful person who is doing her best to cope with the complexities of the world.

I invite you to see your family members this way. If you don't believe in God, perhaps you can either see or remember how others respond to your family members. My own mother has driven me close to insanity, but I have some friends who adore her and seek out her wise counsel for a variety of problems.

It's tough to transition a lifetime of irritation into lighthearted empathy, and I don't expect we'll be perfect at it right away. But the alternative is going mad with irritation, and giving your disease a reason to get you drinking again. With that in mind it's certainly worth a try.

November 14

I try to gear up for some gratitude for my life every single day. I have a so many things for which I am grateful, including my sobriety, that it's usually quite easy for me to rattle off a list of my top ten.

Some days I have the time and the inclination to go deeper. In this month of thanksgiving, see where you can go when you open the floodgates of gratitude. For example, can you find pure gratitude for the people who made the chair you're sitting in, the designer who envisioned it and the truck drivers who delivered it? Can you say a small "thank you" to the hard working folks at the power plant that diligently work to ensure your lights turn on when you flip the switch?

Can you thank the animal that gave its life for your dinner, thank the farmer who grew the vegetables, and the worker who picked them by hand? I'll bet if you can do all of those things, you can also find deep gratitude for the men and women who fix your local roads or the kind souls who feed the hungry in your community, all so you don't have to. Maybe you're grateful for the people who make your computer, your kitchen appliances and construction tools. These are all things you don't have to make yourself!

Going this deep with gratitude brings your day to life with all of the possibilities for creating good feelings. Look around. What are you really grateful for today?

November 15

In order enjoy a fully realized sobriety we must find a way to be grateful for our struggles.

You may have heard the story about the butterfly struggling to break free of its cocoon. A young girl felt sorry for the delicate creature so she snipped open the cocoon with scissors to help it break free. The butterfly emerged, but its wings were small and deformed. It was unable to fly. The process of breaking through the cocoon builds the butterfly's strength, and when the girl made it easier she essentially clipped its wings and doomed it to a flightless life.

I have heard the term "grateful alcoholic" and I fully embrace this philosophy. I am so grateful that I reached what my friend Em calls "the gnarliness" so that I can fully actualize a life of strength, forgiveness and gratitude. I am grateful I have lived an alternative life of ugly, drunken fear simply so I know how miraculous it is to emerge into gratitude and joy. Like that butterfly, my struggles rebuilt me into a person who faces fears, rejoices in kindness and commits to being useful to others. For that I am truly grateful.

November 16

You are at the precipice of one of the most difficult times on the calendar for sober people. We are about to launch full-steam ahead into a holiday season that will find stepping into the emotional landmines of travel, family, holiday parties and lots and lots of work.

Before rushing headlong into the holidays, take a little time to clear out the emotional gunk that comes along with sobriety. Now is the time to identify and address those in your life whom you have not yet forgiven (and find a way to forgive). Now is the time to solidify your plan for how you will handle drinking situations that challenge you. Today is the day to create a gratitude list on which you can rely when you are surrounded by things that don't make you grateful.

For those of you that are newly sober, and perhaps experiencing a sober holiday season for the first time, try to shore up a list of sober friends who will take your call no matter what. You also need your go-to phrase for why you're not drinking. You can be totally honest and tell people that you are an alcoholic (this is what I have started doing—and it really changes the direction of the conversation!). Or, you can say you stopped for health reasons, you're in training, or you're not feeling well. It's up to you how you handle it. Just be ready to handle it.

November 17

There's a real possibility that the people you'll face during the holidays have drinking problems worse than yours. Some of them may be family and friends for whom you care deeply.

Since getting sober I have had to fight to keep quiet with some of the people in my life who seem hell-bent on ruining their lives with alcohol and drugs. But I do maintain my silence because the minute I sound smug, self-righteous or sanctimonious, the drunks in my life go running for their bottles. Any small attempt I have ever made to try to convince anyone they should join me on a sober journey has resulted in zero converts. They have to want it themselves.

Instead, I quietly live the best sober life I can. If any of these people recognize something in my new life that they want to have, I will do anything I can to help them. But until then, I focus on my own sobriety, my own gratitude and my own continual striving for a more gracious life.

November 18

If you remember the television show *Friends* you may recall an episode where Phoebe dates a super-positive guy played by Alec Baldwin. This character finds the good in absolutely everything, including a traffic jam where he exclaims that the brake lights are "aglow with the light of a million fairies." Now that's gratitude!

We all love being around positive people, but if you find yourself tipping into the kind of mania that finds you calling a regular old apartment "a third-floor paradise," maybe you've gone too far. Keep acknowledging the positive things around you that make you grateful: a co-worker's extra effort, your dog's wagging tail or the delicious meal your kids made for dinner. But make sure that you are authentic in your feelings and that you don't go overboard by trying to completely alter your reality.

November 19

Sometimes gracious behavior requires doing nothing at all. Or, perhaps being gracious requires *saying* nothing at all.

When I was drinking I had no reason to keep my mouth shut. I was half-cocked or hungover most of the time so I never bothered to censor myself. If I thought it, I said it. My opinions were so important that you had to hear them *right now,* and if I forgot what I was saying mid-sentence I would ramble on to another topic and tell you exactly what I thought about it, you, your pets, the president, my doctor, your doctor and the doorman. I talked and talked and talked until I passed out or fell asleep. In the process I managed to alienate everyone and start silly arguments that went nowhere and benefitted no one.

In sobriety I practice silence as part of my commitment to gracious living. Officially it's my way to remember that if I don't have anything nice to say I shouldn't say anything at all.

I am not suggesting that you allow yourself to be a doormat. But in most cases I have found that an event, holiday or evening with friends is so much more memorable, relaxing and fun if I stay sober and stay silent unless I am adding kindness to the conversation. Not only do I no longer have to wake up in the morning panicked over what I said while drunk the night before, I no longer have to worry about what I said when I was sober!

Give it a try. Next time you feel that blunt opinion coming up, remind yourself of your gracious sobriety and keep it to yourself. It's lovely to see the results of this kind of behavior, and if it works for you, I suggest you carry your gracious, measured silence into every interaction.

November 20

Treat yourself graciously throughout the holidays starting now. Your gracious behavior, newfound kindness and willingness to serve others—all rediscovered in your sobriety—are a profound gift to those around you. I would like to suggest that graciousness also a gift you can give to yourself.

Schedule time to unwind from the holidays' hectic pace, and then keep the promise to yourself. You can then use your success in looking out for yourself as a springboard to keep your promises to other people. If you make time to care for yourself, you will be less likely to extend yourself with commitments you may not be able to keep up with.

A cornerstone of gracious sobriety is the ability to keep promises to others. You can practice by keeping promises to yourself. By making judicious decisions about what you are capable of managing throughout this busy time and keeping promises, you will keep resentments at bay and ensure that you have a safe and sober season.

November 21

Are you flying somewhere between now and the end of the year? It's prime travel time, and transportation hubs are flooded with people trying to get to their families or their vacation destinations. One thing all of these places have in common, be it an airport, train depot or bus stop, is temptation.

Before I got sober, a trip to the airport was a great reason to get loaded. I would try to arrive early so that I could have a few drinks before boarding. I would drink on the plane and have more drinks when I landed.

If we're traveling alone, it's even easier to duck into a bar at the train station, toss back a few and head to the bar car. Who is ever going to know? Traveling offers the perfect veil of anonymity for the heavy drinker. So what do we do when we find ourselves alone, with a layover or transfer, surrounded by bars?

Here's what you do: **Get on the paging system and ask for Friends of Bill W. to meet you at your location**. Within minutes, sober people from all over the world will find you and help ease your difficulty.

For those of you not familiar with AA, Bill W. is the founder of the Twelve Steps and Alcoholics Anonymous, and his "friends" will drop everything to be with you if you need them. You need not be a "member" of AA to ask for this help. It may feel weird, but it works, and these people will keep you sober no matter where you are.

Write it down if you have to. Practice saying it beforehand. But before you travel, know that you can put a call out for Friends of Bill W. that will be like sending up a bat signal in Gotham. Real sober heroes are all around you and ready to do whatever they can to help.

November 22

*"I slept and I dreamed that life is all joy. I woke and I saw that life is all service. I served and I saw that service is joy." —*Khalil Gibran

As I little kid I would pout and wail when my mother told me I had to finish all of my "work" before I could have "fun." It took me decades to understand that the work can be the fun part if you let it.

Like Gibran says, life is truly service (or work), and it is through this service we find joy.

Before I got sober I was unwilling to accept that service was a good thing. I was always put out, burdened and resentful of the work I was asked to do or my obligations to others. Why wouldn't they all]leave me alone so that I could drink in peace, and have the all "fun" I deserved to have??

Sobriety offers us the chance to make a shift from feeling burdened to feeling blessed. We may not always be perfect in our practice, but readjusting the thought pattern from feeling annoyed to honored-to-be-asked is transformational. I no longer look forward to "down time" quite the way I used to since my "down time" consisted of drinking, sitting around, drinking, watching TV, smoking, drinking and passing out. I like to be busy now, in service to my employers, my family, my dog, my friends and my soul.

As I have embraced this idea more deeply my service is now what I do for fun and my fun is now my service. I've discovered a beautiful flow from one project to the other where I am serving, working, building and creating a life of unimaginable joy.

November 23

Let's all agree to disagree without being disagreeable. Dinnertime is rapidly approaching, and although our sobriety has prepped us to be gracious, grateful and brimming with thanksgiving, many of us face the probability that we will get dragged into some kind of family fracas.

It's a tradition as old as Thanksgiving itself. Family members fly in from all over with the sole purpose of trying to convince you that your religion, politics, job choice, parenting, etc. are all wrong and you should do it their way.

You've got bigger turkeys to baste this year. Make a promise to yourself that you will respectfully disagree with the rabble-rousers and do so without name-calling, yelling, flinging insults or throwing punches.

Do not sink to their level. Grab on to your sobriety life raft, explain that you agree to disagree and then get back to the real reason you've gathered with these people in the first place—gratitude for the multitude of gifts you've been given.

November 24

Have you heard of a book called *Random Acts of Kindness*? Over a million copies of this little tome have been sold because it delights readers with sweet and simple ways to help others, spread goodwill and create happiness.

The idea has created an international kindness movement, with the Random Acts of Kindness Foundation working to create opportunities to teach kindness, live kindly and research the positive effects of kindness.

Since we're sober and grateful for our new outlook on life, let's use this opportunity to offer others a reason to be thankful. Some easy ideas inspired by the randomactsofkindness.org website include:

- Paying a bridge toll for the car behind you.
- Putting change in an expired parking meter.
- Ask someone else about his or her holiday plans and family traditions.
- Leave a used book or magazine behind on a plane, bus or train when you're traveling.
- Remember someone who has to work on Thanksgiving or the day after, and offer to help them or just be extra nice when you encounter them.
- Pick up trash when you see it on the sidewalk.

Giving back can be as easy as we make it! If you are feeling grateful for your sobriety this Thanksgiving, make a simple gesture like the one above to expand this fabulous feeling into the world.

November 25

"Silent gratitude isn't much use to anyone."—G.B. Stern

It's a practice that's gone by the wayside, but might I suggest that we all write thank you notes for the gifts and invitations we receive this season.

In sobriety we've learned that writing our fears, gratitude and forgiveness helps to solidify our growth. By sending a thank you note, we give the person to whom we are grateful a tangible expression of how much their gesture meant to us.

The notes can be brief, but as long as they are sincere, the recipient will be made to feel very special.

Make it easy for yourself. Go out today and buy a stack of notecards you like and some stamps. Make sure you get addresses from the friends and family you would like to thank. Then write one or two sentences and drop them in the mail. It's so much easier than you think, and you truly will brighten someone's day.

November 26

Flip to any newspaper food section or log on to any culinary blog and you'll find thousands of ways to deal with your Thanksgiving leftovers.

What they aren't going to help you with are your emotional leftovers. Sobriety during the holidays can create a vortex of emotions ranging from resentment at not being able to "join in," to profound gratitude and joy for finally being able to "join in."

We take the good with the bad with sobriety, and we live life on life's terms without the crippling crutch of addiction to smooth things over or dull us down. That can mean that when we pack up our bags after a family gathering we may be taking home more than our dirty clothes and toiletries.

Make time to process what your sober Thanksgiving was really like. If it was painful to you, focus on what's really hurting and create an action plan to face these hurts through meditation, writing, talking with a friend or professional counseling. If you experienced joy and warmth in the embrace of your friends and family, spend equal time discovering ways to create more of these experiences in your life. Maybe the after-dinner walk around the block was meaningful to you. Perhaps you enjoyed being with people during the football games on TV. Can you make things like this happen in your life more frequently? Do you desire more time with your family? Do you desire less time with them?

Don't waste what you learned during your sober Thanksgiving—whether it was your first or your fortieth. Those leftovers can make magic if you let them.

November 27

In this month of Thanksgiving, I find myself being grateful for just being here. Looking back over my life with sober eyes, it is so clear now that my disease wanted me dead.

Before sobriety, I was resentful, prideful, angry, selfish and self-pitying. And those were just the emotions I dealt with on a daily basis! In addition, I was exhausted, woozy, dry-mouthed, wobbly, slurry and unable to remember conversations. When things got really bad I would sit in my car wondering if it would be better to let the dogs out before I filled it with carbon monoxide or if it was kinder to take them with me. Driving over bridges would feel like opportunities to end things quickly. I took to wandering through the streets at night, drunk and unable to sleep. Everything in my life suffered as a result of my drinking.

First, my disease made me happy. Next, it made me miserable. Then, it tried to kill me.

I am grateful for so many things in this new life: my family, my work, my home... But most of all I am simply grateful for the chance to be grateful at all.

November 28

We may not be blessed with money or material possessions. We may not even have extraordinary talents to share. Perhaps we don't have creativity to give or great wisdom to offer. But the one thing every human can give, no matter whether he has infinite treasures or merely the breath in his body, is thanks.

November 29

What does gracious living look like for you? Does what you're currently doing live up to the "death bed" test? In other words, when you look back on your life from your deathbed will you be pleased with how you spent your days? If not, let's create a plan that gets you there.

Here's an example of my "road map" to gracious living. It's essentially the top ten things, in no order, that help me feel content and fulfilled at the end of each day.

1. Sobriety
2. Gratitude
3. Moving my body: Yoga, Running, Skating, Walking
4. Creating a clean, organized environment in which to live
5. Serving others
6. Being curious
7. Staying in touch with nature
8. Desiring fewer possessions
9. Setting and achieving goals
10. Kindness

There are probably a handful of other practices I could include on my list, but I believe that if I stick to the ten things above I won't have anything to regret on my deathbed. That was not the case before I got sober. I was given another chance to create a life to be proud of. I invite you to spend today creating your own road map to gracious living so you can be guaranteed a regret-free rest of your days.

November 30

That we dedicate only one day per year to thanksgiving seems silly when you think about it. We've explored the beauty, difficulty, challenge and satisfaction that come from a life of gratitude, giving and gracious living for an entire month, and we've barely scratched the surface.

As you transition into the remainder of your sober year, remember to stay rooted in your gratitude. When you dedicate yourself to feeling thankful, giving to others and surrounding yourself with loveliness in all its forms, resentment and anger simply melt away—and your sobriety gains strength.

Let's take a moment today to thank November for its many gifts: the gatherings, the struggles, the learning opportunities and the magical moments are all equally powerful tools to help us shape the sober lives we envision for ourselves.

December
Inspiration Celebration

December 1

Author Sarah Ban Breathnach describes December as a "month of miracles." For those who struggle with addiction, December may have been the only month of the year we thought of anyone other than ourselves. This alone was miraculous for me before I got sober.

I'm sure this isn't what she meant, however. December has a way of bringing out the best in people. We give what we can to charity. Most of us put great thought into the gifts we give others, as well as the presentation of those gifts. We gather with friends and family for merry good times. The world is aglow with lights and decorations.

So what can we do to capitalize on this miraculous month? We must first recommit to our sobriety.

Spend some time today envisioning a season of sober celebrating. Write an action plan in your journal that will help you stay clean, sober and miracle-ready.

Then, and only then, will you be able to fully participate in the miracles this month has is store. Give this gift to yourself. Then go out and give your immeasurable gifts to the world.

December 2

Let's get really real about the holidays: it's an insane time for most alcoholics and addicts. In between the parties, shopping, gift giving, sales, errands and other responsibilities there is also enormous pressure to make some serious merry. And that means booze is everywhere.

You won't be able to open the paper without seeing wine pairings for your favorite holiday meals. A trip to the store becomes navigating a minefield of pretty little packages filled with poison, stacked RIGHT THERE in the front. Your boss or your friends may even give you bottles of wine, beer or liqueur as a holiday gift.

Plus, let's add in all of the trauma that surrounds the holidays for most of us. My guess is that if you're reading this book, your childhood holidays weren't exactly something out of a Norman Rockwell painting.

It's enough to drive you to drink.

Remember that there is no simple answer to holiday complications, but the solution to staying sober is this: Don't drink. Not ever. Not for any reason.

Leave if you have to. Go for a walk if you have to. Go to bed early if you have to. Call a sober friend if you have to. Exercise if you have to. Lock yourself in the bathroom if you have to.

Do whatever it takes to stay sober, and you will be handsomely rewarded with a month free of hangovers, nights you don't remember, DUIs, out of control behavior and regret.

Sobriety is the gift you should give yourself this holiday season. It's the blessing you deserve.

December 3

What's not to love about holiday lights? I love them in the windows of the local merchants, draped over my neighbors' trees, lining the avenues of my hometown... Everything is better with holiday lights, whether they are for a non-denominational winter celebration, Christmas, Hanukah or Kwanzaa.

When I sobered up holiday lights took on a whole new meaning for me. Not only were they no longer swirling around in a sickening kaleidoscope, but they transformed into a symbol of all the addicts who still suffer. Each tiny light is a prayer for those of us who struggle with addiction: those who are recovering and those who are still suffering.

There are millions of us. Some of us find a lasting recovery; others never will. Let those lights remind you that you are not alone, and that your sobriety shines like a love letter to all those who have struggled.

December 4

"If you can't get rid of the family skeleton, you might as well make it dance."—George Bernard Shaw

I wish I could take this advice. I'm not ashamed of my alcoholism, and you'd better believe I am proud of my recovery, but my family does not acknowledge my journey at all.

Oh, they know I am sober, but they do not mention it, ask me about it, care about it, know about my writing or have any idea what I have learned through this process.

The only reason I am bringing this up now is because it may be useful to you during family gatherings. You may have a family that is the exact opposite: they relish the chance to humiliate you for your past behaviors or make light of your struggles.

Either way, it doesn't matter. We cannot control how other people respond to us, in our sobriety or in anything else. My family won't say a word; your family may be unable to shut up about it. Both are sides of the same coin, and both spring from deep insecurities that have *nothing to do with you.*

Unless you are smothered with warm hugs, congratulations and interest in your journey and process (and if you are, please email me, because you will be the first I've met), don't take others' reactions to your sobriety personally. Don't take it personally when they don't mention it. Don't take it personally when they gab on about it. Don't take it personally when they try to shove drinks down your throat.

The only thing you can control is whether or not you drink. Focus on being the best sober you possible. Let the rest go, and enjoy the holidays.

December 5

"How wonderful it is that nobody need wait a single moment before starting to improve the world."—Anne Frank

Let's improve the world. Let's start right now. As a sober person, you know *exactly* what this means. One moment you were caught in the grips of a destructive condition, the *very next* you were in recovery.

That's exactly how it happens. We take and take until it hurts so much that we must learn to give. It's the difference between meeting our friends at the bar or going home to take the kids to the park. It's the instant we decide to pick up that plastic bag rather than let it wind up in the storm drain. It's the one time we pick up the phone when our mom/grandfather/uncle calls rather than letting it go to voicemail.

What can we do right this moment, in this month of miracles, to improve the world?

December 6

FOMO. Perhaps you've heard of it? It's an acronym that means "Fear of Missing Out," and the holidays can be a FOMO-palooza for those of us in recovery.

FOMO is the nasty little glitch that not only leads us to getting boozed up and making bad decisions, but it's the same mechanism that gets us into debt, causes us to overeat and makes us tag along with friends on a holiday getaway rather than working on our business/book/music/creative project. FOMO is problematic because it comes from a desire to live up to someone else's wishes for your life.

If you're feeling a FOMO coming on, relax, it's normal. But you don't have to give in to it. It's possible that FOMO fueled your alcoholism, but you can turn that FOMO around and let it be the engine behind a robust sobriety.

Create a FOMO on sincere, chemical-free interactions with your friends and family. Nurture a FOMO on getting a gorgeous nights' sleep. Transform your FOMO into the fear of missing out on an actualized life, hangover-free mornings and achieving your life-long goal. Get a good, solid FOMO on having your dreams come true.

Find your own FOMO.

December 7

I was always the drunkest person at my own parties. I would announce this fact to people before, during and after the party so my guests knew that I became the fool so they didn't have to.

Somewhere in the recesses of my brain I believed that I was responsible for everyone else's good time. I would make my guests' favorite foods, make sure I was playing music they liked and serve their favorite wines and cocktails, no matter what the expense. I would then proceed to become the sloshiest in the room so that no one else ever was. I was responsible for their fun and if they didn't have *the best night of their lives* I thought they wouldn't like me.

In this season of party, party, party I want to remind you that you are not responsible for anyone else's good time—even if you're throwing the party. You are responsible for your sobriety above all, and then simply treating others with kindness. If they are bored, don't like the food, hate the conversation or whatever then so be it. It's too bad, but ultimately each one of us is responsible for ourselves.

So if you find yourself stressing out about how others are feeling, or if you feel tempted to reach for a drink so that you can turn on the entertainer you used to be, remember that your only responsibility is to be sober for one more day.

December 8

'Tis the season of mocktails! I always have a few mocktail ingredients in the house during the holidays, as well as a few choice bottles of sparkling cider and the like to take along with me. When I was newly sober I can remember being blown away by how well my mocktails were received.

In the world of non-alcoholics there are people who actually don't care to drink at holiday parties. Can you believe it? It's true! And when I come whisking in to an event with a few easy-make mixes the crowd goes wild. (OK, not the whole crowd, and they don't go *wild*, they go *mild*.) But the working moms, the designated drivers and the athletes who are in training for the annual Jingle Jaunt are always relieved and happy to have a fun and festive drink that won't leave them feeling sick the next morning.

Find a few mocktail recipes or pre-made mocktail bevvies that you love. You'll be surprised at how many people will appreciate the gesture.

December 9

The A&E television show *Intervention* has always fascinated me. I have watched nearly every episode with the goal of trying to understand my alcoholism better. I also love seeing the families interact, the patience of the interventionists and then the follow-ups where the featured addict got sober.

I have no idea if this show and its premise are effective for addicts, but I did learn a lot about myself by watching it. There was one man I will never forget. His daughter was the focus of the show, but it was clear that he struggled with alcoholism as well. His way of conquering his alcoholism was to only allow himself to drink between Thanksgiving and New Year's Eve, going cold turkey on New Year's Day, every year.

The alcoholic in me loved this idea, and I seriously considered doing this myself. Why not live it up during the holidays? People who struggle with their weigh allow themselves a few extra treats during the holidays, why can't I have a few glasses of wine?

I changed my mind completely after going through my first sober holiday season. I remembered who gave me what gifts (I would often drink my way through gift exchanges) so that I could properly thank them. I felt great in the mornings. I woke up on New Year's Day and practiced yoga and watched old movies. After I experienced what the holidays were like without drinking there was no way I was ever going back.

Stick it out with sobriety this holiday season. Give yourself the gift of sobriety every single day and the holidays, even with all of their baggage, can transform from something to be dreaded into something to be cherished.

December 10

When I feel out of sorts I evaluate a few things to see where I am getting off track. Am I sleeping enough? Eating enough? Exercising? Staying on top of deadlines?

If any of those things are the problem, I can attack the problem with an easy fix. But there's one thing that's essential to my well being over and above anything on that list, and that is being useful.

I was surprised to find that being useful is important to me. My entire life was centered on what I was or wasn't getting, what was being done to me or how I was being tricked/ripped off/ignored. When I got sober, I discovered that I actually could give to others, and by doing so I would create the sense of well being I had always craved.

Now, I am not "classically" useful. I'm not usually the person people call when they need a ride to the hospital (though I would gladly do this). My weekends aren't filled with volunteering at the soup kitchen (but I totally would). I lend my talents to the organizations and people I care about by helping them with writing projects, creating plans to assist them in focusing on their goals and offering my expertise for free for charities, non-profits and people trying to make a difference. It's what I do best.

For those of us who don't find ourselves being useful in the traditional change-your-bandages and pick-your-mom-up-from the-airport ways we can still be very helpful to those in need, even during the holidays.

Are you good with bookkeeping? Can you clean a kitchen in seconds flat? Identify the talents you have and offer those. It's okay if you don't fit into the mold. You will find, once you've been useful to someone who really needs it with something you're really good at, that you want more and more. It's the thing that will keep you sane, and the thing that will keep you sober.

December 11

"You take your life into your own hands, and what happens? A terrible thing. No one to blame."—Erica Jong

This quote shakes me to my core. I find myself turning to these words again and again because I am continually falling into the trap of blaming others for my unhappiness.

This blame game is something that gets deeply ingrained in alcoholics. How many times have you found a reason outside of yourself for your shortcomings? Is it your mom's fault you can't commit in relationships? Is your boss the one keeping you from moving up the ladder? Do you eat your feelings because your spouse doesn't understand you? Do you drink because the whole world is out to get you?

When you take responsibility for your life you will face moments that are terrible because there is no crutch. There is no one to blame when things spin off. But something miraculous also happens. You gain control and your life becomes manageable.

Why? Because you're no longer waiting for people to change, and you eliminate the disappointment inherent in this expectation. You find your own solutions rather than waiting for someone else to save you. You identify all of the ways you can take charge of your own destiny.

Yes, it's terrible. Terribly empowering.

December 12

Have you started your holiday shopping? Truth be told, I am not a big fan of gift exchanges at any time of year. I don't like giving gifts and receiving them embarrasses me. Plus, my tree-hugging tendencies make me very wary of giving anything that's going to end up in a landfill.

However, I do understand that the basis for a solid sobriety is putting others first. I prefer to give my time, attention and concern rather than stuff. In those situations where gift giving is inevitable, I buy gifts in these categories: Need. Read. Share. Wear.

My stepkids receive at least one gift each in these categories for the holidays. When I must shop for adults, I follow this rule as well and I find that it eliminates all of the handwringing that comes along with finding the perfect thing.

The point here is that these categories keep me from getting crazy during the holidays. Keeping life simple is key to staying sober, especially when there are so many choices threatening to overwhelm us.

December 13

"It is never too late to be what you might have been."—George Eliot

A close friend of mine recently revealed to me that he is approaching his life as if he were nineteen again. He is actually in his mid-forties, and he found himself repeatedly thinking that if "he knew at nineteen what he knows now, he would have approached life very differently." So rather than looking back over his past and wishing he could change it, he simply takes on problems and challenges as if he were the fearless nineteen year-old who now actually knows something.

The result of his new attitude is that he seeks reasons why something will work, rather than shooting down an idea because there are reasons why it "might" not. He creates ambitious action plans and executes them without worrying about what people might think or how his family will react. He looks to the future and sees a wide-open vista waiting to be conquered, like a teenager. He *gets things done.* He is confident, sure of himself and happier than he has ever been.

What did you want to be at nineteen? Did your life get in the way? What would you have done, knowing what you know now, at age nineteen? What's stopping you from doing all of those things today?

December 14

Before I got sober all of my holiday traditions included booze. I couldn't wait for eggnog season. Bailey's Irish Cream was my "sippin' drink." And let's not forget the dinners featuring robust Napa Valley Cabs, obscure Pinots from the Pacific Northwest and a stocking stuffer of Chateau D'Yquem. Hard to believe I can't remember 15 years of holidays...

If this is the same for you, you may be interested in starting your own, new, sober traditions. I support this completely. Consider an ice-skating outing with the kids, or a cookie bake-a-thon. Make a meal from scratch. Write letters to all of your loved ones. Plan a Christmas Day workout to get everyone moving.

Creating your own traditions, and managing your time, in your own way is a smart tactic for maintaining your sobriety through the holidays. And it works for so many people.

I didn't grow up with strong holiday traditions, and I having these events to look forward to doesn't matter to me one way or the other. So I crafted a different strategy: I have no holiday traditions. Every year is completely different, and go with the flow. This way I don't find myself freaking out over who is coming, where I need to be, if I have all the ingredients or if so-and-so can sit next to so-and-so. We open presents on Christmas Eve. Everything else is a nice surprise, and I have stumbled into all kinds of lovely events, tree lightings, caroling, volunteer opportunities and more. I have the tradition of no traditions and that seems to work great for me because nothing has to be perfect.

Create your own traditions, or have none! It's your life, and your sobriety. Do whatever works to keep you sane and sober, during the holidays and beyond.

December 15

"What I don't like about office Christmas parties is looking for a job the next day."—Phyllis Diller

One of my favorite scenes from one of my favorite movies is in Bridget Jones's Diary. It's a quick clip of a soused Bridget at her holiday office party, wearing two party hats like ears, standing on a desk and warbling a karaoke version of an Air Supply song. That was so me. I was the "life" of every holiday party, more than happy to make a complete ass of myself.

This won't happen to me this year, and it won't happen to you. There will be no scenes you wish to erase, no telling your boss what you really think of her, no hooking up with the cute, but totally-inappropriate-for-you intern. There will be no driving drunk to the liquor store because the party is out of booze. And because of that there will be no holiday DUI, no Christmas mug shot and no visit to the bail bondsman.

You will keep your job. You will maintain your dignity and your legal standing. You will stay sober because you deserve to have a holiday season worth remembering.

December 16

Remember when your aunt would show up for your family Christmas party wearing an ugly sweater adorned with reindeer or Santa? Who knew that, one day, ugly Christmas sweaters would be embraced by the hippest members of our society as a "trend?" Ugly Christmas sweater parties are all the rage, and far from an embarrassment, the ugliest sweater is lauded as prize-worthy.

I make this point because I see the same thing happening with sobriety. Far from being something we should be embarrassed about, sobriety is often seen as something to be proud of. Celebrities who get clean often go on to huge success. They say, in Hollywood, having a highly paid "sober companion" is a point of prestige. People are embracing sobriety at a rapid pace. I recently read that the LA rock scene is embracing sobriety, and that its top stars maintain abstinence from drugs and alcohol.

Events like "Sober October" are popping up all around the world. In their book *The Sober Revolution* Sarah Turner and Lucy Rocca write about the trend of women giving up their evening cocktails. Even non-alcoholics are discovering that an alcohol-free life is more productive, energizing, fun and meaningful.

Far from being alone in your sobriety this holiday season, you're on the tip of the trend. I believe that sobriety is the wave of the future. It's more important than ever that you hold on and ride out the holiday storm.

December 17

"One day at a time" is one of the most outstanding concepts from Alcoholics Anonymous. Working on sobriety during the holidays in 24-hour increments has saved my bacon more than once. Even those with a strong recovery program and firm resolve can be harshly tested during December. I continually remind myself that it's just *today*; it's just the *next hour* or the *next 60 seconds* that I have to hold on.

Like a house with a solid foundation is built one brick at a time, decades of sobriety are built one day at a time. Keep getting through the holidays one 24-hour period at a time, and you should emerge with beautiful memories of a holiday season spent in sobriety.

December 18

Are you planning on giving yourself a gift this year? If you are, I have a suggestion.

Get a beautiful gift box or bag—something that delights you. Find some lovely ribbons or arty tape. Make a huge bow in your favorite color, or cover the packaging in stamps or stickers. Be ready to create a presentation so astonishing, you would be thrilled to receive it.

Get some notecards, small sheets of paper, index cards or Post-its. Spend an hour or so writing down everything that you're currently upset about, every single one of your worries and all of your disappointments. Catalog every single one of your resentments. Make a detailed list of all of your greatest fears.

Put them in your gift package, wrap it in the most pleasing way imaginable, and put this gift away to open next year.

Everyone who does this exercise has a slightly different response based on his or her own experience. But the one thing everyone shares is that, after another year of sobriety and 12 more months of exploring your creativity, your potential and your capacity to give, virtually none of the things you put in your box today will still matter one year from now.

What a gift!

December 19

Take exquisite care of yourself. In my readings about Buddhism, I once came across some instructions for cleaning. The direction that struck me was that I was to handle something "as gently as if it were my own eyes." That's about as gentle as one can be, I would think.

Treat yourself as gently as you would your own eyes. Be delicate with yourself. Stay clean, refreshed and shielded from the sun (or snow blindness, depending on where you live). Rest when you need to. Take in beauty. Be open to surprise. Shut tight when you're in danger. Blink when you need a second.

Your sobriety is as important as your own eyes. Be cautious. Be gentle. Be present. Be well.

December 20

I once had a crash course in how to handle surprises. The holidays, no matter how well we plan them, are FULL of surprises, but with the proper attitude you can handle them well and soar through each unexpected event sober and just fine.

I like my routine. My routine is designed to help me maintain sobriety by allowing ample time for work, exercise, reading, meditation and serving others. I had been solid in my routine for months when I came across a rabbit in the middle of the road.

This was no ordinary rabbit. It was a domestic bunny, white from the tip of its ears to its fluffy tail. It was lost. It was exhausted and hungry. Long story short, this rabbit came home with me.

The rabbit instantly caused chaos. The dog freaked out. We ran around town all day, hanging flyers, posting online, calling the shelters and getting the word out on Facebook to find its owners. We had to buy a hutch and a whole bunch of other rabbit accoutrements. The rabbit, as adorable as it was, pooped everywhere. The amount of attention a house rabbit requires is akin to that of a newborn baby. My routine was shot to hell.

After about three days of misery, an inability to work and an existential crisis, I realized that my attitude, not the rabbit, was the problem. Rather than falling farther down the rabbit hole, so to speak, I decided that I was going to accept this situation as temporary and have as much fun with this rabbit as possible.

I'm so glad I did. We found a home for the rabbit in two weeks, and during that time we played together, learned some tricks, had cuddle time, shot some hilarious videos and otherwise had fun with Bun-Bun.

Life is going to throw you surprises, and they aren't always something you'd wish for. (Sometimes they poop all over your house.) Try to see these things as temporary, live your best, sober life through each one and you'll start to see surprises in a whole new light.

December 21

Have a glorious winter solstice! It's the shortest day of the year in terms of sunlight, and around the world people gather to celebrate at mystical places like Stonehenge, Goseck Circle and Tulum. The primary purpose of these celebrations is to offer gifts to the sun, or the god that represents the sun, so that the days will become longer.

Guess what? It always works. No matter what, starting tomorrow the days will add a few more minutes of sunlight until the longest day of the year on June 21.

The winter solstice is a lovely metaphor for sobriety. We've had our darkest day. Now we must simply be patient, stay sober, and watch the days become brighter and brighter, one after the other.

December 22

Are you laughing all the way? Staying sober through the holidays is enough to make anyone run screaming, so I like to remind myself that the holidays don't have to be so *heavy.*

Let's make some merry. Here are my top recommendations for you to have your own holiday ho-ho-ho:

Love Actually
I watch this every year, and I always forget how funny it is! (It is also very romantic.) Bill Nighy as the aging rocker Billy Mack is enough to restore anyone's holiday spirit.

A Colbert Christmas
This definitive holiday special features Jon Stewart, Elvis Costello, John Legend, Toby Keith, Feist, Willie Nelson and a hungry bear.

The Stupidest Angel by Christopher Moore
What happens when the angel sent to grant your Christmas wish is an idiot?

Christmas Time in South Park
Not for the easily offended. If you enjoy beyond bawdy humor there's simply no way you can watch this and not laugh.

The Santaland Diaries by David Sedaris
Listen to this on audio if you can (usually available from NPR online). Sedaris recalls his hilarious experiences as a shopping mall elf named "Crumpet."

Elf
A classic Christmas tale of Buddy the Elf who wasn't. Bonus: David Sedaris's sister Amy is in this movie, and they refer to another elf as "Crumpet." Coincidence? I think not.

Friends "The One with the Routine"
This is more of a New Year thing, but I watch this annually so I can witness Ross and Monica do their incredible dance on Dick Clark's New Year's Rockin' Eve.

Sentimental, sappy, gooey holidays are all fine and good for some. I like mine with a side of good, healthy giggles.

December 23

"When the going gets tough, the tough take a nap."—Tom Hodgkinson

Drinking helped me deal with having a house full of people. When folks were on their way I simply popped a cork and I did fine. Now that I am sober, being around people all day for several days in a row exhausts me.

In fact, I recently had an overnight guest who was here for less than 24 hours. By the time she left I felt as though I was in the throes of one of my worst-ever drinking days hangovers. She was a delightful guest, but without a buffer, filter or chemical coping mechanism I was "on" the whole time. I got wiped out.

As a result I am committed to napping. If the house is filled with guests, I schedule a naptime no matter what so that I have time to rest and recharge. My naptime is non-negotiable. Once I decide that 2:00 or 3:15 is the time I am going to retire to my room for a couple of hours, I don't let the last-minute plans to go to the movies or the impromptu shopping trip to veer me off course. Everyone can go without me. I need my nap.

Schedule yourself a couple of hours of holiday naptime if you need it. There's no reason to exhaust yourself because people want you to do things their way. Take a nap, and emerge from the holidays relaxed and renewed rather than unfocused and frazzled.

December 24

"What we achieve inwardly will change outer reality."—Plutarch

Sobriety is an inward change unlike any other. You have accepted that your machinery needs adjusting. You have committed to clearing out the gunk so that you can know yourself fully. Your outward reality is changing because your inward experience is clearer, more compassionate, more patient and more loving. As a result, your actions are all of these things, too. Your inward transformation not only changes your attitude, it quite literally changes the experience of everyone around you.

On this eve of the celebration of Christ's birth, let's take a moment to appreciate his teachings and the inward change they require. Before we can do unto others what we would have them do unto us, we must develop a core of self-love and self-respect. Before we can turn the other cheek, we must surrender to faith in kindness. Before we can share our riches with those less fortunate, we must cultivate a heart of gratitude for all the blessings we have been given.

What changes have you embraced? What are you still working on? Is there room in your heart for a deeper transformation? How has your external experience changed because of your inward work?

December 25

Those of the Christian faith celebrate the birth of new possibilities today. The appearance of Christ in the manger heralded the dawning of a new era of compassion, inclusiveness, sharing and love.

As someone who woke up one day as a raging alcoholic and who woke up the next day in recovery, I believe in the power of new beginnings. I believe that we have the transformative power of Christmas available to us every single day. Why wait for one day a year to commemorate the enormous power of humans to change?

As you spend the day in the warm embrace of your family, at the movies with friends or in reflective solitude, take a moment to acknowledge the rebirth of your own precious heart, and its infinite capacity to love and be loved.

December 26

There's a reason during times of great stress we remind others to "just breathe." Conscious breathing relieves anxiety, brings us into the moment and offers us a chance to find clarity in chaos. Now that we're on the tail end of the holiday hurrahs, let's all take a moment to do just that.

Place your right middle finger between your eyebrows. Close your left nostril with your fourth finger. Breathe out. Breathe in. Close your right nostril with your thumb. Breathe out. Breathe in. Repeat for as long as you'd like.

This simple exercise instantly calms and balances your system. You can do it anywhere, anytime. Plus, it's chemical free and doesn't cost a dime. Soothing breathing for sober people—*ahhhhh*...

December 27

"I've learned that people will forget what you said, people will forget what you did, but people will never forget how you made them feel."—Maya   Angelou

There is a certain person in my circle with whom I spend a lot of time by virtue of the fact that we are related. I have no choice. This person is at every family gathering.

On the surface this person is pleasant, has a sweet tone of voice and smiles a lot. I could never understand why, after I left this person's presence, I always felt like I needed to run screaming around the room. I assumed it was because I am impatient, self-centered and bad at drawing this person out. That was until someone else asked me why I allowed this person to continually insult me and complain about everything.

On reflection I realized that behind the smile is a person who makes negative comments, complains and is jealous of others. Like Maya Angelou said, I didn't remember what she said, but I knew for some reason she made me feel awful.

Are there people like this in your life? In your quest to be polite, present and sober are you discovering people with whom you'd like to limit contact? Are there others who make you feel amazing that you'd like to know better?

December 28

Just a few days remain in this calendar year, and it's a great time to think about what the next twelve months might bring for you. I got sober in January, so I know the power of the mental break that the end of a year can bring. I also started some of my favorite hobbies and tackled some lifelong dreams in January, so I also believe in the power of resolutions.

If you're new to sobriety, it's possible that you want to recommit to staying the course. And that's enough.

Maybe you're ready to add a few things to your sobriety, like quitting smoking, drinking more water or reading that novel you never thought you could finish.

The point is that if you decide in the next few days to invite a New Year's resolution in, take it slow. Take it one day at a time, if you will. Be gentle with your expectation and know that if you never do anything but stay sober then you've done enough.

December 29

"The secret of change is to focus all your energy not on fighting the old but on building the new."—Socrates

We can't change the past.

This is very depressing news for those of us who wasted a lot of years getting wasted.

The good news is that since we are sober today, since we are making changes in our lives *today*, our tomorrows promise to be better than we could even imagine.

We can't change people.

This is depressing news for those of us surrounded by toxic humans.

The good news is that we can change ourselves. We can become the people we'd like to have around us by becoming kinder, more generous and by staying sober in every moment.

Forget about the past. Forget about changing people. Focus all your energy on building the best life you can. You've already seen the power of choosing sobriety. Keep choosing, keep building and keep reminding yourself that you are exactly where you are supposed to be.

December 30

New Year's Eve is tomorrow, and next to Super Bowl Sunday it's one of the biggest drinking nights of the year. What's your plan?

You're not the only one who wants to remain sober on New Year's Eve. In fact, over 200 cities in the US celebrate "First Night," an alcohol-free, family-friendly festival designed to promote the arts. The original First Night was held in Boston in 1976 and was such a massive success, the idea caught fire around the country.

If you're lucky enough to live in a city with a First Night Festival, then you have an event tailor-made for you. Not only can you attend (the celebrations are usually free) but you could be one of the volunteers behind the scenes.

If you're interested in this kind of event, check your local newspaper to see if there is a First Night planned, or if any other local organizations are hosting a sober event.

If you're planning on staying in, treat yourself to something special. Get a box of those pastries you love, or splurge on the fancy take-out. Make homemade cocoa. Re-read your favorite book. Or, do absolutely nothing. You deserve an evening of absolute relaxation.

Then, whether it's after midnight or hours before, go to bed knowing you aren't going to be one of the unlucky ones waking up on the first day of the New Year wishing you could have a do-over.

December 31

My wishes for you in the coming year:

Stay sober.
Seek inspiration in unlikely places.
Find the silence in the noise and the beauty in the mess.
Appreciate the power of humble people.
Open your mind to the possible.
Let go of the habits, behaviors, patterns and thoughts that no longer serve you.
Expand your connection to others.
Stay sober.
Move forward fearlessly.
Keep your promises, but be careful what you promise.
Live simply.
Grow your gratitude.
Be your own best caretaker.
Serve.
Allow yourself to be served.
Face your pain so it doesn't overwhelm you.
Recognize that good people admit to and learn from their mistakes.
Stay sober.

Let's move forward.

Resources

January

The Alchemist, Paolo Coelho
A simple, but surprisingly effective, story of one boy's journey to find his treasure.

SleepFoundation.org
Here you'll find every bit of information you'll ever need for getting a good night's sleep.

halelrod.com
Learn how Miracle Mornings® can transform your life.

The Sobriety Handbook: What You Need to Know to Get Sober and Stay That Way, Meredith Bell
My final book on sobriety, it's a short, helpful read that outlines the steps you'll need to take to stay sober.

Meditations, Marcus Aurelius
A glimpse into the mind of a great warrior, emperor and philosopher, this tome is timeless in its wisdom.

MrMoneyMustache.com
This blog is one that I visit frequently reconfirm my belief that conventional wisdom is not always the most useful.

February

Groundhog Day
A must-watch for anyone trapped in addiction. It's funny, touching, and most of all, it addresses the idea that change must come from within.

Unclutterer.com
My go-to resource for tips and tricks about how to live a more orderly life.

Rumi: The Book of Love, Barks, Coleman, Jalal al-Din Rumi, Coleman Barks and John Moyne
The definitive poet on all things love-related, Rumi's words offer comfort in any situation.

March

The Places that Scare You, Pema Chödrön
Pema is the master of mastering fear. This book offers specific, meditation-based guidelines for transforming your fear into love.

Comfortable with Uncertainty, Pema Chödrön
Practical solutions for facing your fears.

A Course in Miracles, Foundation for Inner Peace
Since the 1970s *A Course in Miracles* has been overhauling lives with its direct wisdom and miracle-based philosophy for living.

To the Lighthouse, Virginia Woolf
A peek into the inner workings of a group of people who meet at a beach house, Woolf deftly reveals the fears and longings of each guest and how they respond to them.

How to be an Adult, David Richo
This book should be required reading for everyone over the age of 18. Filled with a-ha moments, this book more than delivers on its title.

How to Survive the Loss of a Love, Peter McWilliams, Harold H. Bloomfield and Melba Colgrove

This book has been on my shelf since the 1990s, and I still turn to it when I experience loss of any kind.

April

On Writing, Stephen King
If you're looking to become a better writer, look no further than this guide by one of the world's most prolific and talented authors.

The Creative Habit, Twyla Tharp
Tharp's ingenious work shows how we can all create a habit of creativity in our daily lives.

Steal Like an Artist, Austin Kleon
Easy to read and filled with insights into the creative process, Kleon's book provides instant inspiration.

Redroom.com
Where writers gather to talk about writing.

The Artist's Way, Julia Cameron
This guide has saved many an artist from going over the edge. It's beloved by millions for its simple, no-nonsense advice.

NaNoWriMo.com
The home of National Novel Writing Month, this is an online support system for writers who want to get things done.

May

Zenhabits.net
Weekly visits to this brilliant site will keep you on track in your sobriety and your life.

Easy Way to Control Alcohol, Allen Carr
Carr's books have inspired so many people to get sober.

Food Rules: An Eater's Manual, Michael Pollan
Short and to the point, there's no better quick guide for shaping your diet.

Living Juicy: Daily Morsels for Your Creative Soul, SARK
Invitingly drawn and beautifully written, there is inspiration on every page.

The Freedom Manifesto, Tom Hodgkinson
This is the book that started it all for me. I picked it up before a flight and read it cover to cover. Then I read it again and again and again.

The Book of Idle Pleasures, Dan Kieran and Tom Hodgkinson
There no more delightful way to spend a day than leafing through this delightful book about simple joys.

June

The Power of Myth, Joseph Campbell
Looking for your bliss? Start here.

July

The Declaration of Independence
An everlasting symbol of liberty. When was the last time you read it?

MyYogaOnline.com
This subscription-based online resource makes it easy to incorporate healthy changes into your life, on your schedule.

Kumare
Watch this movie to discover the power you have within yourself to make lasting and positive change. Kumare.org

Soberistas.com
An online gathering place for sober people to share their stories, experiences and wisdom.

Stitches: A Handbook of Meaning, Hope and Repair, Anne Lamott
Approachable insights on how to put yourself together after you've fallen apart.

The Big Book of Alcoholics Anonymous
Referred to by a friend of mine as "The Magic Book," it's one of those books that you can open randomly and find the phrase you need to get you through the day. Even if you're not in the program and have no interest in it, it's a compelling read for alcoholics.

August

You Are Here, Thich Naht Hahn
Simple wisdom for overcoming challenges abounds on every page.

The Happiness Project, Gretchen Rubin
Rubin spent some time researching happiness and then applying her findings to her daily life. Was she happier? You'll have to read to find out.

AstrologyZone.com
Free monthly horoscopes from the nation's favorite astrologer, Susan Miller

Bright-Sided: How the Relentless Pursuit of Positive Thinking has Undermined America, Barbara Ehrenreich
A realistic antidote to the happy-face movement, this book is far from pessimistic. In fact, you'll feel more in control and, dare I say positive, about challenges after reading it. It never hurts to be realistic!

The Diving Bell and the Butterfly: A Memoir of Life in Death by Jean-Dominique Bauby
Also a feature film, this is the memoir of a successful man crippled by terrible disease. He wrote it by blinking one eye to dictate the words. If this story doesn't make you feel like you can write your own book, I don't know what will.

LifeHacker.com
A fun website filled with great do-it-yourself ideas and brilliant suggestions for handling all kinds of problems

September

Help, Thanks, Wow: The Three Essential Prayers, Anne Lamott
Prayer made easy—and often funny—is what you'll find in this charming, slim volume.

The Power of Now and A New Earth, by Eckhart Tolle
Interesting reads by a modern-day mystic who emphasizes living in the moment and maintaining our connection to spirit.

One Breath at a Time: Buddhism and the Twelve Steps, Kevin Griffin
One of the books I refer to time and again, this is a beautiful guide to incorporating meditation practice into your sobriety.

Living a Course in Miracles: An Essential Guide to the Classic Text, by Jon Mundy, PhD.
If you've attempted to read the *Course*, then you know it's weighty and confusing. This book cuts through all of the difficulty and makes it easy to understand the importance of sending your ego packing.

LaughterYogaUsa.com
Looking to get your laugh on? This website will help you find local laughter yoga classes.

October

I'm Good Enough, I'm Smart Enough, and Doggone It, People Like Me, Stuart Smalley
Before he was a Senator, Al Franken played a seeker named Stuart Smalley on *Saturday Night Live*. This book is a hilarious satire of the self-help movement and a fun way to get out of your negative thought patterns.

The Dark Side of the Light Chasers, Debbie Ford
Embrace your dark side to let the light in.

November

A Return to Love, Marianne Williamson
A bestseller for a reason, this guide offers deep wisdom for overcoming fear, finding the good in others and surviving when things don't go the way we want them to.

RandomActsOfKindness.org
If I'm feeling down, I like to pop by this site to see how I can quickly help others, and in return, make myself feel better.

December

Simple Abundance, Sarah Ban Breathnach
Breathnach's book is a gorgeous exploration of the ways we can improve our lives without overcomplicating them.

Zero-Proof Cocktails: Alcohol-Free Beverages for Every Occasion, Liz Scott
Discover 100 ways to drink like an adult at your next celebration.

Intervention

Watch it online at AETV.com. I daresay you'll see yourself on the screen.

The Sober Revolution: Calling Time on Wine O'Clock, by Sarah Turner and Lucy Rocca
You are not alone. Learn about all the ways in which people all over the world are embracing joyful sobriety.

About the Author

MEREDITH BELL is a former wine industry executive who did the unthinkable and quit drinking. She is the author of *Seven Days Sober: A Guide to Discovering What You Really Think About Your Drinking* and *The Sobriety Handbook: What You Need to Know to Get Sober and Stay That Way.*

Meredith lives in Sonoma County, California.

You can visit her online at sevendayssoberbook.com, or contact her at sevendayssober@gmail.com

Also by Meredith Bell

NEW!
The Sobriety Handbook: What You Need to Know to Get Sober and Stay That Way
The sober journey can be fraught with emotional upheaval, confusion about program options and fear of the unknown. This easy-to-understand guide takes the mystery out of the work of sobriety, and lets you know exactly what you need to do next.

UPDATED & REVISED
Seven Days Sober: A Guide to Discovering What You Really Think About Your Drinking
Have you had enough? If your embarrassing behavior haunts your memory or your three-martini habit leaves you feeling debilitated rather than exhilarated, it's time to take a break. Try Seven Days Sober to discover if sobriety works for you.

sevendayssoberbook.com
greenrabbitmedia.com

Credits:

Front cover design and illustration by George M. Dondero

Manufactured by Amazon.ca
Bolton, ON